Tourism in Transition

Tourism, Retailing and Consumption

Series Editors

Gareth Shaw, Department of Geography, University of Exeter

Dimitri Ioannides, Department of Geography, Geology and Planning, Southwest Missouri State University

Consumption has become an important theme in geography and the social sciences and within this broad debate two key areas of concern are tourism and retailing. Yet to date there is no series that brings together these closely related topics under a unifying perspective. *Tourism, Retailing and Consumption* will provide such a perspective.

The series will provide core texts for students of geography and related disciplines at first degree level. It will be wide ranging in scope and cover both historical and contemporary debates in tourism, retailing and consumption. A number of more specialized texts suited to post-graduate study will also be included.

Tourism in Transition

Economic Change in Central Europe

Allan M Williams
and
Vladimír Baláž

I.B.Tauris *Publishers*

LONDON ● NEW YORK

Published in 2000 by I.B.Tauris & Co. Ltd
Victoria House, Bloomsbury Square, London WC1B 4DZ
175 Fifth Avenue, New York NY10010
Website: http://www.ibtauris.com

In the United States of America and in Canada distributed by
St Martin's Press, 175 Fifth Avenue, New York NY 10010

A full CIP record for this book is available from the British Library
A full CIP record for this book is available from the British Library of Congress

ISBN 1-86064-578-X hardback
ISBN 1-86064-579-8 paperback

Library of Congress catalog card number: available

Typeset by Wyvern 21 Ltd, Bristol
Printed and bound by MPG Books, Bodmin

LIST OF CONTENTS

PREFACE

The transition in Central and Eastern Europe most dramatically dates from 1989 but from the late 1960s the highly centralized state planning system had already begun to unravel, especially in Central Europe. The process of transformation after 1989 was subject to external pressure to adopt a neo-liberal 'shock therapy' model of reform which sought to create market economies in very short time periods. However, in practice the process of transition was path-dependent path-creating and was conditional upon national differences in economic and political structures. One of the rewards dangled in front of the participants was potential future membership of the European Union, and the interim judgement on this was delivered in July 1997 when the European Commission recommended that priority should be given to the accession of six applicants, but at the 1999 Helsinki summit this was extended to all the candidates from Central and Eastern Europe. The massive efforts required to reorientate these economies has demanded a high price, in terms of both high unemployment and massive cuts in living standards, and social polarization, especially in the ownership and control of property rights.

Considerable research attention has been given to various facets of the transformation, especially the restructuring of manufacturing and the emergence of financial services, and the construction of democratic institutions. In contrast, the role of tourism has been largely neglected. And yet tourism was often at the forefront of economic changes in the region. A strongly collectivist model of domestic and international tourism was replaced in a short time span with a largely privatized tourism sector, where domestic consumption was increasingly shaped by market relationships, and international demand was shaped by the business and leisure interests of Western Europe. Tourism was in the vanguard of, and sometimes a model for, many reforms, especially privatization, and the liberalization of international trade. Similarly, the decline and polarization in living standards was reflected in the erosion of popular access to holidays, and convergence upon Western European models of international tourism. While there have been a number of studies of particular aspects of tourism development, there has been a surprising lack of detailed analysis of the different interlocking aspects of the transformation in tourism over the transition period as a whole.

The aims of this book are to analyse the changing role of tourism in the process of transformation in Czechoslovakia and in the two independent Czech and Slovak Republics which emerged in 1993 from the 'velvet divorce'. The choice of case study was determined not only by the practical considerations of the privileged data access and language expertise of Vladimír Baláž, but by the particular features of tourism in these countries. First, amongst the central European states, Czechoslovakia had been the most rigidly wedded to central planning, so that – arguably – the scale and the challenge of the neo-liberal project faced by the country was particularly severe. Secondly, tourism in Czechoslovakia was a mosaic of contrasting tourism attractions, some of which were of international stature while others were only likely to survive within a protectionist domestic tourism system. There is therefore the opportunity to study how a deeply socially and territorially segmented tourism system adapted to changes after 1989. Thirdly, the creation of two separate states in 1993 provides a – virtually unique – opportunity to study the impact of divergent state policies in the Czech and Slovak republics on the differential evolution of what had been a single national tourism system for much of the twentieth century.

We would like to conclude this preface by acknowledging the assistance we have received in preparing this study. First and foremost, the book is the product of a one-year research project which was sponsored by the Economic and Social Research Council (Research Grant R000 22 2240). The authors are also grateful to the support provided by the Department of Geography in the University of Exeter, and the Institute of Forecasting (Slovak Academy of Sciences). Karel Machala (Svět Hospodářství daily) and Marta Gáplovská (Hotel Academy of Prievidza) were responsible for the firm-level interviews, while Karel Machala also provided some secondary statistics on tourism in the Czech Republic. Terry Bacon in the Department of Geography helped to prepare the final diagrams for publication. We also gratefully acknowledge the co-operation provided by the officials responsible for tourism in the two countries. In addition, Vladimír Baláž has had privileged access to officials and data sources in the Slovak Ministry of Trade and Tourism and the Slovak Ministry of Economy. This partly explains why the project has been able to analyse previously unpublished data on tourism in Czechoslovakia, and latterly Slovakia. Our access to such data was more constrained in the Czech Republic, although it is also true that the latter has paid less attention to collating tourism statistics; for example, it did not reinstate its domestic tourism survey until 1998. While acknowledging the assistance of all these bodies and individuals, the responsibility for any errors of fact or interpretation in this volume rests solely with the authors.

Allan Williams and Vladimír Baláž
Exeter and Bratislava

1 INTRODUCTION: TOURISM AND TRANSITION

1.1 TRANSITION IN CENTRAL EUROPE: PATH DEPENDENCY AND PATH CREATION

Since 1989 Central and Eastern Europe have been subject to an economic transformation which has been characterized as the 'sharp-shock' economic programme of reforms. This model has been based on the creation of markets, privatization, and trade liberalization, in combination with macro-economic stabilization measures. Although the neo-liberal sharp-shock model which was promoted by Western interests (Gowan 1995) had wide circulation in Central Europe, and certainly influenced the pace and content of reforms, the economic transformation can not be viewed as a rational process of constructing economic institutions. Stark (1992; 1994) argues that there are three reasons for this: that capitalism in the West did not originate by blueprint; that blueprint models are abstracted from social institutions; and (1994, p 117) 'the devastation wrought by communism and the quick demise of its party-states has not left an institutional vacuum . . . these societies will find the materials with which to build a new order in the ruins of the old'. Nielsen *et al* (1995: p 40) take up this point, arguing that although there has been a systemic vacuum there has been no institutional vacuum; instead, a complex institutional legacy serves to shape expectations and patterns of economic behaviour. Stark (1996, p 995) has memorably argued that transformation involves '. . . rebuilding organizations and institutions not on the ruins but with the ruins of communism'.

Because of the importance of the 'ruins' of the state-socialist system (in terms of trade links, institutions, regulation, personal and inter-firm networks) the economic transformations in Central and Eastern Europe can be characterized as path dependent. This does not imply determinism –

1

the course of the transformation was, and is, not shaped by the legacy of the past in any predictable manner. Rather, path dependency argues that the actors in the transformation process are constrained by existing institutional resources, which limit some fields of action while favouring the selection of others (Stark 1994, p 117). For Smith and Pickles (1998, p 15) path dependency is 'institutionalised forms of learning and struggles over pathways that emerge out of the intersection of old and new', while Nielsen *et al* (1995, p 3) refer to the dialectic of structure and strategic action, which is characterized by structural contradictions and strategic dilemmas. Transformation therefore is not 'architectural design but bricolage' (Stark 1994, p 118), constructed from the materials at hand. This book is informed by the central argument that the role of tourism in the process of transformation has to be seen in terms of the 'intersection of the new and the old' and the constraining of actions and policies.

However, this book also considers that – to some extent – the terminology of path dependency is misleading, suggesting that a pathway has been embarked on which stands in opposition to path creation; the latter is understood to imply that '. . . within specific limits, social forces can redesign the "board" on which they are moving and reformulate the rules of the game' (Nielsen *et al* 1995, p 7). It is more useful to consider path dependency and path creation as lying on a continuum rather than as being polar alternatives. This was recognized by Nielsen *et al* (1995, p 6) who argued that few commentators accepted either the extreme voluntaristic pole or the historical determinist role of institution creation. Instead, they advocated a 'path-dependent path-creating' perspective. However, this book is wary of the 'path-dependent path-creating' perspective as being static and failing to allow for the sharply tangential way in which new pathways can strike off from the old pathways in the course of the transformation. Cox (1994, p 396), for example, draws attention to the increasingly distinctive experiences of privatization and to how 'the influence of different national histories and geographical positions combined with the different complexions of newly elected non-communist governments, and the different experiences of reforms under the previous regimes' produced increasingly varied experiences of privatization after 1994.

One of the keys to diversity was the uneven and incomplete nature of market formation which created space for particular interest groups to manipulate the reform process for reasons of self-interest in latter years. The imperative behind this was that privatization provided a one-off opportunity for economic and political elites to accumulate wealth (Cox 1994, p 406). To some extent this approximates to Staniszkis's (1991) notion of the emergence of political capitalism, whereby a new relationship has been forged between political power and the control of capital; privileged access to political power has been used to accumulate power and wealth, especially in the absence of effective regulatory frameworks for privatization. However, political capitalism provides only a partial conceptualization of the processes involved because it fails to take into account 'the autonomous dynamics of the economic' (Burawoy and Krotov 1993). Instead, economic actors have been able to control property rights through the construction and transformation of networks of firms. As will emerge later, there have been important differences in the strength and direction of the influence exercised on tourism by political and economic actors in the Czech and Slovak Republics.

1.2 TOURISM AND THE CHALLENGE OF TRANSITION

The relationships between tourism and the transition process are symbiotic. On the one hand, change in tourism – despite the sector having its own production and consumption characteristics and sector-specific policies – is influenced by the broad sweep of the economic, social and political transformation in Central and Eastern Europe. On the other hand, tourism contributes to the transformation, being relatively open to international competition and to shifts in consumer expenditure, and being in the vanguard of privatization and market liberalization.

Tourism development directly impacts on economies in transition through its net contribution to the current account/national income, and to employment. It is difficult to generalise about these impacts, as they are contingent. The economic impacts are mediated by company structures and (as we shall see) the particular models of privatization pursued, the embeddedness of firms in national and regional economies (Grabher and Stark 1998), and the productive, labour market and capital features of national economies. All these contingencies are important in the transition economies because of the way they have been remoulded in the process of transition.

The contribution of tourism to the net balance of payments surplus has long been recognized in the economic strategies of European governments, particularly in the late-industrializing Southern European economies in the early post-war decades (Williams 1997). Since the late 1970s, the economic potential of tourism has also been recognized in more mature economies facing de-industrialization crises. Tourism earnings can help balance the current account, and finance imports, whether of consumer, intermediate or capital goods. The same considerations apply to the transition economies, where tourism was one of the few sectors capable of generating a surplus on international trade. Although there are considerable problems in quantifying the foreign exchange earnings of tourism, the statistical data available suggest the sector generated foreign exchange surpluses which helped balance the net international deficit, and finance critical imports of intermediate and capital goods. As will become evident later, the growing

3

appreciation of the role of international tourism informed the repositioning of tourism in state policies during the transition.

Employment is the other key aspect of the economic impact of tourism. The data on employment are more problematic even than for income, not least because of the classic problem of defining what constitutes a job in tourism. Much of the debate has centred on the more visible jobs in hotels and catering, leading to the conclusion that tourism jobs are low quality in terms of pay, security and skills. This is necessarily an oversimplification given the range of jobs which tourism supports in public administration, manufacturing, the producer services, retailing and transport (Shaw and Williams 1987). However, the contribution of tourism to employment in the transition economies is given additional weight by the soaring unemployment rates which have been inherent in the sharp shock neo-liberal economic reforms (Williams and Baláž 1998).

The overall contribution of tourism to these economies is dependent on a number of contingent features, including the following:

- The overall balance between the outflow and the inflow of tourists and tourist expenditures. In the transition, the removal of the 'iron curtain' created opportunities for new patterns of international tourist flows; these were particularly marked in countries such as Romania and, until the late 1980s, Czechoslovakia, which previously had been selectively closed to international tourism (Hall 1995). The most significant changes concerned the attraction of tourists from new Western European markets, but there were also changes in international tourism flows amongst the former Eastern block countries. Organized holiday tourism declined amongst them, and there were significant flows for shopping, business and trading purposes (sometimes clandestinely); many of these trans-border flows were generated by the price and supply differences resulting from the uneven speed and form of the transition in neighbouring economies. Some forms of tourism, therefore, were essential lubricants in the structural economic adjustments in the region.
- There are tourism expenditure leakages from national economies, which is partly a function of the structure and ownership of tourism and related industries. Foreign direct investment (FDI) in tourism is relatively small scale in most of Central Europe, but is already strong in sectors such as air transport and (intriguingly) travel agencies. Moreover, FDI can be expected to make an increasingly important contribution in future to the evolution of tourism development and associated international transactions. Ownership is important because it conditions not just whether but how firms are inserted into international markets (Beattie 1991). However, foreign ownership remains relatively muted, and the issue of inter-firm linkages has probably been

of greater relevance in the transformation (Grabher and Stark 1998). In respect of tourism, the key point is that many tourism establishments were embedded within large company structures, and the extent to which these have been privatized or at least commercialized has influenced the contribution of tourism to national and regional economies. This is also related to the methods of privatization (Hall 1995), an issue which is explored later.

• The contribution of tourism to the national economy is dependent on the regional structure of the industry, for it is essentially a mosaic of regional complexes providing different types of tourism services. The national economic performance of tourism can, in fact, be disaggregated into a series of, often contrasting if linked, regional performances. If Stark (1996, p 995) is correct in asserting that path dependency implies '. . . rebuilding organizations and institutions not on the ruins but with the ruins of communism', then these 'ruins' are territorially situated and differentiated. The performance of the national tourism sector is the outcome of how regional territorial complexes were inserted into a changing global order, albeit that these global–local relationships continued to be mediated by national states. The corollary of this is that the changing territorial organization of tourism has contributed to the overall process of uneven regional development during the transformation. Whether the net effects of tourism development have been to encourage regional convergence or divergence is one of the key questions addressed in this volume.

Tourism not only contributes to economic transformation but has also been shaped by this series of linked economic, political and social changes. Three main dimensions of the transition have significance for tourism: the broad raft of stabilization and market-creating reforms which constitute the 'sharp-shock' economic transition strategies applied in Central Europe; the re-internationalization of the economies; and strategies for privatization. These have fundamentally changed the macro-economic climate for tourism, radically redistributed property rights and exposed the sector to globalization.

• The sharp-shock economic reforms were based on a particular version of liberal capitalism, with four main constituents: market liberalization, privatization, currency convertibility, and trade liberalization. These were combined with macro-economic stabilization measures, involving limiting the money supply and budgetary controls. The new economic model was based as much on theoretical ideals as actual practices of economic management in Western Europe. Moreover, the model was implemented with only scant regard to domestic and international economic realities. It did not take into account, for example, the existence of restrictive practices in world trade, political and social structures in

Central Europe, or the actual as opposed to the assumed role of the state in the liberal democracies of Western Europe. For example, the model discouraged state subsidies, yet these were routinely deployed by Western European governments (Gowan 1995). But the fundamental weakness in this neo-liberal strategy was that while tough budget controls stemmed the flow of public resources to companies, there were few mechanisms (such as modern financial institutions) to redeploy factors of production to new enterprises. The result, not surprisingly, was a collapse in production and living standards, with serious consequences initially for domestic tourism, and for the ability of entrepreneurs to restructure existing tourism establishments or to invest in new ones. The economic recovery in the second phase of the transformation saw increasing social polarization and changes in leisure time, leading to the creation of new markets and to recovery in domestic tourism, although this remained highly uneven.

- A distinctive model of international tourism had developed within Central Europe during the period of state-socialist central planning, with most flows being channelled either to neighbouring 'friendly' countries or to the Black Sea resorts. This system was no longer viable after the removal of passport and visa barriers to international mobility, and the emergent globalization of tourism in Central Europe. A new system emerged – particularly for holiday tourism – which was centred on Western Europe, for both inbound and outbound flows. Tourism development in individual countries and regions, in this period, depended on their ability to adjust to these major shifts in international markets brought about by the general liberalization of international movements.

- Privatization has revolutionized the conditions for the production and provision of tourism services. With few exceptions, tourism has been in the vanguard of privatization and demonstrates many of the advantages and disadvantages associated with changes in property rights, the availability of new sources of capital and entrepreneurship, and economic performance. The type of privatization programme has a major effect on the resultant forms of property ownership, prices paid, capital structures and firm performance. The privatization programmes have been shaped by competing social and political interests, characterized as a form of political capitalism (Staniszkis 1991), and have been economy-wide rather than being tailored to the specific conditions and requirements of tourism.

If tourism in transition can be seen as path-dependent path-creating, then it is to be understood in terms of the intersection of national economic and social reforms with globalization. The next section considers some of the key features of global shifts in tourism.

6

1.3 GLOBAL CHANGES IN TOURISM PRODUCTION AND CONSUMPTION

While the evolution of tourism in Central Europe in the post-1989 period has to be understood in terms of the overall transformation of the regional economies in this period, there were also important changes in global tourism. The re-internationalization of Central European tourism was taking place at a time of significant shifts in global conditions for the production and consumption of tourism. In the 1990s, Central Europe was seeking new markets and engaging foreign investment under very different conditions to those which had prevailed in, say, the 1960s when the heady expansion of mass tourism had occurred in Mediterranean Europe.

The most remarkable feature of the demand for tourism has probably been the rapid growth of the post 1950s period. In the absence of consistent and accurate statistics on domestic demand, the most reliable indicators are the number of international tourists, which increased from 25 million in 1950, through to 69 million in 1960, 160 million in 1970, 429 million in 1990, and 592 million by 1996. The World Tourism Organization (WTO) estimates that the number of international travellers will increase from just over 600 million in 1997 to more than one and a half billion in 2020. Europe has been in the vanguard of the expansion of tourism, and it is estimated that in the EU 55–60 per cent of the population take at least one holiday of four overnight stays per year; 65 per cent of all these trips have national destinations, while 22 per cent are spent elsewhere in the EU, and 13 per cent are outside of the EU (Commission of the European Communities 1993a, p 52).

Central Europe has, therefore, been reinserted into international tourism markets which have experienced a long cumulative boom whilst current demand growth remains relatively strong. However, there have been changes in consumption within this expansionary framework. The dominant trend in Western European tourism in the 1960s and 1970s was the expansion of mass tourism, but in recent decades this has been challenged. Lury (1996: p 94) argues that consumption (in the broadest sense) has been reshaped by three broad sets of changes: greater flexible specialization in production; availability of a wider range of commodities, with shorter life cycles given more rapid changes in fashion and greater differentiation by market segments; and more individualized and hybrid consumption patterns. Consumer preferences have also become more volatile, and consumption is more fluid. With respect to tourism, Fayos-Solá (1996, p 406) argues that:

> The New Age of Tourism is characterized primarily by the super-segmentation of demand, the need for flexibility of supply and distribution, and achieving profitability through diagonal integration and subsequent system economies and integrated values, instead of economies of scale.

7

One element in this shifting mosaic of consumption has been a change in the nature of holidays from being '. . . an annual ritual of considerable cultural significance into just one element within a more universally market-orientated society' (Soane 1992, p 23). There has not been absolute decline in traditional long-stay holidays in mass tourism destinations. This is evident in Montanari's (1995) estimate that some 160 million international tourists visited the Mediterranean in 1994 and the forecast that this will at least double by 2025 (Croall 1995, p 9). However, mass tourism is facing a challenge from the rapid expansion of more individualized and flexible forms of tourism, sometimes termed post-modernist or post-Fordist (Urry 1990; 1995). There has, for example, been growing interest in mega events, in cultural tourism, heritage tourism and rural tourism. To some extent these involve the exploitation of place differences, rather than similarities as in mass tourism.

The urban tourism market encompasses two distinctive strands: cultural tourism and business/conference tourism. In Europe an estimated 48 per cent of urban tourism trips are associated with business/professional reasons, compared to only 27 per cent for leisure and recreation (Grabler 1997). Both urban business and leisure tourism are continuing to expand, and are often intertwined. An additional supply-side twist has been given to the expansion of urban tourism by the prominent role this has acquired in the economic development and diversification strategies of many urban areas (Law 1993). In addition to these newer markets, there are also more traditional centres for cultural tourism based on diverse attractions ranging from archaeological remains, through outstanding architectural settings, to museums and art galleries. This is a continuing tradition associated with Europe's diverse heritage, and the growth rate for such trips in the 1990s has been estimated at 15 per cent per annum (Economist Intelligence Unit 1993).

There has also been expansion of various forms of nature-based tourism; this has been fuelled by environmentalism, the growing negative reaction to mass tourism, and the general social reconstruction of valued landscapes and cultures (Urry 1990). There is also, at least in Northern Europe, evidence that many forms of rural tourism constitute a search for idealised, rural societies and values which have long ceased to exist in the economically most developed parts of Europe. Central Europe has the potential to capitalise on this relative shift from standardized mass tourism holidays to more individualized forms of culture- and environment-based tourism. As will be seen later, the attractions of Prague and the Tatras mountains, in particular, can be partly understood in terms of these shifts in European tourism consumption.

While Europe provides the immediate context for understanding the re-internationalization of tourism in Central Europe, there is also the need to take into account globalization processes. This is evident in the statistics for international destinations: between 1950 and 1996, the number of international tourists in Europe increased twenty-two fold, but the region's share of world tourism fell from a peak of 71 per cent in 1975 to 59 per cent in 1996. It is significant that the erosion of the European share occurred at a much faster rate in the period 1990–94 (0.75 per cent per annum) than in the 1980s (0.3 per cent). This has a double significance for Central Europe. First, the globalization of markets points to the potential importance of non-European markets but, secondly, the declining relative share of Europe points to the increasing pressures of global competition.

In addition to these consumption-related shifts, there have also been changes in the organization and production of tourism services. There has been marked concentration in recent decade in the face of intense competition in an increasingly internationalized industry. One of the most impressive features of European tourism has been the growth of major tour operators. These companies have international activities, but their markets are mostly national. However, the largest British and German tour operators have recently been expanding into new foreign markets within Northern Europe. Internationalization or concentration is also evident in the hotel sector where, Go and Pine (1995, p 133) argue, most large corporations are orientating 'towards greater internationalization, co-operation and concentration'. Within individual domestic markets, such trends are creating intense competition and forcing many small companies to become more specialized. A number of significant factors, in combination, yield competitive advantages to transnational hotel groups. According to Go and Pine (1995, p 8) these include branding, the need for adequate resources to respond quickly to new or changing market conditions, organizational and managerial economies of scale, and the advantages available from global travel reservation systems which require large initial capital investments.

The above features highlight the increasing transnationalization of tourism capital, which has been particularly strong in the business tourism sector for hotels, and in the inclusive tour sector for holiday tourism. This is the context within which transnationals have been displaying increasing interest in investing in tourism in Central Europe. However, these concentration and internationalization tendencies should not be exaggerated. Instead, as Viceriat (1993) points out, independently owned hotels represent some 90 per cent of establishments within the EU, and an estimated 80 per cent of bed capacity. But there are polarization tendencies within the small and medium-sized tour company sector. Many small hotels are finding it increasingly difficult to compete, especially if they lack facilities such as private bathrooms, bars and swimming pools which are becoming standard expectations. These smaller establishments have to compete, instead, in terms of price by cutting their margins to the minimum, often through exploitation of unpaid family labour. On the other hand, many small establishment have thrived by offering individualized and high quality services, sometimes in combination with a distinctive product such as a quality restaurant, or organized sporting and leisure activities. These changes present Central Europe with both opportunities and challenges.

1.4 THE CZECH AND SLOVAK REPUBLICS: CASE STUDIES OF TOURISM IN TRANSITION

There are superficial similarities between the economic and political context in which tourism has developed during the transformation in Central Europe to events in Southern Europe, two decades earlier. The overthrow of the colonels in Greece, the army officers' coup in Portugal, and the dismantling of Francoism in Spain were all political ruptures which precipitated largely unanticipated economic and political transformations (Williams 1984). There are also some striking economic parallels between the economies of the Central and Eastern European applicants and the Southern European countries at what may prove to be similar points in their candidatures for EU membership. Elsewhere (Williams *et al* 1998) we have illustrated this by comparing Portugal in 1977 (the year in which it lodged its application for EU membership), to the Czech Republic, Slovakia and Hungary in the mid-1990s; all three countries had similar population sizes, agriculture was relatively more important in the Gross Domestic Product (GDP) of Portugal, and there were only minor differences in their GDPs per capita, relative to the poorest existing member of the EU.

There are, however, obvious and critical differences between central Europe in the 1990s and Southern Europe in the 1970s, and these illustrate the particular circumstances of the role of tourism in transition. First, the degree of re-internationalization required was far less in Southern Europe, particularly in Spain. Both Spain and Portugal had Association Agreements

Fig. 1.1 Slovakia: administrative areas

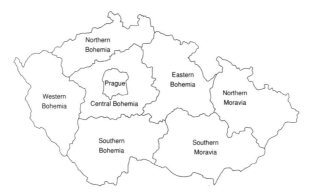

Fig. 1.2 Czech Republic: administrative areas

with the EU from the early 1970s, and Greece from the early 1960s. In addition, the neo-liberal economic transition model offered far less protection to firms in central Europe than had been available in the more protectionist economies of Southern Europe, both prior to accession and during their 5–7-year post-membership transition periods. The economies of Southern Europe had also been far more open to FDI during the periods of dictatorship, especially in the 1960s (Hudson and Lewis 1984), than Central Europe had been prior to 1989.

Secondly, the Southern European countries, like the Central European ones, also needed to implement market reforms and dismantle the remnants of central state controls over their economies (see Williams 1984). These had been exacerbated in the case of Portugal by the massive nationalization of banks and industrial companies in the 1974–6 period. However, in contrast, there had been no central planning in Southern Europe. Instead, a high level of protectionism, monopolies and strategic state ownership, in some sectors, coexisted with functioning, if deformed, markets, private ownership of large parts of the economy, and dense networks of small and medium-sized enterprises. Neither the scale nor the speed of the economic reforms in Central and Southern Europe were comparable.

The above conclusion also applies to tourism. The political transformation in Southern Europe caused a brief hiatus in tourism development (Williams and Shaw 1998b) but did not in itself fundamentally change most of the conditions for growth. Instead, these countries, since at least the mid-1950s, had experienced sustained growth in mass tourism, centred on the sunshine-sea-sand product, which had been based on Northern Europe demand and was articulated through highly-organized international tour companies (Williams 1995; 1997). After the mid-1970s there were changes as domestic tourism expanded in Southern Europe, and these countries increasingly became the origins as well as the destinations of international

11

TABLE 1.1 *Slovakia and the Czech Republic in 1996: basic statistics*

	Slovakia	Czech Republic
Area, km^2	49,000	78,864
Population density per km^2	108	131
GDP per capita in US$ (exchange rates)	3,247	4,882
GDP per capita in US$ (purchasing power parity)	7,486	10,569
Economically active population (%)	48.2	50.2
Life expectancy, years: male (female)	68.4 (76.3)	70.0 (76.9)

Sources: Štatistický úrad Slovenskej republiky (1994–1998); Český statistický úřad (1993–1998a).
Notes: The GDP per capita data refer to 1995.

tourism flows. But the changes were evolutionary and the tourism sector was already highly commodified, not to say transnationalized, prior to the 1970s. In contrast, tourism development in Central Europe in the 1990s occurred against a background of an initial collapse in domestic demand, the dramatic loss of traditional international markets, re-engagement with Western European international markets, and wholesale privatization of tourism provision as part of a concerted attempt to create a market economy in a short time span.

The study of tourism in the course of the transformation in Central Europe therefore provides an opportunity to analyse the role of the sector in one of the most remarkable periods of economic, social and political transformation in modern European history. Conditions existed for the wholesale reconstruction of the tourism industry and the role that it plays in these economies and societies. And yet the discontinuities should not be overemphasized, for many form of tourism production and consumption have shown a remarkable persistence in the course of the transformation. The transformation of tourism, as of the larger economy, was in Nielsen *et al*'s (1995) terminology a 'path-dependent path-creating' process. Or, to paraphrase Smith and Pickles (1998, p 15), the pathways of tourism in the transformation emerged from the inter-section of the old and the new.

While the analysis in this volume is set in context of the transformation in Central Europe as a whole, it focuses mostly on the Czech and Slovak Republics. Both before and post their emergence as separate states after the velvet divorce, they provide contrasting case studies of divergent pathways of transformation, in terms of their general economies and tourism in particular. These differences are not immediately evident in the basic statistics for the two countries (Table 1.1), except that the Czech Republic has GDP per capita levels which are some 50 per cent greater than Slovakia. But these data do hint at the different histories of economic development in the two countries, differences which were narrowed but not eliminated by their long period of political unification and shared experience of central planning. As will be seen in the next chapter, the transformation process has brought about further convergence and divergence between the two countries. The remainder of the book is devoted to exploring these differences.

2 ECONOMIC TRANSITION AND TOURISM

2.1 CENTRAL PLANNING AND MARKET ECONOMIES

The collapse of state-socialism and central planning in Central and Eastern Europe was one of the defining moments, or series of moments, in the second half of the twentieth century. Marxist and Leninist ideals of creating a society based on social engineering and central economic planning had long since turned into a nightmare of political and economic persecution in the 1930s (in the Soviet Union) and 1950s, with a long hangover in the 1970s and 1980s. After 1945 each Central and Eastern European country developed its own model of central planning and state-socialism, rooted in historical legacies and social and economic contingencies; these had varying degrees of economic success. Yet, in 1989 it only took a few months to dismantle state-socialism across the region. There were many reasons why state-socialism failed to compete with the market economies and democratic societies in Western Europe. The underlying cause, however, was the ineffectiveness of central planning. In contrast, decentralized decision-making and the linking of decisions, information and motivations provided market economies with greater flexibility in the face of globalization and shifting demand in the late twentieth century. The differences between market and centrally planned economies in terms of flexibility were evident in several respects:

- Market economies tend to have relatively short information flows, linking customer preferences, purchases and production. In centrally planned economies, it took far longer to modify production structures to meet changing needs and demand. There was little contact between producers and final consumer, but frequent conflicts between the suppliers and consumers of intermediate goods. With the increasing sophistication of production, it became more difficult to balance the production inputs and outputs.

- Goods and services were sold for fixed prices in centrally planned economies, so that individual producers had little scope to adjust prices in order to balance demand and supply. Most prices lost their signal, control and allocation functions and became merely vehicles for administrative information in the process of production redistribution. This led to a 'hoarding and stockbuilding economy' (Mygind 1994, p 76). Excess demand for products, whose quality was greater than their artificially set price, was reflected in empty shop shelves and long queues. On the other hand, products with real prices greater than their administrative ones remained unsold. There were, for example, long queues at those socialist travel agencies which sold the limited numbers of trips to Western Europe.

- Market economies apply budgetary pressures on individual enterprises, for which profit (in the short or long term) is a major, and usually the main, success indicator. Bankruptcy is the normal outcome where an enterprise is unable to meet its liabilities, although there are exceptions when states support 'strategic' industries. In centrally planned economies, the volume of production was given more priority that production efficiency, and most failing enterprises were subsidized by the state for decades rather than years.

- Decentralized corporate governance in market economies gives enterprises considerable flexibility in adapting to change, whilst innovation can secure above average rates of profit. In contrast, innovations in centrally planned economies were sometimes considered to be harmful; they caused short-term disruption of production, and could threaten the organization of, and power within, the controlling bureaucracy, thereby endangering the dominant interest groups.

- Market economies seek to balance conflicts between the owners of capital and employees through the use of instruments of motivation and negotiation between the owners of capital and employees' organizations. In centrally planned economies, where the owner was the anonymous state, a large part of an employee's nominal wage was set in advance and had only a limited relationship to the actual output. This was matched by a high degree of job security, which contributed to low work discipline and poor productivity. A popular saying that 'the state pretended to pay the workers and the workers pretended to work' was an apt description of the 'principal agent–capital owner' relationship. Poor service in state-socialist hotels, for example, was closely related to poor wages in the industry.

- Finally, there was a large distance, both physically and in terms of interests, between the state bureaucracy and the mass of alienated individuals. The petrifaction of the ruling class of communist party

15

bureaucrats, in combination with extensive popular apathy, heralded the demise of state-socialism in 1980s. This class had little to say to most of the population and they found little support during the 1989 crisis.

This short overview of the main differences between the market and centrally planned economies is necessarily generalized, and cannot detail the national and temporal nuances of state-socialism. But it does provide the essential background for understanding the development problems of transition economies. These are distinctive economies, characterized by elements of market economies operating alongside persistent components of state-socialism. This is true, for example, of the power of the state bureaucracy over state-owned, but also some privatized, enterprises. It is also evident in the lack of accountability of decision-making by state bureaucrats and some enterprise managers. There also are remnants of state-socialist social programmes in many transition economies. In tourism, for example, many enterprises still provide social tourism for their employees under schemes which are broadly similar to those which had existed under state-socialism. The creation of elements of a market economy has not meant that model Western-European market economies have been created in Central and Eastern Europe. Instead, many key elements – such as financial institutions and market regulation – are, at best, weakly developed even after a decade of transformation. In this respect, the path-dependency path-creation perspective provides an useful conceptual framework for the analysis in this book.

2.2 THE TWILIGHT YEARS OF STATE-SOCIALISM

While we generally argue the importance of path dependency as opposed to path creation in this book, this is not to say that the Central and Eastern European economies were a uniform economic system. There were important differences in the extent to which they embraced, initially, the sequence of economic models imposed by the Soviet Union and, latterly, economic reforms.

Eastern Germany (GDR) and Czechoslovakia were ruled by grey-haired and grey-minded hard-liners who implemented rigid central planning and ruthless suppression of political opposition. Their economies, however, were relatively stable, with low levels of GDP growth, but also low (officially, at least) inflation, budget deficits, trade balances and foreign debts. Both countries could draw on their industrial heritage and educated labour force. High investment levels in the 1950s and 1960s, and extensive use of labour (generated by rapid urbanization, industrialization and population growth), enabled high rates of production outputs in the 1960s and 1970s. These were reflected in relatively substantial improvements in living standards. The GDR and Czechoslovak governments also implemented extensive social programs, including subsidized cheap holidays for all members of society. These had a legitimation function in the face of unrest emanating from the deteriorating economic situation and political persecution in the 1980s. In their own terms, these governments were relatively successful and stable in 1989 and few commentators could have predicted their imminent downfall.

An important shared problem of Czechoslovakia and the GDR was that of concealed or suspended inflation. Increases in nominal wages and social payments were higher than increases in real production. In a system of fixed prices, people could not consume as much of their incomes, as they wished. The income/consumption gap was characterized by two developments: forced savings, the so-called monetary overhang, and shopping trips to those state-socialist countries, which applied some elements of the market economy and had larger supplies of consumer goods. A large proportion of Czech and Slovaks trips to Hungary in the 1970s and 1980s, for example, were to buy consumer goods imported to Hungary under the loans provided by Western governments. In this way, international travel helped to balance demand and supply inequalities within the centrally planned economies.

In contrast to the GDR and Czechoslovakia, Hungary enjoyed a reputation as being the 'merriest barrack in the socialist camp' after the 1960s. Kádar's government pursued a relatively liberal cultural policy, and the strong reform wing in the communist party introduced selected market and democratic reforms. The Hungarian government made significant investments in the agricultural and service sectors, and allowed limited entrepreneurial activities. Similar policies were applied by the Polish government after the abolition of martial law in 1983. There was a more liberal economic policy for small-scale private entrepreneurs, whilst responsibility was formally decentralized to state-owned enterprises with respect to inputs and outputs and the powers of workers' councils were enhanced. Inevitably, the co-existence of these reforms with overarching central planning of the economy generated tensions. The prices of goods and services produced in the private sector were higher than production prices in the planned sector. This led to an overall increase in inflation (which was higher than in the GDR and Czechoslovakia), reductions in purchasing power, lower savings rates, and the outflow of labour from the planned to the private sector. The private or the 'second' sector in Hungary was largely submerged in the shadow and black economy, mostly to be found in retailing, hotels and restaurants, where it accounted for higher turnover levels that the respective planned sectors (Böröcz 1996). The Hungarian and Polish governments also tried to import Western technologies and thereby became heavily indebted. Large parts of their international loans were expended on importing consumer goods, and both countries became ensnared in the 'interest trap' and had large trade deficits in the late 1980s.

The economic peak of state-socialism was in the 1960s and 1970s, when strong output growth was generated by sharp increases in capital investment and labour, together with extensive education and research programmes in certain fields (e.g. in physics research, connected with armaments production). This growth model was only sustainable over the short term, whilst the sources of growth (labour, in particular) were abundant. The state-socialist countries, however, failed to effect the transition to the more intensive phase of economic development (Vintrová 1993, p 79). They were not able to 'step over the shadow of central planning' and sustain a level of innovation, which would have been generated by market forces in market economies. Instead, central planning degenerated to complex negotiations amongst different parts of the economic administration, wherein each group sought to secure or protect specific privileges. Dogmatic political control was waning, power shifting to technocrats and professional managers. At the same time, an informal economy emerged, filling some of the gaps caused by the deterioration of the central economy. However, these changes could not remedy the underlying economic weaknesses. By the later 1980s, the centrally planned economies had low growth rates, low capital productivity and increasing internal and external economic imbalances.

The major early experiments in introducing market reforms and democracy (Hungary 1956, Prague Spring 1968, Poland 1981) were crushed by the Soviet Army and domestic quislings. But, by 1989 the Russian ruling classes were no longer able to govern their own country let alone their larger empire. With Soviet military and economic powers in decay, state-socialism disappeared within a few months in Central Europe. A popular saying that 'socialism is just a diversion on the way from capitalism to capitalism' became a reality. But this had different meanings in different countries. As noted earlier, Hungary and Poland – compared to Czechoslovakia – had '... gone, a considerable way, even before the end of 1989, towards dismantling central planning, decentralising enterprise management, and developing markets for intermediate goods' (Fogel and Etcheverry 1994a, p 12).

Before 1939 the former Czechoslovakia had been one of the most developed countries in Europe, although industrial development had been concentrated in the Czech regions. After 1948 a rapid industrialization programme was implemented in Slovakia, partly in order to proletarianize a region previously dominated by peasant agriculture. There was state investment in a number of new enterprises, particularly in the capital goods sectors, oil processing and armament production. But after forty years of central planning, communist ideology and economic and political subordination to the Soviet Union, the country faced relative economic decline by the 1980s, in what were to become the twilight years of state-socialism. While there is no question about the relative economic decline in Czechoslovakia in the 1980s, it is important to realize that its effects were not evident in unemployment or in absolute reductions in living standards. Instead, the latter continued to improve although at rate below that prevalent in Western Europe, especially after 1975. Despite mounting economic difficulties, the state had been able to protect living standards and reduce the income gap between the Czech and Slovak regions, even in the 1980s. This partly explains the relatively cautious Slovak attitudes to radical reforms, for there were real fears that living standards would decline in the transformation. These fears were well based.

At the start of the post-1989 transformation, the Czechoslovakian economy was markedly different to those of Hungary and Poland. Czechoslovakia had become more strongly embedded within the Council of Mutual Economic Assistance (CMEA) than either Poland or Hungary, and was more isolated from global economic shifts (Landesmann and Székely 1995a). Its economy was more dominated by central planning, and there was almost no legal and institutional basis for a market economy. 'Unlike Poland and Hungary, it would have . . . to tackle the complete transformation of a centrally planned economy into a market economy' (Fogel and Etcheverry 1994b, p 37). However, the more rigid adherence of Czechoslovakia to the state-socialist economic model also meant that it entered the transition period with lower inflation and less monetary overhang than the other two countries.

2.3 TOURISM UNDER STATE-SOCIALISM

Czechoslovakia was the most industrialized country in the Eastern block, and the sectors which symbolized this, as well as being the largest contributors to national income, were machinery, metal and oil processing. In contrast, service industries – including tourism – were considered to be of relatively minor importance. This social and political construction of the economy – which was also reflected in its structure to some extent – can only be understood in terms of two main considerations:

1)   There was a long industrial legacy, especially in the Czech part of the republic which had constituted the industrial core of the Austrio-Hungarian empire, and had been the world's tenth largest industrial producer on the eve of the Second World War. After 1948, Czechoslovakia became the leading supplier of (relatively) sophisticated industrial products for the other members of the CMEA, the Eastern European trading block. A large share of industrial production was exported to Western markets – Western Europe alone accounted for some 40 per cent of Czechoslovakia's exports (Federální statistický úřad 1989a).

2) There was an ideological legacy, rooted in the Marxist theory of production. According to this, only the production of material goods could be considered a real and/or efficient form of production. In the service sector, in contrast, only those activities directly supporting the production of goods (including transport) were considered to be productive (see Hall 1984 on the different but relevant experience of Albania).

Tourism was classified as being 'unproductive', that is, as an 'inefficient' activity, and had a low priority in the national development strategy. Instead, during the 1950s and 1960s, tourism was mostly considered to be a social activity. Its main role was conceptualized as being 'to regenerate the labour force' and 'to satisfy the demand for recreation' (Hall 1991a). The nature of that recreation, of course, was supposed to be based on the 'socialist way of life'. Holidays, for example, were to be spent with other members of the worker collective, and a parallel tourist industry was established to serve these needs (Carter 1991; Veyret 1963). Trade-union and company-owned recreation centres were constructed and, by 1985, there were 3147 centres with 61,790 beds; the rapid expansion of these facilities is indicated by the fact that there had been only 1845 centres in 1975. The prices in company-owned tourism facilities were highly subsidized, either directly by the state or indirectly by the parent firms. There was also a parallel commercial tourism sector, the main function of which was to provide low cost holidays for domestic tourists and for visitors from other communist countries. Both the prices and quality of the tourism services were planned with these goals in mind: the outcome was high volumes of nights spent, and modest quality levels.

In terms of economic policy, tourism had been recognized as an industry in its own right in 1963, when the Czechoslovak Government Committee for Tourism was established. Its main functions were to advise on the regulation of the tourism industry and to represent Czechoslovakia on international tourist bodies. When, in 1968, the Czechoslovak Socialist Republic was made a federation, responsibilities for tourism development were transferred to the Czech and Slovak Ministries of Trade (later the Ministries of Trade and Tourism) and the Czech and Slovak Government Committees for Tourism. There was limited decentralization in 1974, when District Tourist Enterprises were established by District Councils, charged with the responsibility for the development of regional tourism infrastructure, sports facilities and information centres. Regional tourism development plans were prepared by the tourism units of the District Councils. Despite their limited financial and personnel resources, they contributed significantly to the creation of a more sophisticated tourism industry in many Czech and Slovak regions.

In the early 1980s, the state-socialist economic system encountered deep-set systemic difficulties (see Section 2.1). Czechoslovakia's basic industries failed to innovate and became less competitive in western markets, so that exports were depressed and there was an acute shortage of convertible currency. Yet, reconstruction of the Czechoslovak industrial base required massive imports of western technology. It was at this stage that tourism began to be viewed as a potential resource for bridging the foreign currency gap, and there was a perceptible shift in its ideological construction. Incoming tourism, generating foreign exchange, was reclassified as 'productive' rather than 'unproductive' This was significant because, in the centrally planned economy, the allocation of both investment and personnel resources was determined by the priorities established by the central Communist Party. There was investment in new hotels, particularly in Prague. By the late 1980s, limited foreign capital participation in hotel construction was even permitted, through joint ventures, although these were far less common than in Poland or Hungary (Hall 1991b, p 64). However, the Czechoslovak regime, considered the most rigid in the Eastern block, was unable to 'step over its own shadow', for a large influx of western tourists would be a conduit not only for foreign exchange, but also for liberal and market economy ideologies. This highlighted the production and ideological contradictions which persisted in the economy down to 1989.

The XVIth General Meeting of the Czechoslovak Communist Party (XVI. zjazd Komunistickej strany Československa 1981) had set out priorities for tourism development:

a) development of mass sport and tourist activities, with the aim of regenerating the labour force;
b) promotion of friendship between nations;
c) generation of foreign exchange, particularly in the spa and transit tourism sectors;
d) improved utilization of hotel, restaurant and spa facilities;
e) development of more sophisticated tourism services.

A number of tourism policy instruments were designed to achieve these goals:

a) price regulation linked to the goals of social policy;
b) promotion and information activities;
c) regulations and administrative measures;
d) infrastructure development;
e) vocational training;
f) tourism research and planning.

Some of these instruments were contradictory. For example, the regime invested substantially in marketing abroad in order to attract more foreign tourists, and the expenditure on marketing abroad (Kč 14.95 million) in 1989 was far higher than it would be in the early transition years – being

21

only Kč 8.56 million in 1992. Yet the insistence that Western tourists should make a compulsory minimum daily amount of foreign exchange was highly unpopular, fostering the image of a greedy and unwelcoming destination. This depressed tourism foreign exchange receipts which were less than one-seventh the level that would be realized by 1992 under transition conditions. Social policy considerations also contradicted the goal of maximizing foreign exchange. In 1976–80, for example, the Tourism Fund spent Kčs 810 million on tourism infrastructure development, marketing, information and related activities (Medved 1984), which far exceeded the corresponding state expenditure in the 1990s. Yet the resultant poor quality services in cheap hotels, constructed primarily for domestic tourism and for foreign tourists from other state-socialist countries, did not match the expectations of Western tourists.

The volume and structure of tourist flows to and from Czechoslovakia in this period were mostly determined by political considerations (see Hall 1991a, p 89 for the comparable experience of Poland). Visitors from Western countries accounted for only 5 per cent of total flows. Tourist exchanges with three neighbouring state-socialist countries (the German Democratic Republic, Poland and Hungary) alone accounted for 90 per cent of all flows. While the economic objective of increasing convertible currency receipts was given priority in West–East exchanges, ideological priorities informed the intra-Eastern block exchanges. These were to 'promote international friendship' and a 'better understanding of brother nations'. In practice, tourism policies diverged from these ideals. After the Solidarity movement had secured a position of real political power in Poland, the Czechoslovak authorities imposed complex barriers on travel to that country, and the need to develop a 'better understanding of brother nations' was set aside. Instead, a system of special permissions was introduced for trips to Poland, so that after 1982 such tourism exchanges were severely reduced (Figure 2.1).

Administrative barriers were also utilized to limit tourist exchanges with Western countries (see Böröcz 1990 for the comparable experience of Hungary). For example, every potential traveller had to apply to the Czechoslovak State Bank for a foreign exchange allowance. There were no transparent or equitable criteria for allocating such allowances, and few applicants were successful. Moreover, securing such an allowance represented only the first step in a formidable series of travel barriers. A potential traveller to the West had to obtain seven recommendations on his/her reliability from the local committee of the Communist Party, the army, the police and other bodies. There were also visa barriers to be overcome for, with the exception of Finland, there were no free-travel agreements with Western countries. This sophisticated system of travel barriers effectively torpedoed the 1975 Helsinki Agreement which was supposed to guarantee free travel in Europe.

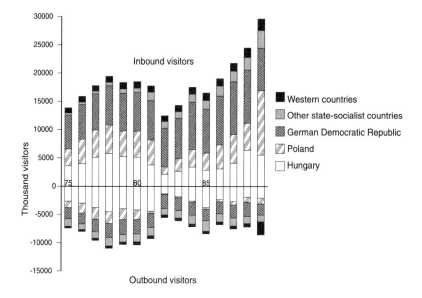

Fig. 2.1: Inbound and outbound travellers at the frontiers of the Czechoslovak Socialist Republic in 1975–89.
Source: Federální statistický úřad (1986–1993).

To what extent can state-socialist tourism policy be judged to have been successful? In terms of its contribution to the international tourism account, the assessment is positive. In the late 1980s, tourism foreign exchange earnings increased rapidly. Tourist inflows were far larger than outflows (Figure 2.1), and the system of administrative controls ensured there was a positive balance in exchanges with Western countries. The volume of foreign exchange allocated to travel to Western countries was determined centrally and planned in advance, usually being set at a level equal to about one-quarter of the expected income from foreign tourism (Figure 2.2). However, the total volume of convertible currency income was relatively low. Tourist exchanges with other state-socialist countries generated considerable foreign exchange, but not in widely convertible currencies. Not surprisingly, travel intensity (expressed in the terms of nights abroad per domestic resident) was only 1.6 in 1988, while the same ratio was 11.9 for Austria, 3.3 for the UK, and 6.3 for France. The Czechoslovak ratio was

23

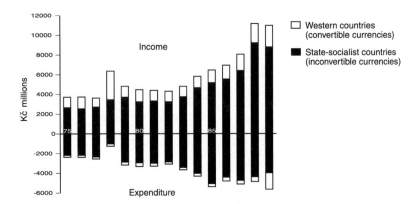

Fig. 2.2: International tourism income and expenditure in the Czechoslovak Socialist Republic in 1975–89.
Source: Ministerstvo obchodu a cestovného ruchu Slovenskej republiky (1990).

close to that of Portugal (1.8) in 1989, even though the latter was relatively isolated, geographically.

A critical assessment of state-socialist tourism policy is not entirely negative. There was virtually universal access to holidays in domestic tourism establishments, although the service levels in these were relatively modest. This was one of the first features of domestic tourism to be threatened during the transition to a market economy.

2.4 THE ECONOMIC TRANSITION AND TOURISM

As discussed in Chapter 1, the sharp-shock economic reforms were based on a particular version of liberal capitalism, with four main constituents: market liberalization, privatization, currency convertibility, and trade liberalization. The new economic model was a neo-liberal construction based as much on ideals as the actual practices of economic management in Western Europe. Moreover, the model was implemented with only scant regard to domestic and international economic realities. Yet there were critical variations in the strategies adopted in different countries, reflecting economic and political circumstances in each country, and the distribution of interests and power between the state, civil society and individual economic agents. There were also differences in the speed of the shock therapy. Poland and Hungary had some previous, if selective, experience of the market economy, and had functioning if limited private sectors. In contrast, the private sector was virtually absent in Czechoslovakia where it was argued that, therefore, there was a need for very rapid transformation. After the parliamentary election in June 1990, the new Parliament agreed a fun-

24

damental economic and social strategy, 'The Scenario of Economic Reform'. This was prepared by V. Klaus, who later became the Czech Prime Minister, and it was strongly rooted in neo-liberal ideology. The document set out milestones for achieving price liberalization, tight monetary policy, balanced budgets, currency convertibility, trade liberalization and privatization within a period of one to two years. Although these proved unrealistic, they established the framework for the transformation.

2.4.1 The first phase of economic and social transition (1990–93)

The years 1990–93 constituted one of the most difficult periods in Czech and Slovak history. With the start of the economic transformation, gross domestic product decreased by 2.6 per cent in Slovakia and 1.2 per cent in the Czech Republic in 1990. This was only a foretaste of the catastrophic declines of 16.2 per cent and 14.2 per cent in 1991 (Table 2.1). The relatively small decline in GDP in 1990 was mainly the outcome of changes in the external environment, such as the disintegration of CMEA trade and the Gulf War. In contrast, the sharp decrease in 1991 originated in three main considerations: the final collapse of CMEA, price liberalization and tight monetary policy, which accounted for about one-third each of the overall decrease. The economic transition demanded substantial industrial restructuring and several important industries went into decline. As a result, in the early 1990s services took over from manufacturing the mantle of the leading economic sector – as measured in terms of contribution to GDP (Table 2.1). Tourism played an important role in this sectoral shift.

During 1990 there were two devaluations of the Czechoslovakian currency, the koruna (Kč). In October, the exchange rate against the dollar fell from 16 to 23 Kč, while in December it was further reduced to 29 Kč. The devaluations and increases in selected regulated prices pushed the inflation rate to 9.6 per cent. While historically high, inflation was still considerably lower than in other transition economies. However, devaluation (which of course made Czechoslovakia more attractive to foreign tourists) and the introduction of import surcharges had positive effects on the trade balance. New markets were explored in Western Europe to replace those lost after the collapse of the CMEA. This re-internationalization of trade was given a new institutional framework in December 1991, when Czechoslovakia, Hungary and Poland signed association agreements with the European Union. Meanwhile, in 1992 a Central Europe Free Trade Agreement (CEFTA) was signed in Krakow. These agreements helped to improve international trade with the EU countries and amongst the transition economies (Williams *et al* 1998). In 1992, Czechoslovakia had a negative trade balance of Kč 45.3 billion, but this was offset of by a positive balance in internationally traded services, to which tourism made an important contribution. The aggregate trade statistics are somewhat flattering because they conceal significant shifts in the composition of exports: the shares of technology and machinery declined, whilst the shares of raw material and intermediate goods increased.

Czechoslovak economic policy in this period prioritized a sound macroeconomic environment over economic growth. The main goals – reduced inflation and a low budget deficit – were achieved in 1991 and 1992. However, a high price was paid for this in the realm of production, particularly in Slovakia. Armament production (see Smith 1994) was particularly severely affected and in this case the impacts of changes in international trade were intensified by poorly conceived conversion programmes. Moreover, rapidly rising levels of unemployment fanned anti-Prague resentment in Slovakia, as did the fact that 93 per cent of foreign investment in 1992 had been in the Czech Republic. While both republics' economies were disrupted by the division, the effects were more marked in Slovakia.

The first phase of transition brought two new and unwelcome developments for the Czechs and Slovaks – rising unemployment and inflation. In state-socialist Czechoslovakia, unemployment did not officially exist, although there was significant overemployment, informally estimated to be around 10-15 per cent. The decline in industrial output led to rapid increases in unemployment. Whereas the secondary sector accounted for almost two-thirds of GDP in 1984, its share had been reduced to 40 per cent by 1993. De-industrialization was accompanied by an increase in the relative and absolute importance of the service sector, including tourism. The removal of central planning forced enterprises to create, or collaborate with, trade and marketing firms, seek out business services, and rely on financial service providers to a much higher level and in more complex ways than had been the case before 1989; Smith (1995) conceptualizes this in terms of mercantile capitalism. Industrial restructuring created new jobs in the service sector in general, and in the above-mentioned branches in particular (Tables 2.1 and 2.2). The labour force shed from state-owned heavy industries was partly absorbed by service firms in the private sector. However, total employment continued to decline, and the impacts of unemployment were socially and territorially differentiated (Williams and Baláž 1999). Several regions in southern and eastern Slovakia had unemployment rates in excess of 20 per cent.

Prices had been stable in state-socialist Czechoslovakia due to prudent macroeconomic policies and strong price controls. Consumer prices rose by only about 1–2 per cent per annum on average. Even as late as 1990, about 85 per cent of GDP was price regulated, but most prices were deregulated after January 1st 1991. This generated monthly price leaps of 25.8 per cent and 20.8 per cent, respectively, in what were to become Slovakia and the Czech Republic. The total 1991 increase in consumer prices was 61.1 per

TABLE 2.1   *Major features of GDP in Slovakia and the Czech Republic, 1985–97*

	1985	1990	1991	1992	1993	1994	1995	1996	1997
					Slovakia				
GDP (US$ billion)[2]	6.78	8.16	10.21	9.95	11.22	14.11	17.42	18.22	18.80
GDP per capita (US$)[3]	1,313	1,539	1,933	1,874	2,099	2,638	3,248	3,387	3,490
GDP annual growth (%)	4.0	−2.6	−16.2	−6.3	−3.7	4.9	6.8	6.9	6.5
Sectoral share (%):									
Primary[4]	6.4	7.4	5.7	5.6	7.3	7.5	5.6	5.2	n.a.
Secondary[5]	61.5	59.1	60.1	54.3	39.7	37.3	38.8	40.9	n.a.
Tertiary[6]	32.0	33.5	34.2	40.1	53.0	55.2	61.2	53.9	n.a.
Privatized GDP:									
% of total GDP[7]	0	5	27	32	39	58	63	77	83
					Czech Republic				
GDP (US$ billion)[2]	16.1	19.0	25.1	28.4	31.2	42.7	49.7	54.9	47.6
GDP per capita (US$)[3]	1,556	1,833	2,438	2,754	3,024	4,130	4,812	5,314	4,624
GDP growth (%)	0.1	−1.2	−14.2	−7.1	0.0	2.6	4.8	4.4	1.0
Sectoral share									
Primary[4]	6.9	7.2	5.6	5.1	5.2	5.8	5.2	5.0	n.a.
Secondary[5]	60.0	58.3	61.3	42.9	43.0	40.7	41.4	40.6	n.a.
Tertiary[6]	33.1	34.5	33.1	52.0	51.8	53.5	53.4	54.4	n.a.
Privatized GDP:									
% of total GDP[7]	0	5	9	28	45	56	64	80	85

Sources: Štatistický úrad Slovenskej republiky (1994–1998); Štatistický úrad Slovenskej republiky (1991–1998c), Národná banka Slovenska (1993–1998a), (1993–1998b) and (1993–1998c); Český statistický úřad (1993–1998a) and (1993–1998b).
Notes: 1 = end of period; 2 = in the period 1948–1992 the Material Product System was used. Data for 1980–1992 were recalculated from the MPS (National Income) to the System of National Accounts (the GDP system); all data are in current prices; 3 = computed via exchange rates; 4 = includes agriculture, forestry and fishing; 5 = industry (including mining and quarrying and water, power and gas supply) and construction; 6 = services and other items (including indirect taxes); 7 = all enterprises where the state stake is less than 50%. Data for 1997 were preliminary; n.a. = not available.

cent (Table 2.3). Price inflation effectively devalued the savings of most of the population. Tight monetary and fiscal policies subsequently brought inflation under control but the reduction in real savings could not be reversed, and this had significant implications for domestic tourism (see the budget indicators in Table 2.3).

Privatization was a key element in the sharp shock model of economic transition. In 1991–3, two privatization programs were completed. The Small Privatization programme was based on public auctions. Almost 10

TABLE 2.2   *Employment and wages in Slovakia and the Czech Republic, 1985–97*

	1985	1990	1991	1992	1993	1994	1995	1996	1997
					Slovakia				
Unemployment rate (%)[1]	0.0	1.5	7.0	11.7	12.9	14.6	13.8	12.8	13.0
Employment (in thousands)[2,3]	2,425	2,459	2,152	2,040	2,118	2,096	2,138	2,014	2,194
Sectoral distribution (%):									
Primary[4]	15.4	13.6	12.3	12.1	9.4	10.2	9.4	8.6	8.6
Secondary[5]	45.4	44.1	44.0	39.2	37.8	36.9	36.5	35.9	39.2
Tertiary[6]	39.2	42.3	43.7	48.7	52.8	52.9	54.1	55.5	52.2
Average monthly wage, Sk[7,9]	2,920	3,286	3,792	4,530	5,380	6,285	7,195	8,154	9,226
Average monthly wage, US$	95.5	109.8	132.1	151.0	163.2	222.1	243.3	255.6	265.1
					Czech Republic				
Unemployment rate (%)[1]	0	0.7	4.1	3.1	3.6	3.2	3.1	3.5	5.2
Employment (in thousands)[2]	5,267	5,351	5,059	4,927	4,853	4,885	5,012	5,126	5,117
Sectoral distribution (%):									
Primary[4]	12.0	11.8	10.0	8.6	6.8	7.0	6.3	6.0	5.7
Secondary[5]	47.1	45.4	46.5	44.8	44.6	42.2	43.5	41.0	41.0
Tertiary[6]	40.9	42.8	43.5	46.6	48.6	50.8	50.3	53.1	53.3
Average monthly wage, Kč[7,8]	2,920	3,286	3,792	4,644	5,817	6,893	8,172	9,676	10,834
Average monthly wage, US$	97.3	110.0	133.0	164.3	199.5	257.4	307.9	356.5	308.8

Sources: Štatistický úrad Slovenskej republiky (1994–1998); Štatistický úrad Slovenskej republiky (1991–1998c), Národná banka Slovenska (1993–1998a), (1993–1998b) and (1993–1998c); Český statistický úřad (1993–1998a) and (1993–1998b).
Notes: 1 = end of period; 2 = includes self-employment; 3 = end of period; 4 = agriculture, forestry and fishing; 5 = mining and quarrying, water, power and gas supply, manufacturing and construction; 6 = services and other items; 7 = period average; 8 = for 1985–1992 data are in Kčs. The data for 1997 are preliminary.

thousand retail units, restaurants and small enterprises were sold to domestic investors. Meanwhile, in the first wave of the *Large Privatization*, vouchers were used to distribute state property more widely amongst the population. Foreign investors were not allowed to participate in either of these privatizations (see Williams *et al* 1998). There is, however, evidence that many domestic investors and investment privatization funds were

TABLE 2.3 *Inflation and the budgetary balance in Slovakia and the Czech Republic, 1985–97*

	1985	1990	1991	1992	1993	1994	1995	1996	1997
				Slovakia					
Inflation rate (%)[1,2]	2.2	9.7	61.1	10.0	25.6	13.4	9.9	5.8	6.4
Budget balance: US$ million[3,4]	x	−15.7	−358.8	−280.2	−698.2	−730.6	−280.7	−801.2	−1065.4
Percentage of GDP	x	−0.19	−3.51	−2.82	−6.22	−5.18	−1.61	−4.40	−5.7
				Czech Republic					
Inflation rate (%)[1,2]	2.3	9.7	56.7	11.1	20.8	10.0	9.1	8.8	8.5
Budget balance: US$ million[3,4]	x	20	−537	−59.7	37.7	361.4	271.3	−55.3	−453.3
Percentage of GDP	x	0.1	−2.1	−0.2	0.1	1.0	0.6	−0.1	−1.0

Sources: Štatistický úrad Slovenskej republiky (1994–1998); Štatistický úrad Slovenskej republiky (1991–1998c), Národná banka Slovenska (1993–1998a), (1993–1998b) and (1993–1998c); Český statistický úřad (1993–1998a) and (1993–1998b).
Notes: 1 = consumer price index; 2 = end of period; 3 = includes the balance of central and local government and social funds; 4 = for the period 1985–1992, only the budgets of (what were to become) the Slovak and Czech Republics are considered, and the balance of the Czechoslovak federal budget was not taken into account; the data for 1997 are preliminary.

backed by foreign capital. Despite numerous difficulties, widespread fraud, and lack of experience amongst purchasers, these programmes were to be the cornerstones for the creation of the private sector – as is evident in the data on both GDP and employment.

The sharp-shock strategy created a relatively sound macroeconomic background for the latter phase of the economic transition. However, its social consequences were controversial. Rising unemployment and inflation rates, especially in Slovakia, generated considerable popular resentment. Decreases in living standards were also exploited by some populist politicians, and were instrumental in the 'velvet divorce' between the Czech and Slovak Republics in 1993, although it should be noted that the division of Czechoslovakia was imposed by the federal parliament, without the plebiscite which had been promised. The social frustration resulting from the social and economic difficulties of the transition also provided a background for undemocratic practices by the Slovak government after 1993.

Tourism in the first phase of transition

Macroeconomic developments influenced tourism in Czechoslovakia in two different ways. In international tourism, devaluation of the Kčs in 1990, the signing of economic and tourism agreements with the EU countries, and market economy reforms opened the way for an influx of foreign visitors. Privatization and the establishment of literally thousands of new tourism businesses also improved the supply of tourism services. Czechoslovakia became an attractive and low-cost destination. Whilst 29.6 million foreign visitors came to Czechoslovakia in 1989, 71.7 million visitors came to the Czech Republic and 12.9 millions to the Slovak Republic by 1993. International tourism receipts increased sharply and their share of GDP increased from 0.4 per cent in 1989 to 3.5 per cent in 1993 in Slovakia, and from 0.7 per cent to 5.0 per cent in the Czech Republic (Table 5.1). As discussed later, in policy terms international tourism ceased to be seen as an annex to production and was recognized as a dynamic sector of the national economy in both countries. International tourism receipts had a major role in offsetting trade balance deficits and improving international currency reserves in this period.

When the independent Czech and Slovak Republic were established in 1993, international tourism balances provided for 27 per cent of National Bank reserves. The domestic economy, however, experienced a deep recession. Sharp cuts in living standards inevitably reduced domestic tourism expenditure (see Chapter 7). Real incomes declined more in Slovakia than in the Czech Republic, and this was reflected in the relative levels of domestic tourism activity.

2.4.2 The second phase of transition (1993–7)

The Slovak Republic

The Slovak Republic came into being on 1 January 1993 and immediately faced a number of economic challenges. The Czechoslovak currency union was to be short-lived, and Slovakia introduced its own currency. As early as March 1993, the Slovak government – in the face of declining exports and foreign confidence – devalued the Slovak koruna (Sk) by 10 per cent. Devaluation and an import surcharge further boosted the 1993 inflation rate to 25.6 per cent. Nevertheless, these measures also had positive results. After 1993 exports rose rapidly (Table 2.4), leading to significant output growth. In 1994, GDP grew by 4.9 per cent, marking a sharp turn around from the continuous decline over the previous four years. In the course of re-internationalization, the EU became Slovakia's main export market. Export-led growth was replaced by domestic consumption-led growth in 1995, and investment and state consumption-led growth in 1996. Most of the success in macroeconomic stabilization can be ascribed to the prudent monetary policies of the National Bank of Slovakia. By the end of 1996 the inflation rate had fallen to 5.8 percent and increased only slightly in the following year. The tight monetary policies of the National Bank, in the period 1994–1997, meant that the Slovak inflation rate was the lowest amongst the transition countries.

Privatization continued apace and, in 1996, the second wave of the Large Privatization programme was completed, with the sale of some 300 enterprises. The direct sales of enterprises to national 'government-friendly' investors also came to and end, not least because of the lack of transparency, the exclusion of foreign participants, and the massive discounts secured by 'friendly' interest groups had been heavily criticised both in Slovakia and abroad.

In 1996 and 1997 Slovakian growth continued but with marked imbalances. High levels of state expenditure on infrastructure conflicted with the tight monetary policy of the National Bank, and there were acute capital shortages, particularly in the private sector. At the same time, the poor reputation of the Slovak government deterred potential foreign investors, so that the level of FDI per capita (Table 2.4) was the lowest in Central Europe (Williams et al 1998). High interest rates on the money and capital markets (inter-bank rates reached 30 per cent in 1997) also dampened private sector expansion, and contributed to the unbalanced growth. Rising wages and interest rates were reflected in increasing production costs, and reduced competitiveness amongst Slovak exporters. Together with high levels of domestic consumption, this generated a massive trade deficit equivalent to 11.1 per cent of GDP in 1996. In the same period, high levels of government spending created a major budget deficit (Table 2.3). The combination of trade and budgetary deficits threatened future economic development. As a result, an import surcharge was imposed in 1997 which helped to dampen imports and reduce the trade deficit to 7.7 per cent of GDP by the end of that year.

There were impressive growth rates in this period (6.5 per cent in 1997) but these were unbalanced, being led by domestic private consumption and state fixed investment. Structural reforms in 1994–6 had an effect on the restructuring of GDP; some 52 per cent of the 1996 increase was generated by small enterprises in the wholesaling, retailing and repair sectors, and this was fuelled by domestic demand growth. Industrial production, on the other hand, grew more slowly, except for basic metals and transport equipment. The tertiary sector became dominant, and the share of manufacturing decreased to levels comparable to the Organization for Economic Co-operation and Development (OECD) countries. In both 1996 and 1997, the GDP growth was achieved by increasing material inputs with lower levels of value added (Okáli et al 1997).

The economic boom in 1994–7 was mainly evident in production, but

TABLE 2.4   *The external economic relations of Slovakia and the Czech Republic, 1993–7*

	1993	1994	1995	1996	1997
	Slovakia				
Trade balance, US$ million	−828	130	60	−2,023	−1,424.6
Percentage of GDP	−7.4	0.9	0.3	−11.1	−7.7
Current account, US$ million	−522	729	652	−1,865	−1,297
Percentage of GDP	−4.7	5.2	3.7	−10.2	−6.9
Foreign currency reserves, US$ billion[2]	0.5	1.7	3.4	3.5	3.5
Total foreign debt, US$ million[3]	3,682	4,285	4,770	7,800	9,896
Percentage of GDP	32.8	30.4	27.4	42.8	52.6
Total foreign direct investment, US$ billion[4]	326.3	528.3	740.0	1,326.2	1,511.2
Total FDI in US$ per capita	61.0	98.8	138.0	246.5	280.5
FDI as percentage of GDP	2.9	3.7	4.2	7.3	8.0
	Czech Republic				
Trade balance, US$ million	80	−769	−3,606	−5,810	−4,065.1
Percentage of GDP	0.3	−1.8	−7.3	−10.6	−8.6
Current account, US$ million	114.6	−49.0	−1,362.3	−4,475.8	−3,155.8
Percentage of GDP	0.4	−0.1	−2.7	−8.2	−6.1
Foreign currency reserves, US$ billion[2]	3.8	6.1	14.0	12.4	9.8
Total foreign debt, US$ million[3]	8,500	10,700	16,550	20,410	21,400
Percentage of GDP	27.2	29.5	33.3	37.2	44.9
Total foreign direct investment, US$ million[4]	2,102.6	3,215.1	5,807.0	7,106.3	6,844.6
Total FDI in US$ per capita	203.6	311.1	562.1	687.9	664.6
FDI as percentage of GDP	6.7	7.5	11.7	12.9	14.4

Sources: Štatistický úrad Slovenskej republiky (1994–1998); Štatistický úrad Slovenskej republiky (1991–1998c), Národná banka Slovenska (1993–1998a), (1993–1998b) and (1993–1998c); Český statistický úřad (1993–1998a) and (1993–1998b).

Notes: 1 = consolidated balance, including non-convertible currencies; 2 = reserves of the National Bank at end of period; 3 = debt guaranteed by the state and the National Bank of Slovakia (Czech National Bank) and debts of commercial banks and private enterprises. Data for 1997 were preliminary; 4 = cumulative sum, end of period. FDI is primarily calculated in Kč and then re-calculated to US$. Shifts in the exchange rate between the Kč and US$ caused a nominal decrease of absolute volume of FDI despite a real increase of US$ 1275.2 million in 1997.

did help to reduce unemployment. Rapid economic growth helped to generate new jobs. These were mainly in the service sector (Table 2.2), and in small enterprises (with less than 25 employees). The overall unemployment rate decreased to 12.8 per cent in 1996, rising slightly to 13.0 per cent in 1997. There were also some improvements in long-term unemployment rates, and some amelioration of regional disparities: the number of Slovak districts with unemployment rates exceeding 15 per cent decreased from 18 to 11 in the same period. However, there were persistent regional disparities. While the major industrial centres (Bratislava, Košice, Žilina) enjoyed low levels of unemployment, the rural and peripheral districts in the east and south experienced further employment decline and net outmigration.

The economic transformation has also been influenced by external conditions, and more specifically by price/wage differences in neighbouring more-developed economies. Most exports from transition economies are channelled to developed ones, and there is also considerable labour movement to these via either commuting or legal/illegal migration, As a result of such cross border movements, there have been convergence tendencies; wages and prices have been forced up in Slovakia and, to a far lesser extent, have been depressed in the adjoining regions in Germany and Austria. In addition, since 1993 the exchange rate between the Sk and the US$/DM has been broadly stable, because the Sk has been pegged to a currency basket (60 per cent DM and 40 per cent US$). Therefore, all increases in Slovak prices automatically generated a revaluation of the Slovak currency. Imports from Germany and Austria became cheaper but Slovak exporters were adversely affected. While Slovak imports rose by 20.8 per cent, exports rose only by 2.5 per cent in 1996. The introduction of import surcharges in 1997 belatedly helped to narrow the trade deficit.

The widely publicized undemocratic practices of the Slovak government and corrupt privatization practices deterred foreign investors and FDI was very low (Table 2.4). Most foreign investment was concentrated in Bratislava (63.7 per cent by 1996), and in the car, metals and chemicals sectors. After 1995, the share of FDI and loans in total capital inflows decreased relative to short-term capital deposits of a speculative nature. This helped the National Bank of Slovakia to build impressive international currency reserves but, on the other hand, the commercial sector borrowed large volumes of short-term loans from abroad, so that the total national debt increased to US$ 10 billion by the end of 1997.

The economic recovery in this second period of the transformation was, of course, generally beneficial to tourism. The recovery in domestic household expenditure and the devaluation of the currency improved demand conditions. However, foreign investment continued to be deterred by the political climate, and there were still high if relatively stable levels of unemployment. In addition, the high level of government spending on infrastructure contributed to a capital shortage and a rise in interest rates (30 per cent on government bonds) which affected the other sectors of the economy. Small and medium-sized enterprises were affected, because they often lacked their own sources of capital and found it too expensive to borrow from commercial sources. This, of course, had an impact on tourism, where the large numbers of small and medium-sized enterprise had to rely on shadow economy sources of capital. Arguably, therefore, investment in hotels and other tourism facilities was one of the victims of the financial market repercussions of high levels of state expenditure on infrastructure such as new motorways.

The Czech Republic

There were high expectations of economic growth in 1993, the first year of the independent existence of the Czech Republic, but these were only partly fulfilled. While foreign trade with Western economies stimulated economic growth, devaluation of the Slovak currency (providing a competitive advantage for Slovakia) depressed Czech export potential to an important trading partners. Recession in the main EU markets and the costs of establishing an independent state also impacted negatively on the economy. By 1994 there were signs of recovery. While growth was lower than in some transition economies, it was based on sounder macroeconomic fundamentals of a low inflation rate and a limited budget deficit. The main sources of growth were private consumption (accounting for about 60 per cent of total growth), fixed investment and exports. In terms of industrial structure, the major increases in output were in the service sector.

Privatization continued throughout this period and had largely been finished by 1995. The Czech government completed the planned Second Wave of the Coupon Privatization and made a number of sales to foreign and domestic investors; tenders and direct sales were the preferred methods. The Czech economy became one of the most privatized in Central and Eastern Europe. The Czech government, unlike the Slovak one, tried to project the image of a transparent privatization environment, with equitable access for all types of investors. In 1997, however, this image was severely damaged by disclosures concerning the illegal contributions made by privatizing interest groups to the ruling party.

Since 1990 the Czech Republic has enjoyed the lowest unemployment rate in Europe. This is in sharp contrast to the experiences of the other transition economies, including Slovakia, where unemployment was well above the EU average (see Williams and Baláž 1999). Location and accessibility contributed to this, as is evident in the regional distribution. Other than in Prague, unemployment rates were lowest in Western and Southern Bohemia. Commuting to Germany and Austria became commonplace in these border regions, and business ties also existed across the frontiers; in short, they enjoyed the competitive advantages of relatively low wages and production costs combined with access to product markets. These regions also have relatively diverse production structures, including tourism. In contrast, Northern Bohemia and Northern Moravia had severe problems related to declining mining activity and severe accumulated environmental problems. These regions had the highest unemployment rates in the Czech Republic.

By 1995 there was strong economic recovery, and GDP growth of 4.8 per cent was recorded; growth was mostly generated in the manufacturing sector, and construction and fixed investment became the most rapidly expanding elements of GDP. Fixed investment alone accounted for 45 per cent of the 1995 increase in GDP, and private consumption for 55 per cent (Šujan 1996) (Tables 2.1 and 2.2). The fixed investments sucked in imports, and the trade deficit exceeded Kč 100 billion (US$ 3.3 billion). As in Slovakia, there was little improvement in the structure of trade, which remained highly dependent on low value-added goods. The trade deficit was partly offset by the positive balance on the service sector account, including tourism, and the total current account deficit was only Kč 50.2 billion. Reducing inflation proved more difficult than expected due to an influx of foreign capital, high rates of GDP growth and increases in nominal wages. This was despite conservative monetary and fiscal policies which had produced a budget surplus by the end of the year.

The second phase of economic transition in the Czech republic witnessed significant changes in foreign investment. In 1990–92, official loans provided by the World Bank and International Monetary Fund (IMF) to the Czechoslovak government accounted for a major share of total foreign investment. The loans were mainly used for stabilizing the exchange rate and to support the central bank's international currency reserves. After 1993 foreign investment became more diversified in favour of FDI and the private sector. A number of FDIs were carried out as part of the privatization process, via direct sales of Czech enterprises from the National Property Fund portfolio or via portfolio purchases on the Prague Stock Exchange. German and USA capital were of major importance. Large volumes of foreign capital helped to finance some fixed investments but, most of all, the international currency reserves. In 1995, for example, the total Czech National Bank reserves exceeded 30 per cent of GDP.

The GDP growth rate fell in 1996. A 12.4 per cent increase in fixed investment was the main growth factor, followed by an increase in domestic private consumption. Exports grew more slowly and the trade deficit increased to US$ 5.8 billion. Only about a third of this deficit was covered by a surplus on international traded services. The main causes of the slow-down in exports were recession in Germany and revaluation of the Kč (which had been pegged to a DM/US$ currency basket since 1993), so that the price competitiveness of Czech goods against the DM worsened by 8 per cent in 1996.

There were only minor reductions in inflation due to the pressures in the private consumption sector. In 1996 the Czech government increased several regulated prices, but nominal household income increased by 19 per cent and real wages by 8 per cent. Real prices grew three times more than labour productivity in this period (Hájek 1997). As a result of the trade deficit, covered mainly by short-term loans, considerable speculative capital was attracted. In 1996 the Czech National Bank widened the floating rate of the Kč to 7.5 per cent and this deterred speculative short-term capital flows, so that the international currency reserves of the central Bank fell. The Czech government followed a prudent budget policy and there was only a minor deficit in the government budget. The unemployment rate increased to 3.5 per cent, but remained low in comparison to other European countries – both in the east and the west.

1997 proved to be a more difficult year, and the GDP growth rate fell to just one per cent due to: declining domestic demand, an absolute decrease in fixed investment, monetary turbulence resulting from the transition from a fixed to a floating exchange rate, and disastrous flooding in the late Spring. The current account deficit fell but remained relatively high being equivalent to 6.5 per cent of GDP. Real wages still outstripped labour productivity growth, but the gap between these rates narrowed. At first, the gains in real income had a positive influence on tourism spending, but individual travel plans were disrupted by the floods.

In previous years, the pegging of the Czech currency to the US$ and the DM had been affected by unfavourable movements in their exchange rates. Most imports were paid for in US$ (Russian oil and gas, in particular), while exports were mainly channelled to Germany. Increases in the US$ purchasing power against the DM made Czech imports more expensive, while exports became less competitive. This depressed enterprise profitability and, consequently, the taxation revenues accruing to the state. In addition, the combination of an influx of speculative capital and inflation overvalued the Czech koruna. By May, the Czech National Bank could not resist further attacks on the currency, so that the koruna was floated and devalued by 10 per cent. Meanwhile the decline in productivity and exports in the first half of 1997 had pushed the unemployment rate to 5 per cent, the highest level since 1989. Despite this, the IMF still criticized Czech enterprises for overemployment (Dostálová 1997). However, exports recovered in the second half of 1997 assisted by the devaluation, the economic boom in Western Europe, and the increase in production resulting from the earlier high level of fixed investment.

Tourism and the second stage of transition

While there were major increases in international tourism in the first phase, the second phase brought more positive results for domestic tourism. The

36

economic recovery after 1993 brought about improvements in living standards and, as a result, increasing tourism expenditure in both Republics (see Chapter 7). Improvements in living standards were more marked in the Czech Republic than in Slovakia, and this was mirrored in higher growth in domestic tourist nights. In the period 1993–6, the numbers of nights spent increased almost threefold from 7.8 to 23.1 million in the Czech Republic and almost doubled from 2.9 to 5.0 million in Slovakia.

The development of business and foreign trade with the EU, and within CEFTA, helped to increase both the volumes of business travel and international tourism receipts. By 1997 the share of these receipts in GDP had increased to 7.7 per cent in the Czech Republic and 2.9 per cent in Slovakia (Table 5.1). The Czech share of official receipts was one of the highest amongst the OECD. If the estimated actual receipts (considered to be 2.5 times larger than those computed by the National Banks – see Chapters 3 and 5) of at least US$ 13 billion are taken into account, this share could have been as high as 27 per cent of GDP. The shares of tourism receipts in exports were also unusually high in comparison to the OECD countries. Tourism became increasingly important for both countries as a source of international currency and for employment generation. The share of the hotel and restaurant sector in total employment, for example, increased from 1.3 per cent to 1.8 per cent in Slovakia, and from 2.0 to 3.2 per cent in the Czech Republic.

While there were large increases in fixed investment after 1994, the tourism sector was not a major beneficiary of this. The reported shares of the hotel and restaurant sector in total investment were lower than their shares in total value added and employment. This can be explained by three factors. First, privatization converted large numbers of state-socialist non-commercial tourism facilities to commercial use, and the supply of tourism services was sufficient to match demand without extensive new investment. Second, the Czech and Slovak Republics have had a strong industrial tradition. After initial decreases in 1990-3, the share of the secondary sector in total GDP stabilized and manufacturing has retained an important role in both national economies. Manufacturing, power supply, financial services and telecommunications attracted most new investment after 1993. Third, much of the construction work in small businesses and the tourism industry tended to occur in the shadow economy, so that real investment outlays were probably far higher than reported.

The Czech and Slovak tourism balances made a major contribution to the National Banks' reserves in 1990-3. With the increasing influx of foreign capital, the role of tourism decreased but remained important. After speculators attacked the Czech currency in 1997, the Czech National Bank's reserves fell dramatically due to major outflows of short-term capital, so that tourism receipts regained some of their former prominence. For example, the tourism balance of US$ 1267.3 million generated 12.9 per cent of the official Czech reserves in 1997.

2.5 TOURISM POLICIES DURING TRANSITION

2.5.1 Tourism policies and the state

There are a number of reasons why the state does not leave tourism to the actions and decision-making of individual tourism capitals. The most significant of these is that individual capitals can not guarantee the conditions for the reproduction of the tourism industry. In addition, the economic and social logic of state intervention in tourism is reinforced by cultural and environmental considerations, relating to the differences between individual and collective costs and benefits. Both the logic and the form of state intervention in tourism have changed over time in response to local, national and global considerations.

There have been at least five distinct phases in the evolution of state tourism policies since 1945 in the capitalist European countries (OECD 1989; see also Williams and Shaw 1998a). Each of these stages has its own priorities and tourism policy instruments:

1) *the state as promoter.* In most European countries, this stage occurred in the 1950s. After the Second World War, most Western European economies were confronted by hard currency shortages, and trade imbalances. State promotion of tourism was a means of increasing inbound tourism and revenues. Linked to this, there were measures to eliminate negative passport, customs and police barriers to trans-border movements.

2) *the state as stimulator.* The state was increasingly required in the 1960s to provide the infrastructure required to meet growing tourism demand, including motorways and airports. In addition, a number of new tourist resorts were constructed with significant financial assistance provided by the state, both in the Alps and on the Mediterranean coast.

3) *the interventionist state.* In the 1960s and 1970s, a surge in the prices of tourist services prompted governments to implement price controls to promote the longer-term international competitive position and collective interests of their national tourist industries.

4) *the state as co-ordinator.* In the 1970s and 1980s, sustainable development, job generation and regional development became the dominant themes in national tourism development policies.

5) *the non-interventionist state.* During the 1990s, the capacity of the state to intervene on behalf of any economic sector has been constrained by the rolling back of 'the frontiers of the state', due to both an ideological

onslaught from the neo-liberal right and the dictates of global competition and macroeconomic strategies (focused on interest rate reductions and public borrowing reductions). In many European countries, the state has tended to withdraw from active intervention in tourism.

The above scheme is necessarily idealized and particular forms of state-intervention took place in different periods in different European countries. Each country has applied its own mix of tourism policy objectives and instruments. These, however, can be seen in terms of three major conceptualizations of tourism development (Kaspar 1986).

1) *laissez faire*. The state creates and maintains only the principal framework for tourism development, and no individual industry is prioritized. The basic components of *laissez faire* in respect of tourism development are: free trade, free competition and minimalist currency, customs and visa regulation. This approach is prevalent in the Anglo–American economies in particular.

2) *dogmatic concept*. The development of tourism is subordinated to declared objectives. This approach is characterized by the precise division of responsibilities amongst the various tourism policy bodies (federal state, member republics, municipalities, etc). The model has been applied in many developing countries and also in Germany and Austria (Würzl 1988).

3) *as a sum of pragmatic interventions*. Tourism development responds flexibly to political and economic events. Swiss tourism policies are considered to typify this concept.

In addition, Freyer (1990) recognizes two other concepts:

4) *a marketing theme*. The borders between policy and marketing are often indistinct, especially at the regional and local levels. If modern marketing can be described as a strategic influence on markets, then 'public tourism-marketing' is synonymous with tourism policy.

5) *as a universally planned goal*. This concept has been applied in some underdeveloped regions. The state creates all the principal conditions for tourism development, such as infrastructure, investment in accommodation, and financial support for private investors. A 'weak form' of this approach is similar to the 'dogmatic concept', a 'medium–strong' version was evident in France in the 1960s and in Spain and Portugal. A 'strong form' was similar to tourism development policies in centrally planned economics.

In general, national tourism policies are most important in those countries where a relatively large proportion of GDP is accounted for by tourism and where governments have, or had, an interventionist rather than *laissez faire* approach to economic policy. This brief review poses two major questions to be considered in this section. Was the general development of Czech and Slovak tourism policies similar to the models in Western European countries? And, were there similarities between the tourism policies in the 1950s and 1960s in the EU countries and the tourism policies applied during transition, or did the Czech and Slovak Republics adopt more sophisticated tourism policies, similar to those which can be found in the EU member states in the 1990s?

2.5.2 Tourism policies during the first phase of transition (1990–93)

The 1990–93 period was the most dynamic in the history of tourism in both Republics. The re-internationalization of the economy, following the lowering of the Iron Curtain, and progress towards a market economy, radically transformed the political and economic context of tourism development. Most of the major changes were brought about by market mechanisms, rather than by tourism policy. During 1990–93 most of the state-socialist tourism system disappeared, but its replacement by a new market system was incomplete and uneven; as ever, new pathways were constructed from the ruins of the old system.

Perhaps the most important change was the privatization of tourism enterprises (see Chapter 4). In addition, the National Ministries of Trade and Tourism were abolished, and responsibilities for tourism development passed to the Tourism Units of the Ministries of Economy. These Units had limited responsibilities and had low status within their parent Ministries. The counties and districts, as self-governing regions, were dissolved, and the Tourism Units of the District and County Councils also disappeared. District Tourism Enterprises were liquidated and most of their property was privatized. This meant that the elaboration of regional tourism development plans and investment in regional tourism infrastructure were severely disrupted for several years.

In 1990, several important laws concerning tourism were abolished – the National Committees Law, the State Statistics Law and the Domestic Trade Law in particular – as part of the dismemberment of the state-socialist economic system, but they were not replaced by a new regulatory system. This contributed to a deterioration in the quality of tourism statistics, low levels of professionalism in many newly-established tourism businesses, the disappearance of regional tourist policies, and the collapse of tourism development in some regions. However, a weak regulatory framework did not prevent the development of the tourism industry. On the contrary, there was a major boom in tourism development in both parts of the federation.

Slovakia

After 1989, international tourism was one of the most successful sectors of the Slovak economy. Both the numbers of foreign visitors and the volume of tourist receipts increased rapidly. There were also changes in the structure of international demand, with increased numbers of German and Austrian tourists. This success was not easily secured because, after 1989, tourists from the former GDR (previously a major market) preferred new destinations on the Mediterranean coast. As a result, many Czech and Slovak hotels had very low occupancy rates in the summer of 1990. Tourism managers had to develop new tourism products and markets so as to regain market share. Short stays, second and third holidays and skiing programs were emphasized, and this helped to regain markets which had been lost in Germany.

The above account raises the question of whether the success of tourism was the result of sophisticated state tourism policies or a self-generating process? It can be argued that both general framework and industry specific factors were important in the rapid transition of the Slovak tourism industry (Baláž 1995b). First, framework factors (tourism-industry non-specific) resulted in a favourable change in the overall social and economic situation of the country. As such, changes in the tourism industry were a by-product of the wider transition. The more important developments were: maintenance of economic and social stability; gradual incorporation of the Slovak Republic into wider European structures; removal of passport and visa barriers; establishment of a market economy; major privatization programmes.

The most significant developments were probably the removal of passport and visa formalities and privatization. In 1990 non-visa tourist exchange agreements were signed with 18 countries, including Austria, Germany and Italy. Five other countries followed suit in 1991, and by 1992 agreements were in place with most European states. The resultant changes in visitor flows generated a considerable increase in international tourism receipts (see Chapter 3). At the same time, privatization speeded up the establishment of market structures in the tourism sector.

The second major set of influences were tourism-industry-specific. A series of governments after 1989 were, not surprisingly, preoccupied by the general challenges of transition. Macroeconomic stabilization, privatization, price liberalization, export-reorientation, employment policies and the creation of market institutions were the main priorities in the period 1990–92. In 1992 the 'velvet divorce' and the creation of an independent Slovakia became the political priorities. Therefore, whilst there were official proclamations concerning the importance of tourism for the economy of Slovakia, there was little effective state intervention in the sector. Moreover, state tourism policy has been inconsistent. There have been seven governments in Slovakia, 1989–96, and almost every succession has been accompanied by changes in the Ministry of Economy staff, including the tourism section. There has also been a psychological barrier to overcome, stemming from the material and ideological legacy of the state-socialist period: Most of the Economy Ministers were former directors of major Slovak industrial enterprises, and they had little understanding of the service sector.

A number of reports on tourism were prepared for the Slovak government in this period, mainly concerned with generating jobs and international tourism receipts. The framework for the future development of tourism was provided by a 1993 report prepared for the Ministry of Economy of the Slovak Republic (Ministerstvo hospodárstva Slovenskej republiky 1993). It set out the following priorities: increased international tourism receipts; primary support for urban tourism, spa tourism and mountain tourism development; and job generation and regional economic development.

The report identified a number of obstacles to tourism development including: inadequate infrastructure, particularly motorways and telecommunications; poor-quality tourism services; the negative impacts of the introduction of a 25 per cent value added tax in January 1993; the lack of financial resources for marketing abroad and developing tourism information programmes; and the lack of a basic tourism law. The Ministry proposed the following measures to enhance tourism development:

● higher subsidies for the Tourism Development Programme; (TDP)
● creation of a Tourism Marketing Agency;
● preparation of a Tourism Law;
● implementation of the Tourism Information Programme.

While these measures were well-intended, their implementation was constrained by lack of resources. State sponsorship of tourism marketing abroad was limited to Kč 13 million in 1991 and only Kč 8.56 million in 1992. The TDP provided subsidies for up to 70 per cent of the interest on loans to the tourism industry. However, the total aid provided to hotel and restaurant development projects in 1991 and 1992 was only Kč 13.5 million (US$ 0.5 million), which subsidized investments of Sk 217 million (US$ 7 million). The Programme generated 836 full-time jobs and helped to create 824 new beds in hotels and similar establishments (Table 2.5). Ironically, these subsidies were drained from the remnants of the pre-1989 Tourism Fund – a very concrete example of using the ruins of the past to rebuild organizations and institutions (Stark 1996, p 995).

The failure of the Tourism Law provides an example of how a well-intended transfer of know-how could conflict with the realities – and the path dependent nature – of a transition society. The state-socialist tourism system had been centrally regulated. Although the founders of particular tourism entities may have been different (the state for the *Interhotely*

TABLE 2.5   *The Tourism Development Programme in the Slovak Republic, 1991–7*

	1991	1992	1993	1994	1995	1996	1997	Total
Number of projects approved	4	60	60	46	31	52	60	313
Total subsidy (Sk million)	4.68	12.96	19.62	27.55	18.79	59.90	79.08	218.37
Total investment generated (Sk million)	x	216.18	197.46	258.98	145.76	609.23	992.88	2,420.49
No. of new beds	95	729	700	223	268	615	770	3,400
No. of new jobs	86	750	600	654	337	690	1,751	4,868

Source: Slovenská záručná banka (1998).

chains, co-operatives for the *Jednota* chain, municipalities for the District Tourist Enterprises, etc), the regulations enacted by the Ministry of Trade and Tourism applied to the tourism sector as a whole. After 1989, most tourism businesses were either privatized or were new enterprises established by private bodies. Ownership of the District Tourist Enterprises passed to the municipalities. In 1992, therefore, the Ministry of Economy found that is no longer had any property rights in the tourism sector it sought to regulate, for the private sector was outside the Ministry's responsibilities, whilst the regional tourism councils had been disbanded.

In the course of 1992 the Ministry prepared two versions of a Tourism Law, which was mainly concerned with organizational and financial matters. The Law proposed the creation of regional tourist organizations, and it was planned that membership would be compulsory for all bodies involved in tourism, from hotels to transport enterprises. The membership fees would be divided between the organization and the state, to help fund tourism development in Slovakia. The compulsory membership scheme was adapted from Austria, and it is not difficult to understand why this was the preferred source for the transfer of know-how and an institutional model. Austria has one of the highest levels of international tourist receipts per capita in Europe, shares a common history with Slovakia and has a broadly similar culture and mountain landscapes. In addition, the idea of compulsory membership conformed with the mind set of the Ministry staff, most of whose members had been socialized within a central planning system. The proposed scheme was, however, quickly rejected by the private sector, not least because of its association with central planning and regulation. They considered that the Tourism Law constituted a return to centralized control and were generally opposed to *any* form of regulation. After numerous protests, the Tourism Law was quietly laid aside.

In summary, tourism-non-specific considerations were more important than tourism-specific ones in the development of the sector. Despite a lack of capital, weak state intervention, and legislative opaqueness, the tourism industry expanded rapidly in this period. The results of this *laissez-faire* phase of tourism development were ambiguous. About 14,000 new tourism businesses were established during 1990–93, and they valued the lack of regulation as a lack of bureaucracy. On the other hand, most new entrepreneurs had little experience of managing tourism businesses. While a special diploma was required for employment as a cook or a waitress, no licence and/or special qualification was required to establish either a travel agency or a hotel. One of the implications of this was perpetuation of poor, but now also overpriced, service in many tourism establishments.

The Czech Republic

Tourism policies in the Czech Republic resembled those in Slovakia, confirming the policy overhang from the unified Czechoslovakia. The Czech government was also preoccupied with the management of the societal transition, and paid little attention to tourism. A *laissez-faire* approach was considered to be most effective for tourism development, and this was probably true in the particular circumstances at that time, despite its imperfections. As in Slovakia, tourism-industry-non-specific general framework factors were of major importance for tourism development in this period.

Since 1989, successive Czech governments have following a liberal economic policy line. No industry has been given a preferential status in state policy. In fact, tourism has experienced a reduction in its relative importance, as measured in terms of regulatory structures. The Ministry of Trade and Tourism was abolished and, in 1992–96, tourism was regulated by the Tourism Section of the Ministry of Economy. The Section was responsible for licensing tourism businesses, negotiating international co-operation agreements, consultancy activities, marketing abroad and subsidising tourism development loans. The Ministry initiated a programme for subsidizing the interest on tourism loans, but this was underfunded. In 1993, the Czech Travel Centre was established as a tourism marketing agency, having several foreign affiliates. In May 1993, the National Information and Reservation System (NIRES) programme commenced which, originally, was planned to cover most tourism development in the Czech Republic, including the following projects:

- a supply-side study;
- promoting Czech tourism abroad;
- establishing a system of information and reservation centres;
- a study on tourism legislation;
- for establishing regional tourism information centres;

- establishing a database centre, including the supply of software and hardware;
- a communication network.

The total planned budget of the NIRES programme was an impressive Kč 391.7 million (US$ 14 million), to be co-funded by the Czech government (Kč 70.2 million), various development programmes (Kč 104.5 million), and the EU Phare programme (Kč 217 million). The project preparation was completed in October 1993, and in the same year the Ministry secured a grant from the United Nations Development Programme. The latter funded selected NIRES activities, particularly consultancy activities, the establishment of and/or unification of 30 tourist information centres, and industry information and reservation systems. NIRES was connected to the Amadeus, Start, Magellan and other world information and reservation systems (Vitáková 1994). However, it was expected that most of the planned activities would be carried out, using Phare assistance. As in Slovakia, the pathway of tourism development was essentially path-dependent path-creating in this period, and this was due as much to the general economic and political overhang, as to specific conditions in the tourism sector.

2.5.3 Tourism policies during the second phase of transition (1994–7)

Slovakia

The creation of an independent Slovakia on 1 January 1993 did little to facilitate tourism development. The new state had a weak image in foreign tourism markets, and faced competition from neighbours with stronger images – the Czech Republic and Hungary. Many Czech tourists – previously a very important market – were reluctant to visit Slovakia as a result of anti-Slovak commentaries in some nationalistic newspapers. Meanwhile, economic recession and a decline in living standards continued to depress domestic demand. 1993 probably represented the nadir of modern tourism development in Slovakia, but 1994 was a turning point. Some of the emotions generated by the 'velvet divorce' began to fade, and Czech tourists rediscovered favoured holiday destinations in Slovakia. Economic recession was replaced by a boom, and as living standards improved for the first time since 1989, so the number of domestic tourist nights started to increase.

Were the changes in the domestic and international tourism environment accompanied by significant changes in tourism policies? The 1994 report on tourism development, prepared by the Ministry of Economy of the Slovak Republic (Ministerstvo hospodárstva Slovenskej republiky 1994), basically confirmed the findings of the 1993 report. It acknowledged that the rapid growth in international tourist receipts had been generated with only minimal state assistance. These receipts, however, still lagged behind Slovakia's tourism potential. The main barriers to tourism development were seen to lie in the organizational infrastructure of tourism, the economic situation, and at the operational level:

1) weak domestic demand;
2) poor quality tourism services for foreign visitors;
3) lack of tourism bodies, such as national and regional tourist organizations;
4) lack of tourism information systems;
5) high rates of value-added taxes for tourism services;
6) the declining quality of tourism statistics.

The report also investigated the potential for international tourism and considered that the three priorities should be: city tourism (generating about 33 per cent of visitors); mountain tourism (accounting for about 28 per cent), and spa tourism (14 per cent). Taking into account both the above weaknesses and the potential for tourism development, the following measures were proposed:

- amendment of the TDP allowing the participation of both small and large tourism enterprises, as well as municipalities; this made available partial reimbursement of the interest paid on bank loans for tourism development;
- establishment of a Slovak Agency for Tourism, for marketing abroad;
- creation of a National Tourist Office;
- preparation and implementation of a Tourism Law;
- abolition of the 25 per cent value-added tax for tourism services;
- increasing levels of hygiene, personal security, tourist information and overall service standards in tourist centres;
- completing general infrastructure programs, particularly the Bratislava–Žilina–Košice highway construction, so as to provide a motorway route along the spine of the country.

The ambitious programme was to be financed from diverse resources. As would be expected, the report relied on state subsidies for the creation of the marketing agency and National Tourist Office. The major challenge would be how to finance the estimated Sk 2 billion (US$ 670 million) cost of modernizing and reconstructing tourism centres, for this lay outside the realistic scope of domestic investment. High interest rates (17–22 per cent per annum) and the lack of long-term capital loans (due to government demands on the capital markets to fund the budget deficit) were obstacles to even relatively modest investment in the tourism sector. Therefore, the aim was to fund the costs of reconstruction from two sources: foreign investment (including the EU's Phare programme), and domestic loans subsidized by the TDP. The measures proposed in the 1994 report were discussed and confirmed by the Slovak government in 1995. There was an approximately 50 per cent success rate in implementation by 1998.

The TDP has been amended several times, and by 1998 was in Phase III (which generally made more generous provisions for tourism). The most important amendment was the introduction of subsidized loans for artificial snow-making facilities in Slovak ski-centres in response to climatic constraints (changeable weather conditions) on the growing market for skiing holidays. Whereas subsidies for 70 per cent of interest rates and a total of Sk 3 million were available from the TDP for non-skiing projects, subsidies of 80 per cent and a total of Sk 4 million were provided for artificial snow-making projects. The investments in skiing infrastructure effectively extended the winter season by two months.

In total, 313 tourist projects received subsidies of Sk 218.4 million from the TDP by the end of 1997. The overall value of the investment generated in this way was Sk 2420 million (US$ 75 million), and the programme helped to create 4868 new beds and 3400 jobs in tourist facilities. The largest increases in TDP expenditure were in 1997, when subsidies of Sk 79.1 million generated total investment of Sk 993 million (Ministerstvo hospodárstva Slovenskej republiky 1997a). Most tourism investments originated from domestic sources, because the political environment deterred foreign investors. However, limited investment was provided for expert studies and rural tourism by the EU's Phare programme (see Table 2.5). Over time, there was increasing diversity in the range of projects subsidised, particularly in the inclusion of artificial snow-making facilities, as skiing accounted for 15 per cent of all international visits in the period January–March 1997. In 1997, the TDP supported investments in 14 hotels, 22 inns, 12 restaurants, eight skiing areas with artificial snow-making, two supplementary tourist facilities (ski-tows) and two camping sites.

The Slovak Agency for Tourism (Slovenská agentúra pre cestovný ruch, SACR) was established in 1995 as planned, but on a more limited scale than had been anticipated. The nationalistic government, which was obsessed by the notion that the true heartland of the Slovaks was in Central Slovakia (and had limited electoral support in Bratislava), located the agency's headquarters in the provincial city of Banská Bystrica. The agency's activities were constrained by its limited personnel and financial resources. For example, the small 1996 budget of Sk 51 million (US$ 1.7 million) had been further reduced by 8 per cent by the end of the year, in response to the growing deficit in the state budget. The 1998 budget was set at only Sk 45 million, so that a number of planned activities – such as editing a new CD ROM on Slovak tourism – had to be cancelled (Kuča 1997). The Agency also lacked the funds to establish branches abroad, and instead had to base its foreign promotion on negotiating contracts with selected tour operators. Plans could not be realized for including Slovakia in the Panorama Satellite television broadcast whereby television transmission facilities would be installed in 20 resorts, allowing them to make short broadcasts every morning as to the weather, snow and other conditions. These would be used to attract new customers, particularly from Scandinavia, Russia and previously untargeted markets.

The 25 per cent value-added tax on incoming tourism activities was abolished in 1995, as planned. This represented a major victory for Slovak tourism interest groups, such as the Slovak Association of Travel Agents, and the owners of major hotels. This improved the competitiveness of Slovak hotels and travel agents on international markets. However, calls to abolish VAT in the restaurant sector were rejected by the Ministry of Finance which was desperate to increase its tax base to remedy its budget deficit. The favoured status of travel agents and hotels may have been influenced by the ownership interests of leading political interests, a prime example of political capitalism (Staniszkis 1991).

During 1995–6 the Ministry of Economy implemented two major tourist information programmes: the Programme for Establishing Tourist Information Offices and Improving their Services, and the Programme for Local Tourist Information. The latter subsidized the production and distribution of tourist information leaflets for accommodation, attractions and other facilities. The former helped to fund the free distribution of tourist information software to 50 Tourist Information Offices (Ministerstvo hospodárstva Slovenskej republiky 1997b).

The declining quality of accommodation services forced the Ministry of Economy to strengthen its classification criteria. As of 26 December 1995, the amended Regulation of the Accommodation and Catering Establishment Standards No 125/195 implemented more stringent rules for tourist businesses. This regulation was inspired by similar laws in Austria, Switzerland, France and Germany (Janegová 1996). The Slovak Association of Hotels and Restaurants was consulted over its contents and, possibly having failed to examine them in detail, did not object to the new regulations. In addition, the Association only represented a minor part of the hotel sector, and many individual entrepreneurs argued that the new standards were too stringent and that their implementation would force up costs. The Ministry of Economy, however, was determined to implement the new standards, believing that quality levels had to be improved, and they allowed only minor derogations. Tourist businesses reacted to the regulations in two ways. Most made the improvements required to retain their existing number of stars. However, some entrepreneurs decided either to decrease the number of stars or reclassify their hotels as inns, while maintaining the same quality of services.

Improvements have also been made to the quality of tourism statistics. In 1990–3, only accommodation facilities with at least 30 employees and/

or registered in the Business Register supplied statistics. As most new hotels and inns were small-scale enterprises and personal businesses, coverage was far from complete. Since 1994, these businesses have also had to prepare tourism reports. The difference between the old and new statistical bases was approximately 10 per cent in terms of nights spent, which should be borne in mind when interpreting the tourism statistics for Slovakia.

Some improvements were effected in tourism education. While the masters' course in the Tourism and Services Faculty of the Matej Bel University in Banská Bystrica is the longest established in Central and Eastern Europe, its capacity did not match the demand for tourism industry professionals. By 1998, the Bratislava Economic University offered undergraduate and masters courses in tourism economics, and Prešov University offered undergraduate studies in hotel and tourism management. In addition, 17 public and four private Hotel Academies offered courses in hotel, restaurant and travel agency management; all the Academies were required to adhere to national education standards (Bacigalová 1997). The current system of Academies was established in 1990 and was based on the former hotel colleges, which were mainly concerned with practical skills. These courses were based on German and Austrian models. By 1998, some 28 Academies had been planned with the capacity to produce 817 graduates annually. While the numbers of students and the course contents matched the industry's needs, the graduates' knowledge and skills – especially of more sophisticated hotel and restaurant practices, and of foreign languages – were criticized by hotel managers (Svitana 1998). In part this was due to the difficulties of attracting high quality and experienced teaching staff in the face of low wages, and the reluctance of the major companies to provide placements for young trainees.

Tourism was also supported by other forms of state intervention. In 1996 the Slovak government recommenced its highway construction programme, with the aim of adding a further 400 km of new motorway to the existing 200 km by 2002. The extension of motorway links to the High Tatras region has particular significance for the development of tourism in Slovakia. In practice, massive government expenditure on infrastructure and the decreasing efficiency of the Slovak economy (measured in terms of falling exports and wage rises outstripping labour productivity gains) resulted in a financial crisis in the second half of 1997, in consequence of which the motorway building programme was slowed down. Even so, new stretches of motorway have substantially improved connections between Bratislava and selected tourist regions in Central/West Slovakia.

In the later stages of the economic transformation, discussions about the role of tourism in regional development resurfaced. In the 1990–93 period, the overriding concern of tourism policy was the generation of international currency receipts. In contrast, by December 1997 total international currency reserves amounted to US$ 6.7 billion and tourism accounted for only a minor part of these expenditures. The *Concept of the Territorial Development of Slovakia*, prepared by Ministry of Environment (Ministerstvo životného prostredia Slovenskej republiky 1997), identified tourism and transport as the 'two most important territorial development activities of the twenty first century'. It called for a better understanding of the social and environmental aspects of tourism development and marked, in a positive way, a return to pre-1989 concerns about the spatial distribution of tourism (Vláda Slovenskej socialistickej republiky 1981).

The *Concept* document argued that tourism should not be conceived only as a source of income, but also as providing for recreational needs and human development. It therefore proposed to select and rapidly develop tourist zones adjacent to the major cities. These zones were to provide weekend recreational opportunities and decrease tourism congestion in areas with fragile environments. In future, most tourism infrastructure was to be concentrated in urban areas, while the construction of new tourist facilities would be virtually prohibited in the remainder of the country. Spa tourism, cycling, horse riding and golf were considered to be the most environmentally-friendly tourist activities and were to be promoted. Self-governing local and regional governments were also recognized as the main tourism planning and development bodies. While the proposal was well-intentioned, it was also vague in key respects. For example, there were no self-governing regions in Slovakia (and in the Czech Republic) during 1989–97, but only the regional branches of central government, so that there has been little progress in regional planning.

In September 1997, the Slovak government reconsidered the 1994 and 1995 reports on tourism development (Šucha 1997). The 1995 report was amended to propose better collaboration between the state and the municipalities in tourism development programmes. The 1997 report also examined the performance of various kinds of tourism and concluded that mountain tourism and skiing were the most successful and most promising sectors. By 1997, for example, snow cannons had been introduced into 20 winter tourism centres, and the skiing season had been prolonged by several months. The government proposed to amend the TDP, by adding the reconstruction of cable cars and ski-tows to the list of activities. Cultural and discovery travel, on the other hand, were promoted less and accounted only for only minor increases in tourist nights since 1995. Since 1st July 1998, the Fourth Stage of the TDP has been in force, with a total budget of Sk 60 million; this provided subsidies for constructing and reconstructing cable cars and ski-tows.

By 1998, the industry was fragmented and competition predominated over co-ordination and collaboration. Communist hotel chains had been abolished and individual hotels had been privatized, whilst no new hotel chains had emerged. Moreover, tourism regulation was in the hands of the Tourism Unit, the smallest and least important of the nine units created in the Ministry of Economy. Although there were plans to create a Unit of Small and Medium Service Business, and to devolve tourism regulation to the sub-unit level, these have not been implemented. In May 1998, the Tourism Unit of the Slovak Ministry of Economy was merged with its Trade Unit, so that the importance of the tourism industry was reduced to being a Section within the Ministry.

This organizational lacuna was filled to some extent by the industry's own associations. There were two at the national level: The Slovak Association of Travel Agents and The Slovak Association of Hotels and Restaurants. The former included 135 leading Slovak travel agents, while the latter included over 100 hotels. Both bodies were associations of private businesses and neither was sponsored by the state. These were supplemented by other national associations, including the Association of Slovak Information Centres and the Association of Cableways and Ski-Tows (LAVEX). There were also numerous regional tourism associations, whose members were mostly small businesses. The associations were constrained by a number of shared common features: a lack of resources; the restriction of their area of activities to their district; functioning largely as 'debating clubs' of private members; and inadequate co-ordination with the public sector. There are two main reasons for the poor performance of semi-governmental bodies, and in more general terms of governance. First, there were no self-governing regions in Slovakia, in the period 1989–98, so that regional tourist bodies did not have the support or legitimacy of regional governments. Second, the tourism industry continued to be characterized by a *laissez-faire* ethos, due to the massive privatization programmes. After 40 years of a centrally planned economy, many new entrepreneurs were not prepared to accept either state supervision or partnership, and were suspicious of most forms of inter-enterprise co-operation.

The 1997 report on tourism development recognized this problem and drew attention to two Ministry of Economy projects designed to secure enhanced collaboration between the state, the municipalities and the private sector. In the village of Terchová (Žilina district) a local tourism association had been established with the assistance of Swiss experts and the Slovak Tourism Institute. This was proposed as a model for other local tourist bodies. Secondly, in terms of regional tourism marketing, a Tourism Development Agency had been established in the High Tatras; while the Ministry provided administrative support, professional and financial help was granted by the British Know-How Fund. Both bodies had to overcome substantial difficulties arising from the scepticism of Slovak tourism entre-preneurs in respect of any kind of collaboration and regulation.

During 1997 some negative trends emerged in Slovak tourism. The numbers of international tourist arrivals and volume receipts decreased for the first time since 1989. This was partly due to external factors (notably the devastating floods in Central Europe just before the summer season), but tourist surveys also reported the dissatisfaction of foreign and domestic with the low quality of tourism services. It seemed that the initial development potential stemming from the removal of the Iron Curtain, and the introduction of a market economy, had been exhausted. Cheap, but poor quality, services seemed unable to attract a new customer base. Instead, there was the need for a more sophisticated tourism system, better able to compete with tourist industries in other transition countries and in the EU.

The Czech Republic

More liberal economic policies were applied to tourism, in common with the rest of the economy, in the second phase of transition. At the same time, there were strong demand conditions because the Czech Republic had a relatively buoyant domestic sector (related to low unemployment), while Prague was a major international tourist attraction. After 1996 increasing attention was paid to the tourism sector, mainly in response to rising unemployment rates in particular localities and regions (linked to the broader processes of restructuring), and the publicity given to frauds and bankruptcies amongst the major Czech travel agents.

Since 1993, the Ministry of Economy has paid particular attention to co-operation with the private sector, and especially the principal self-regulation tourism bodies, the Association of Travel Agents of the Czech Republic, the Association of Czech Private Travel Agencies and the National Federation of Hotels and Restaurants. Representatives of these associations, together with selected professionals and municipal representatives, form the Tourism Council, which advises the Ministry of Economy. The Council prepares analyses of the Czech tourism industry and drafts proposals for tourism laws and other forms of regulation (Čech 1994). The other significant associations are the Czech Association of Tourist Information Centres (ATIS), the Union of Operators of Ropeways and Tows, and the Union of the Medicinal Spas and Baths of the Czech Republic.

The Ministry's collaboration with the EU institutions and with regional tourist bodies has been rather less successful. In 1993, the Phare administration initiated the TOURISM programme designed to assist tourism development in the transition countries of Central and Eastern Europe. The NIRES programme, initiated by the Czech Ministry of Economy in 1993, was an ideal candidate for assistance under the TOURISM programme, and the Czech regional and industry associations had high expectations for this (Kainc 1996). In 1994, they were disappointed to learn from the EC Commission that the Czech government had not officially applied for assistance. Angry representatives of CATIS accused the Ministry of Economy of deliberately mishandling the application and/or of ignorance. In 1995 the Czech Ministry of Economy prepared a new proposal for Phare assistance of 29 million ECU. The Czech government, however, did not consider tourism development a priority, and the project was not included in the official Czech government proposals to Phare. In Spring 1996, the Ministry, the Phare Czech Office and CATIS prepared a new joint proposal for the 1997 NIRS programme; this broadly covered the same activities as the 1993 NIRES programme, but was also not supported by the Czech government.

Several regional projects, assisted by international experts, were supported by Phare, particularly in the border areas. These projects were mostly concerned with tourism marketing and information, and they suffered from a number of weaknesses including a lack of resources, and duplication due to lack of co-ordination by the Ministry of Economy. In 1994, for example, the Podkrušnohorské informační centrum was established as a regional tourism information and development organization in the Krušné hory mountains. With assistance from German consultants, projects were developed for unified regional networks of information centres, mountain bike routes and the revitalization of spas. Although prepared according to Ministry and Phare instructions, the same Ministry failed to forward these to the Phare administration. The regional tourism organization applied to the Tourism Commission of the Economic Committee of the Czech Parliament, but received no significant assistance (Světoběžník 1996).

In 1996, there was a reorganization of tourism regulation, with responsibility being passed to the Ministry for the Regional Development (Ministerstvo pro místní rozvoj, MMR), established on 1 November 1996 by Law No. 272/1996. By 1998, it had been divided into five sectors, which were sub-divided into departments. There were three departments within the Sector of Regional Policy and Tourism, one of which was the Department of Tourism. The Department had the following responsibilities:

- proposing and implementing measures to strengthen international co-operation, and the image of the Czech Republic abroad;
- participating in the legislative process of approximation EU legislation to the legal system in the Czech Republic;
- collation of statistical information about regional tourism, and evaluation of the quality of tourism services;
- supporting foreign assistance in the development of tourism;
- analysing tourism development;
- evaluation of land zoning around towns and cities from the perspective of the tourism industry;
- responsibility for international agreements, and for bilateral and multilateral international co-operation;
- co-operation with regional associations in supporting regional tourism development;
- providing consultancy services for regional bodies;

- acting on behalf of the state, in administering the assets of the former Fund of Tourism (dating from the state-socialist period) and its outstanding loans;
- founding of the Czech Centre of Tourism, and co-operating in the promotion of the Czech Republic and its regions;
- executing its duties as a founder of ORBIS (responsible for producing books and pamphlets about Prague, Czech music and other cultural features).

The Czech Travel Centre was established in April 1993 as a national tourism marketing agency, modelled on Austrian, German and French experiences (Nejdle 1994). By 1997, it operated as a directly controlled contributory organization of the Ministry for Regional Development, and had nine foreign offices, including London and Tokyo. The main task of the Centre was to create a consistent and attractive image of the Czech Republic abroad, and it also disseminated basic information about cultural and social events, and the historical and natural heritage. Its work was constrained by its relatively modest budget of Kč 76 million (US\$ 2.5 million), which was sourced from state subsidizes, payments by contracting partners and its own commercial activities.

Financial assistance has also been available since 1997 for small and medium tourism enterprises, from the Czech Moravian Guarantee Bank, in the form of subsidized interest on loans for tourism development.

Despite various and mostly small-scale activities, the – essentially neoliberal – Czech government showed little interest in an interventionist tourism policy. Consequently, there was no place for extensive tourism development programmes within its broad policy framework, such as existed in France or Spain (Williams and Shaw 1998a). However, developments in the tourism industry demanded greater interventionism. In particular, a number of medium and large Czech travel agents collapsed in 1996 and 1997, including Prog and Travela, respectively the third and fourth largest agencies in the Republic. About 7,000 Czech tourists were left stranded abroad with invalid air tickets and hotel vouchers (Hospodářské noviny daily, 10 October 1997), and the costs of repatriating them were estimated at Kč 30 million (US\$ 1 million). There were suspicions that the crashes were deliberately planned as part of a scheme to defraud the customers and partner travel agents. A Guarantee Fund had been established in 1996 by several major Czech tour operators in order to finance the repatriation of Czech tourists in the case of travel agency failure. However, the Fund was inadequate to deal with the scale of the claims arising from the bankruptcies of the Prog and Travela agencies.

Faced with angry protests from thousands of stranded tourists, the Ministry for Regional Development speeded up work on a Tourism Law designed to deal with consumer protection. This was partly based on EC

314/90/EEC Travel Package Directive. It proposed that, agencies should be obliged to protect consumer interests, Ministry licensing of travel agencies, and a compulsory insurance scheme. Moreover, agencies involved in outgoing travel would be required to make an initial deposit of Kč 200,000 and to pay an annual fee of 5 per cent of sales to a special Repatriation Fund. Whereas the compulsory insurance was designed to recompense customers for the non-provision of services, the Repatriation Fund specifically funded the return of tourists stranded abroad by the failure of travel agents. The Repatriation Fund was strongly opposed by Czech Travel Agents, because of the way that the earlier voluntary Guarantee Fund had been devastated by frauds amongst a number of tour companies. The Ministry bowed to this pressure and the Repatriation Fund was replaced by a proposal for compulsory bank deposits to be made by the agents for individual package tours. In 1998 there was agreement in principle between the Ministry, the insurance companies and the travel agents concerning the issue of insurance. Each agency was required to sign an insurance contract, which progressively covered an increasing proportion of its business, rising from 25 per cent of turnover in the first year to 42 per cent in the fourth year. In addition, a guarantee deposit of 2 per cent of the agency's turnover was to be made to the insurance company. The final version of the Law was expected to obtain parliamentary approval in late 1998.

While the government and popular opinion blamed the travel agents for these crashes and frauds, the travel agents could justifiably complain of government neglect. The 25 per cent value-added-tax rate, for example, was the highest in Europe. Czech travel agents and hotels called for the abolition of, or at least a decrease in the rate of, the tax (NFHR 1996), but had not been successful by 1998. Persistent complaints about the quality of tourism statistics did, however, lead to the implementation of a new and more comprehensive tourism data collection programme as from 1997.

In recognition of the shared interests of neighbouring Central European states in international tourism, the Austrian Ministry of Economy convened a meeting in 1987 attended by the tourism ministers of the Czech and Slovak Republics, Poland, Hungary, Slovenia, Croatia and Austria. The Austrian government proposed the establishment of The Tourism Area Central Europe–Danube Region, in order to realize the tourism potential of Central Europe's rich natural and cultural heritage. Since 1989 all the above-mentioned countries have tried to generate tourist flows from new international markets, but have been handicapped by weak national tourist images. Moreover, most tourists to the region are likely to want to visit more than one country. The proposed association aims to create a shared image for the region and to develop regional tourism products. The first step in this direction was made by the Austrian National Tourism Marketing Agency, which organized a joint presentation of the Central European countries at the Kyoto (Japan) tourism fair in April 1997. The tourism ministers supported the Austrian proposal and agreed an Action Plan, encompassing the following:

- co-ordination of the policies of the national tourism authorities and tourism marketing agencies, with a co-ordination centre being established in each national tourism ministry;
- co-operation to create a common tourism product, marketed by the major national tour operators at international tourist fairs;
- creation of a Tourism Office, which would encourage national tour operators to prepare common tourism products and a unified tourism reservation system. For example, the Slovak representative lobbied for The European Wine Road (Grellnethová 1997).

2.6 CONCLUSIONS: UNEVEN AND HESITANT INTERVENTIONISM

Since 1989 both republics have experienced difficult periods of economic and social transition. Market economies have been created, virtually in their entireties, in a very short time period. In common with other governments in Central and Eastern Europe, the Czechoslovak – and later the Czech and Slovak governments - have had to cope with numerous problems: for example, the collapse of established CMEA markets, changes in production structures, economic decline, rising unemployment, and widening regional differences. Political problems arising from the 'velvet divorce' further complicated the situation. Unsurprisingly, tourism development was not a priority for Czech and Slovak policy makers in this period. Instead, the rapid growth of the tourism industry occurred despite the lack of state intervention and perhaps even because of the largely unregulated policy environment. Thousands of new tourism businesses were established, many of which quickly collapsed. However, state intervention became more apparent after 1995, when the situation in the tourism market became more stabilized. Not surprisingly, macroeconomic and political considerations were the key to the essentially path-dependent path-creating process of tourism development in this period. However, there were increasing state attempts to steer the tourism industry, and these together with the inherent economic conditions in the sector favoured the development of greater path creation.

Tourism policies in the two republics were broadly similar in the period 1990–97, with the most salient features being:

- *state neglect and market-led development.* Governments, overburdened with the general challenges of the economic and political transitions, gave little attention to tourism development, particularly in the first phase of the transformation. Compared to the pre-1989 situation, the priority allocated to tourism within the state bureaucracy actually decreased. The tourism policies followed by both governments can generally be described as liberal, and the development of the sector was market-led.

- *hesitant intervention.* No major infrastructure or development projects in tourism were assisted by the state in this period. Moreover, except for the relatively small-scale programmes of subsidized tourism loans, there were no important legislative and/or financial initiatives. Tourism policies were more reactive than proactive. The Czech Tourism Law, for example, was prepared as a reaction to the failure of several major travel agents. In Slovakia, work on the Tourism Law was hastened by declining tourism growth during 1997 and by the need to adopt EU standards of tourist consumer protection.

- *marketing and promotion.* Both countries established tourism marketing agencies and implemented tourism information systems. The Czech Travel Centre established several offices abroad, but these were limited in terms of their range of activities and finance. The Slovak Tourism Agency was unable to establish offices abroad and its activities were limited to participation in major European tourist fairs.

- *organisational vacuum.* The state-socialist tourism organization had been abolished by 1990, but little progress had been made in constructing a new organization even as late as 1998. There was a lack of strong regional and local tourist bodies. Since 1990, there have been no laws or regulations pertaining to the promotion of local and regional tourism development. Numerous tourist associations were established in both Republics, but they lacked the support of local and/or regional governments. There was also a lack of co-ordination between the private and public sectors with respect to regional tourism development.

- *regulation and quality.* The absence or incompleteness of regulation was a major problem with regard to the quality of tourism services, especially in the first phase of transition. Weak regulation of accommodation standards, and the limited experience and training of travel agents in the face of very low barriers to entry to the sector, resulted in low-quality services being provided by many tourist businesses.

- *minimal national differences.* There were mostly only minor differences between Czech and Slovak tourism policies. The Slovak approach was slightly more interventionist than the Czech one. In the second phase of transition, both the abolition of the 25 per cent value-added tax, and subsidies from the TDP, proved to be among the more positive and effective tourism policy instruments. They helped to ease some of the financial pressures on enterprises in an economy characterized by acute capital shortages. The more active Slovak investment and marketing policies were a reaction to pressures on the country's international currency reserves and the lack of a clear national tourism image.

In general policy terms, tourism policies and instruments in the Czech and Slovak Republics can be described as partly *laissez faire*. The objectives were mostly concerned with income generation and offsetting deficits in the trade balance, and were broadly similar to those in the developed European countries in the 1950s and 1960s. However, there were signs of a shift to the following stages of tourism policy development. The second stage of transition witnessed major infrastructure programmes which were important to tourism development (such as the construction of motorways). In the EU member states, tourism policies have been progressively shifting from the simple maximization of tourist receipts to the creation of conditions for the competitiveness of tourism enterprises and regions, and from the primary use of promotional instruments to the application of specific models of tourism competitiveness (Fayos-Solá 1996). This shift was also visible in Czech and Slovak tourism policies, but more in the objectives than in the actual instruments applied.

Given the legacy of central planning and the considerable shares of international tourism receipts in GDP and exports, it could be expected that there would be a gradual shift from a 'tourism policy as a universally planned goal' to a medium or strong 'dogmatic concept' of tourism policy and that, in addition, major attention would be paid to tourism policy design and implementation. However, this has not been the case. Strong regulation of the tourism industry was dismantled almost overnight and tourism was not at the forefront of economic policies in the Czech and Slovak Republics. This was due to two main considerations: first, an ideological legacy of neo-liberal economic policies applied in the first stage of transition, which did not permit the prioritization of any particular industries; and secondly, the importance of manufacturing industries and the limited recognition of tourism industries in both the Czech and Slovak Republics in the last 40 years. In contrast, tourism has been of considerable importance for local and national economies in Portugal and Spain since the 1960s at least, and this was reflected in the relatively strong position of the tourism industry within the state administrations and development policies in these countries. In the Czech and Slovak Republics, tourism started to play an important role in the economic and social development only after 1989 and there was little experience of the integration of tourism initiatives into a broader framework of economic, social and environmental policies.

3 TRANSITION AND THE RE-INTERNATIONALIZATION OF MARKETS

3.1 CHANGES IN INTERNATIONAL TOURISM CONSUMPTION AND BEHAVIOUR

Europe has accounted for the dominant share of international tourism in the post-1945 period. This was determined by several considerations: the level of economic development (travel tends to increase with prosperity and education levels), territorial considerations (a large number of relatively small states in close proximity), strong climatic differences between the North and South, good infrastructure and last, but not least, a well-elaborated system of national tourism statistics. International visitor flows have changed in Europe since 1945. The most fundamental change has been a decline in departures to neighbouring non-Mediterranean countries and a corresponding growth in traffic to sun and sea destinations, most of which were also characterized by lower living costs (Pearce 1995, p 46). The development of inclusive charter tours and aggressive tourist development programmes in Spain and other Mediterranean destinations have been of particular note in these changes (Williams 1997).

This broad pattern has been and will continue to be subject to change. Turning to the future, the three most important factors determining the future of tourism in Europe are likely to be (Jansen-Verbeke 1995):

- whether the interest of non-Europeans in Europe as a holiday destination can be sustained;
- the changing preferences of Europeans, and their growing propensity to travel to long-haul destinations outside Europe;
- whether both these threats can be compensated for, to some extent, by the rapid growth in tourist traffic within Europe, generated by growing numbers of cross-border business contacts, more frequent visits to

more spatially dispersed family and friends, more cross-cultural exchanges, and business traffic intensification especially in the economic core of Europe.

International tourism has also been subject to a number of other changes, including a relative shift from mass tourism to more individualistic and flexible forms of tourism consumption (Section 1.3). There has also been reification of nature and of some cultural forms, with corresponding growth in rural and urban tourism, catering for both domestic and international markets.

These comments are based on analyses of international visitor flows in Western Europe and, as such, reflect 50 years of post-war economic, social and political stability and prosperity. This raises the question of whether these findings are also valid for transition countries in Central Europe which have experienced unprecedented changes in their economic, social and political systems since 1989. There are issues here concerning the extent to which international visitor flows in the transition period differed from those in the state-socialist period and from those in Western Europe? While there are superficial similarities in the explosive growth of tourism in Southern Europe in the 1960s and in Central Europe after 1989, the previous discussions (Chapter 1) have emphasized that these are also fundamentally different in a number of important respects: the tourist attractions, the organization of international tourism, the role of cross-border trading and transit tourism, and the structure of both national and international capital ownership. These features are further reviewed in this chapter, although ownership issues are dealt with in Chapter 4. In general, the findings reported here confirm the inadequacy of simple economic models of international tourism flows (see also the review in Sinclair and Stabler 1997), and we tend to agree with Böröcz (1996, p 131) that 'simple push–pull theories, as borrowed from the human ecology and neo-classical economics of labour migration are not satisfactory in the area of leisure migration'.

3.2 CHANGING DOMESTIC AND INTERNATIONAL MARKETS

In the period of state-socialism, the former Czechoslovakia – in common with other Central European countries – was heavily reliant on tourist demand from neighbouring countries. In 1989, 83 per cent of foreign visitors came from just three countries: the GDR, Poland and Hungary (see Hall 1991c, pp 19–22 for comparisons with other CEE countries). These were also the principal destinations for outward tourist flows, and accounted for 59 per cent of outbound Czech and Slovak visitors. This pattern of 'nearest-neighbour' tourist flows, has changed very little since 1989, and trips to/from neighbouring countries accounted for about 90

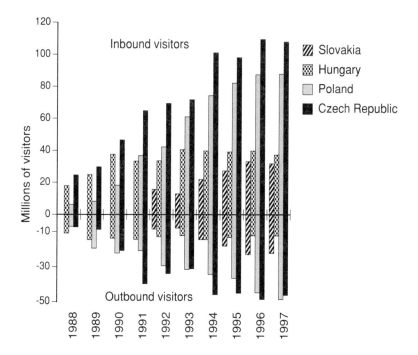

Fig. 3.1: Inbound and outbound visitors in Central Europe, 1988–97.
Sources: WTO (1994); Cestat (1990–98).
Note: the Czech data for 1988–91 refer to Czechoslovakia.

per cent of tourist exchanges in both countries in 1996 (Figure 3.1). The remarkably stable structure of visitor movements in Central Europe has to be understood in the context of a strong degree of path dependency, grounded in geographical, economic and social considerations. Most regions within Hungary, Poland, the Czech and Slovak Republics are easily access-ible to each other (being within a few hours drive), there are strong eco-nomic contacts within CEFTA (which replaced CMEA) requiring business tourism flows, and there are relatively high levels of cross-border friend-ships and marriages which facilitate visiting friends and family tourism flows. In addition, the geographical location of the Czech and Slovak Republics in the centre of Europe has long given them an important role in transit travel.

The overall stability in the geographical structure of tourism flows is deceptive, however, for there have been significant changes in both the volumes of and the purposes of visitor flows. Whereas 29.6 million foreign visitors came to Czechoslovakia in 1989, by 1997 this number had leapt to

107.9 million visitors to the Czech Republic and 31.7 million to Slovakia. The same dramatic shift is evident in outbound tourists. Whilst there were 8.6 million trips abroad from Czechoslovakia in 1989, there were 46.1 million and 22.1 million such trips in 1997 from, respectively, the Czech and Slovak Republics. There were a number of reasons for these increases, linked to the removal of the Iron Curtain, the growth of business tourism in newly opened economies, and the generation of trans-border shopping tourism from Germany and Austria.

There were differences in the national composition of the numbers of visitors and of the total numbers of nights spent by foreign tourists in the Czech and Slovak Republics after 1989. While Germans, Austrians and Poles were the dominant groups of visitors to both Republics, *hotel guests* mainly originated in Germany, the Netherlands, the former USSR, Italy and France; the difference lies in the greater reliance on informal provision amongst the former, as well as a higher level of day visitors. The removal of travel barriers after 1989 also opened up more spatially distant markets, and, for example, there were large increases in the nights spent by tourists from the UK, USA, Israel and Japan. These 'new' markets were still overshadowed by the large numbers of German tourist in Czech and Slovak hotels, but the former groups spent relatively more on accommodation and other tourist services on a per capita basis.

3.2.1 Slovakia

The structure of the nights spent by foreign countries in Slovakia has been subject to concentration tendencies in the period 1993–7; it is not possible to comment on the earlier period due to data inconsistencies. The top five generating countries accounted for 67.2 per cent of nights spent in 1993 but for 74.9 per cent in 1997. The most notable feature was that the market share of the Czech Republic increased from 20.2 per cent to 24.9 per cent, and that of Germany from 20.1 per cent to 26.3 per cent, while the share of Hungarian tourists decreased from 7.4 per cent to 4.5 per cent. There were only minor changes in the other major markets (Table 3.1 and Figure 3.2).

Although the geographical structure of visitor flows was relatively stable, there was a significant increase of 60.9 per cent in the total nights spent by foreign tourists in Slovakia between 1991 and 1997. The statistical data for 1991–3 have to be approached cautiously, because of changes in the numbers of establishments included in the system of data reporting, but the growth in nights spent by foreign tourists is confirmed by data on the numbers of foreign tourists enumerated at the frontiers (Figure 3.1). The main increases in terms of national market segments were for Germany (90.2 percent), Austria (93.5 per cent) and the former-USSR (295.2 per cent). These national markets segments were characterized by different

TABLE 3.1   *Nights spent in Slovak and Czech hotels, and similar establishments, by foreign tourists: by major countries of origin, 1990–7*

Year	1990	1991	1992	1993	1994	1995	1996	1997
				Slovakia				
Czech Republic	x	x	x	362	614	654	746	630
Germany	306	346	378	360	490	743	732	666
Poland	244	310	332	238	544	281	392	317
Former USSR	263	42	64	112	140	150	209	166
Hungary	332	237	176	133	238	175	167	114
Austria	60	62	78	75	105	149	141	120
Netherlands	n.a.	42	74	79	103	85	79	44
Others	731	539	394	433	534	555	602	471
Total foreign tourists	1,936	1,577	1,495	1,792	2.769	2,791	3,068	2,528
Domestic tourists	8,320	4,828	2,791	2,925	3,580	3,043	5,045	5,112
				Czech Republic ('000)				
Germany	3,001	2,878	2,790	2,640	3,151	3,902	5,480	n.a.
Netherlands	n.a.	322	492	618	637	812	1,145	n.a.
Russia	n.a.	41	67	142	209	431	776	n.a.
Italy	n.a.	413	489	446	518	620	723	n.a.
Slovakia	x	x	x	421	541	513	681	n.a.
Poland	475	384	362	503	340	341	644	n.a.
United Kingdom	n.a.	150	187	229	344	373	503	n.a.
Others	3,938	1,942	2,221	2,377	2,869	3,336	4,234	n.a.
Total foreign tourists	7,415	6,129	6,609	7,377	8,611	10,327	14,186	n.a.
Domestic tourists	17,187	8,869	6,872	7,832	9,589	13,906	23,100	

Sources: Štatistický úrad Slovenskej republiky (1991–1998a); Štatistický úrad Slovenskej republiky (1991–1998b), Štatistický úrad Slovenskej republiky (1994–1998); Český statistický úřad (1989–1998a) and (1989–1998b).
Notes: since 1993, Czech tourists in Slovakia have been classified as foreign tourists, whereas previously they were domestic tourists; the numbers of both Czech and domestic tourists are not, therefore, comparable for 1991–3; the same situation applies to Slovak tourists in the Czech Republic; during 1991–3 the data refer only to the numbers of nights spent in accommodation registered in the Business Register in both Republics.

motivations. German and Austrian tourists tended to be motivated by the availability of low-cost alternative holidays. While many German tourists had earlier experiences of Slovak tourist resorts, dating from the GDR period, Austrian tourists 'rediscovered' a country that had become 'a clandestine neighbour' during the Cold War years. Russian and Ukrainian tourists mostly had shopping and trans-border business interests in Slovakia. During the years of state-socialism, it had been relatively difficult for Soviet

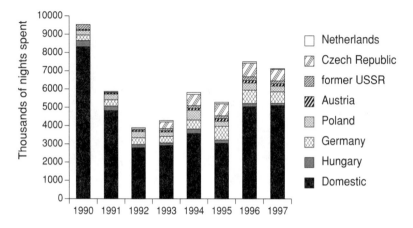

Fig. 3.2: Nights spent in the Slovak Republic, 1990–97: countries of origin.
Source: Štatistický úrad Slovenskej republiky (1991–1998b).

Union citizens to obtain permission for individual international travel even
to other countries within the Eastern block. Most of the relatively small
number of incoming Soviet tourists, therefore, came on travel agency packages. Consequently, the removal of barriers to individual travel stimulated
an influx of Ukrainians and Russians. Most of this travel was for shopping,
smuggling, job-seeking and other shadow economy activities. A weak business infrastructure in the Ukraine also meant that many Ukrainians lacked
access to sophisticated travel agency services in their own country, and
instead travelled to Slovakia to purchase these. Only indirect data is available on this phenomenon, but it seems conclusive: 38,707 out of a total of
217,578 outbound packages sold in Slovakia in 1995 were sold to foreigners,
of which 33,389 were in the City of Košice, located close to the Ukrainian
border. Ironically, this was similar to the pattern of outbound tourism from
Czechoslovakia after the opening of the Austrian borders in 1989. Many of
the Czech and Slovak 'tourists' who went to Austria in 1989 and 1990 were
engaged in shopping or business tourism, or in shadow economy activities.
However, there is also a new elite in the former USSR which has re-
discovered the High Tatras mountain resorts and the Piešt'any spa; again
there are parallels with the many wealthy Czechs and Slovaks who have
rediscovered the Austrian Alps since 1989.

A decrease in the nights spent by Czech tourists in Slovakia was expected
after the 'velvet divorce' in 1993. But language compatibility, familiarity (a
tradition of visiting Slovak resorts since 1918) and low prices have attracted
increasing numbers of Czechs. This is evidence of the importance of path
dependency in international tourism flows in Slovakia, as in the Czech

Republic. Between 1993 and 1997, the nights spent by Czech tourist increased by 74 per cent.

There was no clear trend in the numbers of nights spent in Slovakia by Polish tourists. After an increase of almost 100 per cent in 1994, there was a sharp decrease in the following year so that the aggregate change over the 1991–7 period was a small net increase of only 2.3 per cent. Short trips related to business travel and shopping accounted for a large share of tourist exchanges with Poland. These substantial annual variations may have been due to such factors as changes in customs formalities and in consumer price relativities. Turning to Hungary, there was a 51.9 per cent decrease in the number of nights spent by Hungarian tourists in Slovakia, in 1991–7. Some commentators related this decrease to political tensions between Hungary and Slovakia, but in fact there was a sharp increase in the numbers of Hungarian overnights in 1994, at the height of the tensions between the two neighbours. An alternative explanation is that the volatility in the number of nights spent by both Polish and Hungarian tourists is related to price increases in Slovak accommodation facilities. Whereas a 50 per cent discount was usually given to domestic and Czech visitors, between zero and 20 per cent was offered to Polish, Hungarian and former USSR visitors (tourists from Western countries usually paid the full price).

The numbers of nights spent by domestic tourists stagnated in the early transition period, partly due to the 30 per cent decline in household incomes, 1989–93 (see Section 2.2). In 1994, the decline levelled off and there was a small increase in domestic nights in the following year. There were, however, adjustments in the types of accommodation used. Holidays in hotels had become a luxury for most of the population, and Slovaks sought out alternative forms of accommodation, such as working holidays, short breaks spent at home or in second homes, and visits to friends and relatives; this reduced the economic significance of domestic tourism. Then in 1996 the numbers of reported domestic nights increased sharply to 5 million (and to 5.1 million in 1997), compared to only 3 million in the previous year. While the recovery is partly related to improved living stand-ards in the second part of the transition, most of the increase was probably due to improvements in the reporting of tourist statistics. Whereas under state-socialism all nights spent in commercial facilities had been reported, this was not the case in the 1990s. Privatization had meant that most hotels and inns had been divested from large hotel chains, creating many smaller units. In the period 1990–3, only the tourist accommodation establishments registered in the Business Register, usually with 25 or more employees, were required to report nights spent; this excluded large tranches of small and medium-sized tourism enterprises. But after 1993 the reporting requirements were extended to all tourism accommodation businesses. This created a particular statistical discontinuity at this point in time. However, because many entrepreneurs do not bother to make returns, there are also

TABLE 3.2   *Length of stay of visits to Slovakia, 1994–7: percentage distribution*

| | 1994 | | | 1997 | | | |
	Summer	Autumn	Total	Winter	Summer	Autumn	Total
Transit	32.1	29.9	31.0	18.8	28.3	25.9	25.2
1-day stay	19.9	33.6	26.8	31.7	18.3	29.9	27.2
2–3 days	14.6	19.7	17.2	20.3	17.0	25.0	22.0
4+ days	33.4	16.8	25.1	29.2	36.5	19.2	25.7
Total	100.0	100.0	100.0	100.0	100.0	100.0	100.0
Average length of stay, days	4.1	2.5	3.1	3.2	4.3	2.9	3.3

Sources: Ústav turizmu (1995–1998) and (1997).
Notes: The 1994 data are simple averages for the summer and autumn surveys, whereas the 1997 data are weighted averages for the summer, autumn and winter surveys.

considerable annual fluctuations due to under-reporting even in the mid- and late 1990s.

An important question is whether Slovakia was a tourist destination in its own right or mainly a country to be visited while in transit to other destinations? Transit travel does account for a relatively large share of all trips to Slovakia (Table 3.2), and this is particularly marked in the summer season. This is not surprising, given its central location in Europe, at the cross-roads of both west-east and north-south routes. On the other hand, there was a trend towards longer stays in Slovakia in the period 1994–7, especially for visits of four or more days, while the share of transit visitors decreased.

There are significant differences in the national patterns of tourist visits to Slovakia. German tourists had the longest stays, 4.4 days on average in 1997 (including transit travellers). In contrast, Czechs spent 3.9 days, Poles 2.1 days, Austrian 1.8 days, Hungarians 2.1 days and Ukrainians 1.8 days. There were also seasonal differences in the visiting patterns of each national group. The Polish tourists, for example, stayed 3.2 days in winter but only 2.0 days in autumn. Similar patterns of longer winter stays and shorter autumn stays were also typical for Czech and German tourists, and may be related to the popularity of winter skiing holidays. Austrian and Ukrainian tourists, on the other hand, were mostly motivated by shopping so that there were few seasonal variations in their length of stay.

3.2.2 The Czech Republic

The basic structure of the nights spent by foreign tourists in the Czech Republic was stable in the period 1993–6. The top ten generating countries accounted for 79.1 per cent of all nights spent in 1993 and for 79.4 per

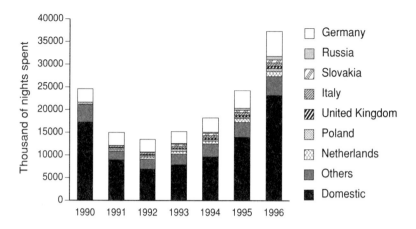

Fig. 3.3: Nights spent in the Czech Republic, 1990–96: countries of origin.
Source: Český statistický úřad (1989–1998b).

cent in 1996 (Table 1.2, Figure 3.3). Within this total, the share of German tourists increased from 35.8 to 38.6 per cent, emphasizing the dominance of this market segment, and of Russian tourists from 1.9 to 5.5 per cent. On the other hand, there were decreases in the share of Polish tourists (from 6.8 to 4.5 per cent) and Austrian tourists (from 4.7 to 3.0 per cent). However, these only represent relative declines for there were significant increases in the absolute numbers of nights spent by all national groups. Between 1991 and 1996, the numbers of nights spent by German, Polish and Italian tourists increased (respectively, by 90.4, 67.8 and 75.1 per cent). However, the most rapid rates of growth were in some of the smaller and geographically more distant markets; overnights by UK and Dutch tourists increased by more than 200 per cent. But the most striking statistic was the massive (1792 per cent) increase reported for Russia, as that county's new rich re-discovered the West Bohemian spas.

The growth in the total number of nights spent in the Czech Republic was not the only positive feature of this period. There was also a significant increase in the average length of stay from 3.4 days in 1991 to 4.1 days in 1996. This increase was mainly accounted for by German tourists, whose average stays were extended from 3.4 to 4.4 days, and by Russians (from 4.0 to 6.2 days). But there was also a more generalized tendency for most national groups to have longer stays in this period.

In general, the national market structure of foreign tourism (in terms of the generation of tourism receipts) was more favourable in the Czech than in the Slovak Republic, and the former also had longer average lengths of tourist stays. This was reflected in the level of international tourist receipts

TABLE 3.3 *Main purposes of travel to/from the Czechoslovak Socialist Republic, 1956–81 (percentages)*

Year	Inbound visitors			Outbound visitors	
	Holiday	Business	Transit	Holiday	Business
Tourist exchanges with state-socialist countries					
1966	95.3	4.7	x	94.4	5.6
1970	90.1	9.9	x	96.7	3.3
1975	83.2	2.9	13.9	92.9	7.1
1981	60.0	3.7	36.3	94.6	5.4
Tourist exchanges with non-state-socialist countries					
1966	93.1	6.9	x	66.4	33.6
1970	86.4	13.6	x	41.3	58.7
1975	63.2	18.9	17.9	44.2	55.8
1981	58.0	23.8	18.2	47.4	52.6

Source: Vládny výbor pre cestovný ruch ČSR (1974–1982).

per inhabitant, which was 3.1 times higher in the Czech Republic than in Slovakia. This was due to two main factors: accessibility to Western markets, related to the long Czech borders with Germany and Austria; and the status of Prague as Central Europe's most esteemed tourism destination, attracting relatively high-income tourists from the EU and the USA.

3.3 THE CHALLENGE OF REPOSITIONING IN INTERNATIONAL MARKETS

In the 1960s, state-socialist Czechoslovakia could be crudely characterized as 'a country of holiday-makers'. Holidays were the principal motivation for both incoming and outgoing tourists (Table 3.3). In the 1970s the situation began to change, as potential tourists from other state-socialist countries were increasingly able to select alternative destinations, particularly the Black Sea resorts. Most incoming tourists stayed in Czechoslovakia for relatively short periods, one to three days, and were mainly drawn from the neighbouring countries of Hungary, East Germany and Poland. While the total number of visitors to Czechoslovakia increased, more than one-third of the travellers were estimated to be 'in transit' by 1981. Business travel was of little importance, because foreign trade was concentrated in a small number of state monopolies. Virtually all the outbound movements from Czechoslovakia in this period were for holiday purposes. The main destinations were either short trips to neighbouring state-socialist countries, or the Black Sea coastal resorts.

There were more marked changes in tourism flows to and from Western countries between 1966 and 1981. In the 1960s, foreign tourists coming to Czechoslovakia had mainly been on holiday, but after the Prague Spring in 1968 and a difficult period of 'normalisation' (the official term adopted by the XIVth General meeting of the Czechoslovak Communist Party to describe developments after 1970), there were changes in the structure of visitor flows in the 1970s. While the total numbers of incoming Western tourists stagnated, the share of holiday-makers declined as the poor reputation of the political regime coloured a bleak national tourism image. On the other hand, the development of East–West foreign trade was reflected in increasing numbers of business visitors to Czechoslovakia. There were also changes in outbound tourism. Those Czechoslovaks who wanted to travel to the West, 'to look behind the Iron Curtain', faced enormous bureaucratic obstacles, and international currency shortages; as a result, there was a decrease in the share of holiday-makers in outbound tourism. In contrast, business travellers, travelling on behalf of state monopolies, had privileged access to simplified administrative procedures and their share of outbound tourism increased after 1970.

As has already been observed, this picture was to change radically after 1989 and the remainder of this section considers in further detail changes in tourist motivations and preferences.

3.3.1 Slovakia

A stronger statistical base exists for the study of incoming tourists in Slovakia than in the Czech Republic. Since 1994, a major annual survey of incoming tourists has been undertaken in the former by the Tourism Institute on behalf of the Tourism Department of the Ministry of Economy (Ústav turizmu, 1995–1998). As the time series for this survey only covers four years, 1994–7, trends cannot be established with any confidence. However, some changes, related to the transformation, can be identified.

The main object of both the domestic and the foreign tourist gaze (Urry 1990) was mountain landscapes (Table 3.4). The second most important attraction was urban and cultural tourism, which are closely interlinked. Except for Bratislava and Košice (which have business and culture tourism), the major tourist attractions were historical mining towns (Banská Bystrica, Banská Štiavnica, Kremnica) and the towns of the Spiš region (Levoča, Kežmarok). Water-based and spa tourism were significant only in the Danube region, the Váh River Valley and the Lower Zemplín region, but they dominated tourist demand in these areas. As the 1994 survey of foreign tourists was undertaken in the summer and autumn, it excluded winter sporting activities, and underestimates the importance of the mountains as destinations. Yet, winter sports are probably the fastest-growing tourist activity in Slovakia. This was reinforced by state intervention: in 1995, the TDP began to subsidize the renewal of some 30 major winter

TABLE 3.4   *The principal visitor interests in Slovakia in 1994 and 1996, and in the Czech Republic in 1996*

Tourist interest:	Czech Rep	Slovakia			
	Foreign visitors	Foreign visitors		Domestic visitors	
	1996	1994	1996	1994	1995
Mountain tourism	x	55.4	51.9	37.3	37.8
Urban tourism	75.0	34.3	33.1	2.7	2.3
Cultural tourism	50.1	32.7	25.6	1.2	1.0
Water-based tourism	x	26.9	23.6	28.5	31.0
Spa tourism	x	24.3	21.0	6.0	7.8
Rural tourism	63.8	16.8	16.2	3.5	5.0
Shopping tourism	35.2	17.9	16.9	n.a.	n.a.
Visiting friends and relatives	16.2	23.6	29.3	13.5	10.7
Skiing	x	n.a.	30.1	n.a.	n.a.
Low-cost eating out	41.5	x	x	x	x
Castle visits	65.7	x	x	x	x
Discovering a different culture	62.4	x	x	x	x
Other	x	n.a.	n.a.	7.2	4.4
Total		x	x	100.0	100.0

Sources: Ústav turizmu (1995–1998); Marcom (1996).
Notes: Multiple response for foreign tourists in each Republic; n.a. = not available; In the Czech Republic, urban tourism includes historical cities, while rural tourism includes rural and mountain tourism. In Slovakia, the figures for 1994 are simple averages for the summer and autumn, while the figures for 1996 are weighted averages for the summer, autumn and winter surveys.

centres in the mountain districts in Northern, Central and Eastern Slovakia.
The seasonal distribution of visitors peaked around July and August during most of the 1990s, and there was no strong winter season with January having the lowest monthly share (Figure 2.1). However, the single-peak seasonal pattern changed in 1997. In the course of 1996 and 1997, several ski resorts were equipped with snow cannon which markedly strengthened the winter season. While the summer was still the strongest season in 1997 (23.3 per cent of foreign visitors arrived in July and August), its relative importance declined compared to the winter. The share of the latter more than doubled from 8.6 to 20.6 per cent in the period 1993–7, whilst the share of summer visitors decreased from 43.3 to 32.6 per cent. A number of factors may have contributed to the relative shift to winter tourism, including a decline in summer transit travel and a growth in Christmas visits to friends and relatives (VFR), but the growing popularity of skiing is probably the main reason; this is confirmed by surveys (Ústav

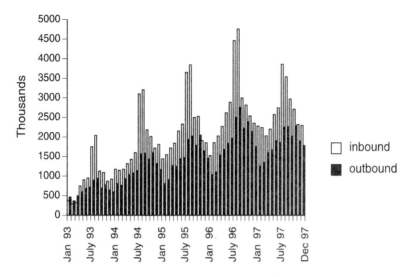

Fig. 3.4 Inbound and outbound numbers of visitors (at frontiers) in the Slovak Republic, for selected months 1993–7.
Source: Štatistický úrad Slovenskej republiky (1991–1998c).

turizmu 1995–1998) which demonstrate increasing international tourist interest in skiing and other winter sports in Slovakia. The outbound flows of Slovaks were distributed more equally during the year, with July and August (10.2 and 10.2 per cent of the total) and October (10.2 per cent) being most important. There were only moderate seasonal changes in the period 1993–7 (Figure 3.4).

There were no major changes in tourist preferences according to the 1994 and 1996 surveys. However, there were more substantial shifts in the purposes of their visits (Table 3.5). While the total volumes of visitors and nights increased in the mid 1970s, the shares of tourists motivated by recreation, discovery and culture decreased. At the same time, there was a sharp rise in business travel, related to the post 1974 economic boom. The renewal of growth in CEFTA, increased foreign trade with the EU (see Williams *et al* 1998), and economic recovery in the Ukraine produced a more favourable economic environment for business travel; as a result the share of business visitors to Slovakia increased from 8.7 to 22.8 per cent, 1994–7. In addition, improved living standards in neighbouring countries, particularly in the Czech Republic and Hungary, stimulated an increase in the share of visits to friends and relatives from 12.3 to 17.8 per cent in the same period.

TABLE 3.5   *Foreign visitors to Slovakia and the Czech Republic by purpose of visit in 1993, 1994 and 1997 (percentages)*

	Slovakia 1994			Slovakia 1997				Czech Republic	
Purpose of visit	Summer	Autumn	Total 1994	Winter	Summer	Autumn	Total 1997	1993	1996
Transit	31.9	29.2	30.6	18.6	28.1	25.9	25.1	20.0	15.0
Recreation	24.5	18.1	20.3	20.3	21.7	9.0	11.6	50.0	55.0
Discovery and culture	13.4	17.0	15.2	4.4	10.4	7.0	7.4	x	x
VFR	11.3	13.2	12.3	15.8	16.9	19.0	17.8	18.0	21.0
Shopping	9.2	11.4	10.3	8.7	8.2	10.7	9.7	20.0	9.0
Business and study	8.4	9.0	8.7	30.0	12.7	24.9	22.8	9.0	21.0
Visits to spas	1.3	2.1	1.7	1.4	2.0	3.5	2.7	n.a.	3.0
Total	100.0	100.0	100.0	100.0	100.0	100.0	100.0	x	x

Sources: Ústav turizmu (1995–1998) for Slovakia; Ekonom weekly (1994) and GfK (1997) for the Czech Republic.
Notes: for Slovakia the figures for 1994 are simple averages for the summer and autumn surveys, while the figures for 1998 are weighted averages for the summer, autumn and winter surveys; for the Czech Republic, multiple answers are possible so the columns total more than 100%; the recreation category includes discovery and cultural travel in the Czech Republic; n.a. = not available.

These broad patterns can be further disaggregated by national market segments:

- Czech Republic: 67 per cent of this market is based on business, VFR and recreation tourism;
- Germany: 62 per cent of this market is accounted for by transit and recreation tourism;
- Hungary: shopping, VFR and transit tourism have a 62 per cent share;
- Poland: transit and recreation have a 67 per cent share;
- Austria: business, shopping and VFR, account for 68 per cent of the market;
- Ukraine: shopping, transit and business are the main reasons for 72 per cent of all trips.

National differences in the purpose of visit are the outcome of particular historical legacies and geographical conditions. Slovakia has long been attractive to Czech, Polish, (East) German and Hungarian tourists for skiing and mountain hiking, because it provided one of the few accessible mountainous regions in Central Europe prior to 1989. There are also historical friendship and family ties across the Czech and Hungarian borders,

TABLE 3.6 *Regions of tourist interest, in Slovakia, 1994–6; by country of origin*

Country of origin	Preferred regions, 1994	Preferred regions, 1996
Czech Republic	Danube Region, Váh River Valley, Bratislava. Kysuce	Kysuce, Váh River Valley, High Tatras
Poland	High Tatras, Orava	Orava, High Tatras
Austria	Bratislava, Danube Region	Bratislava
Hungary	Danube Region, Košice, High Tatras	Danube Region, Bratislava, High Tatras
Ukraine	Zemplín Lower, Košice, Šariš	Zemplín Lower, Košice, Šariš
Germany	Bratislava, High Tatras, Trnava region	Bratislava, High and Low Tatras
Slovakia	High and Low Tatras, Váh River Valley	High and Low Tatras, Váh River Valley

Source: Ústav turizmu (1995–1998) and (1997).
Note: the data for domestic tourists refer to 1995 and 1996.

which generate international tourism. Tourists from Ukraine were mostly interested in shopping and business, and this was related to 'informal foreign trade', smuggling and/or buying and reselling consumer goods. Austrian tourists have a preference for urban tourism and, since 1989, have established strong business and shopping links with Bratislava; in turn, the Western Slovakian cities have established strong business and shopping links with Austrian regions.

There is a strong neighbourhood effect in the regional destinations of foreign tourists within Slovakia (Table 3.6). This is reinforced by the short duration of visits: except for Czech tourists, Slovakia was a second- or third-holiday destination for most foreign tourists. In addition, there are accessibility constraints: some 80–90 per cent of foreign visitors use their own car and, while Slovakia has a generally well-developed road network (Johnson 1997), there were only 200 km of motorway in 1996. As foreign visitors tended to restrict their visits to destinations accessible within two or three hours travel of the gateway entry point, the limited motorway network strongly reinforced the neighbourhood effect. However, German and Hungarian tourists were also likely to visit some of the remoter regions, especially the High Tatras and the Spiš region. German tourists were attracted by the unspoilt natural surroundings (mentioned by 90 per cent), and they also had a strong preference (81 per cent) for individual travel, and for taking several short and medium breaks rather than a single long holidays (37 per cent) (Opaschowski 1990). This reinforced the tendency to more flexible and individualized holidays outside the regions of mass tourism. There was little change in the tourists' regional preferences in the period for which we have data, 1994–6; this is again evidence of path dependency. The main changes were as follows: Czech tourists became more interested in the High Tatras; there was a shift in German preferences to the Piešťany spas (in the Trnava region); and Hungarian preferences shifted to Košice. However, in terms of the overall regional pattern, there was considerable stability between 1994 and 1996, with Bratislava (21.4 per cent) and the High Tatras (20.3 per cent) being the leading destinations.

There were also some changes in the socio-demographic profile of visitors:

- In 1996, 33.7 per cent of visitors originated from within 100 km of the Slovak borders, which was similar to 1994.
- The age structure of the visitors is relatively stable, and is predominantly composed of young and middle-aged adult: in 1996, 59.9 per cent were aged 25–44.
- The visitor profile is relatively upmarket in terms of social status: 16 per cent classified themselves as upper class, 31.6 per cent as upper middle, 32.0 per cent as lower middle class and 6.3 per cent as, what was termed, lower class. There was a shift towards higher status tourists over time, partly due to the growth of business tourism under market conditions (Table 3.5). Slovakia's share of repeat visitors is relatively high (71.5 per cent in 1996), and with the easing of some of the crises of the transformation in the neighbouring countries in the mid 1990s, the visitors from these countries – who tended to have a relatively high status – have returned in large numbers. Such visitors are higher spending and prefer holidays in the autumn and winter seasons. It is not, however, clear whether the shift to a higher status client profile is sustainable, and the results of the 1997 visitor survey indicate counter-tendencies.
- In 1997, both the numbers of foreign visitors and international tourist receipts decreased for the first time since 1989. The total numbers of German visitors increased, but pensioners and housewives accounted for unusually large shares of this group. Similarly, Czech visitor numbers increased, but only due to rapid expansion of VFR tourism. The numbers of Austrian, Hungarian and Polish tourists decreased (Bujna 1998). These shifts are counter to those observed in previous years, and may be an aberration related to the extensive flooding in parts of Central Europe in the spring and summer of 1997.

In terms of the foreign visitors' evaluation of their holidays in Slovakia, they mainly emphasized the natural beauty, the friendliness of the host population, the 'atmosphere' of the country and its rich culture heritage. The landscape quality in the national parks, in particular, reinforced perceptions of an untouched nature (Table 3.7). The urban and cultural heritage of Slovakia are given little prominence in marketing, but constitute promising areas for future tourism marketing. Unfortunately, we can not comment on tourist perceptions of these features, as they were not included

TABLE 3.7 *Foreign tourists' evaluations of Slovakian holidays in 1994 and 1996*

Tourists	Satisfied with (%)		Disappointed with (%)	
Comments on:	1994	1996	1994	1996
Beauty of nature	67.5	n.a	n.a	n.a.
Friendliness	51.4	n.a.	n.a.	n.a.
Atmosphere	41.4	n.a	n.a	n.a.
Currency exchange	42.9	35.8	14.1	9.4
Historical sites	43.6	n.a.	n.a.	n.a.
Language convenience	43.3	29.5	16.6	16.5
Gastronomy	39.8	40.2	12.2	6.8
Accommodation	34.7	33.8	n.a.	n.a.
Price levels	36.1	32.4	14.6	10.9
Transport	33.5	24.0	n.a.	n.a.
Hygiene	33.6	27.8	16.7	20.6
Reliability	32.9	35.3	15.1	11.5
Culture, sports, entertainment	22.9	20.8	10.3	7.5
Quality of service	25.1	n.a.	19.2	n.a.

Source: Ústav turizmu (1995–1998) and (1997).
Notes: multiple response are possible so the columns do not total 100%; n.a. = not available; the figures for 1994 are simple averages for the summer and autumn surveys, whilst the figures for 1996 are weighted averages for the summer, autumn and winter surveys.

in the 1997 survey. Foreign tourists considered that the main disadvantages were an unfamiliar language, low levels of service quality and hygiene, inconsistent standards of accommodation, weak images of Eastern Slovakia, and a lack of marketing information at the local level. Between 1994 and 1996, perceptions of the gastronomy, and the reliability and friendliness of staff in tourist establishments improved.

There were some differences in the evaluations of particular national groups of tourists in 1996. Tourist from the former state-socialist countries (the Czech Republic, Poland and Ukraine) appreciated the language familiarity, and the quality of the accommodation services, but were disappointed by high prices, transport and information services, and the lack of cultural sites. Hungarian tourists were the most negative amongst these. In contrast, Austrian and German tourists were positive about the low prices, the facilities for currency exchange, the accommodation and the gastronomy, but they were disappointed by the hygiene, information and cultural services, transport and language difficulties.

Slovak tourism relies on established markets, and in 1996 repeat visitors accounted for 71.5 per cent of all visitors. This share was highest for Czechs (92.1 per cent), which is not surprising given the recent partition of Czechoslovakia and the 70 years of shared coexistence of the two Republics. There was also a high level of repeat tourism from Hungary (88.8 per cent), which can be explained by a long common border, limited possibilities for travel during the years of state-socialism, and large volumes of VFR travel. Repeated visits were important but at a lower level for Germans and Poles. In contrast, the share of first-time visitors were relatively high for countries such as Denmark, Sweden, UK, France, Italy, and Belgium. The expansion of new markets seems to have proceeded despite rather than because of Slovak tourism marketing abroad. Only 10 per cent of foreign tourists obtained information on Slovakia via travel agents, tourist fairs or advertisements in the media.

One of the most informative questions in the survey concerns whether the tourist felt able to recommend Slovakia to others. The answers are relatively encouraging, but far from overwhelming, and show national variations as can be seen in the following data: Poland (69.6 per cent), Germany (61.4 per cent), the Czech Republic (57.8 per cent), Austria (52.5 per cent), Ukraine (49.4 per cent) and Hungary (47.1 per cent). Another useful index is the proportion of visitors who expressed a wish to visit Slovakia again in future; in this case, there was a relatively positive endorsement; visits to the mountains (51.9 per cent), cities (33.1 per cent), skiing (30.5 cent) and VFR-related travel (29.3 per cent) were the main focus of interest. There were also variations by nationality: for example, the main interests of the Czechs were in the mountains, VFR and skiing, while those of the Austrians were the cities, mountains and shopping.

3.3.2 The Czech Republic

The first inbound tourism surveys in the Czech Republic were commissioned by the Ministry of Economy, and undertaken by ECOMA Ltd, in 1992 and 1993. These surveys included about 3000 visitors at the Czech frontiers. Since 1994 incoming surveys have been undertaken by the GfK agency and are based on samples of 7300 visitors. The GfK surveys also had more interview points, interview days and questions than the ECOMA survey so the results are not strictly comparable. In addition, a special survey of travel motivations was undertaken by the Marcom agency. These surveys identify broad trends in tourism in both Republics, although comparisons between them must be approached cautiously.

The seasonal distribution of tourist flows to the Czech Republic has a single peak in the summer. However, the winter–summer season differential is smaller than in Slovakia, due to the relatively greater importance of cultural, business and spa travel in the Czech Republic. Similarly to Slovakia, the curve of the seasonal distribution of tourist inflows flattened in the period 1993–7: the share of the summer season (July–September) decreased from 32.5 per cent to 29.3 per cent, while that of the winter season (January–March) increased from 16.6 to 29.3 per cent. This was due to investment in winter tourism attractions, including the staging of more

76

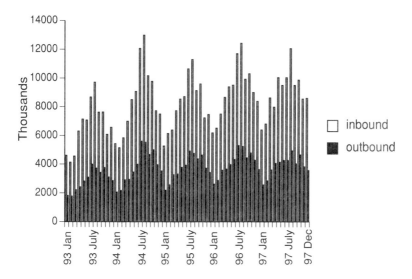

Fig. 3.5 Inbound and outbound visitors (at frontiers) in the Czech Republic, by month 1993–6.
Source: Český statistický úřad (1993–1998b).

cultural events, the development of ski resorts, and increasing numbers of spa visitors.

The numbers of foreign visitors have grown more slowly than international tourism receipts. This is partly accounted for by a shift to higher income tourism, one indicator of which is the larger proportion of visitors coming by air and staying in relatively expensive Prague hotels. While visitors from neighbouring countries remain the major market, there have been increasing numbers of intercontinental visitors (from Japan, the USA and Israel in particular).

The Czech Republic's market profile is strongly grounded in its rich historical and cultural heritage and there is a pervasive image of beautiful cities in the tourist gaze (Simonian 1995a, Marcom 1996). Prague is a major attraction and accounted for almost one half of all foreign overnights in the Czech Republic in 1996. Spa towns, such as Karlovy Vary and Mariánské Lázně, have also been poles of attraction. As in Slovakia, differences in the principal tourist interests were segmented along nationality lines (Table 3.4) in 1996:

- historical cities were attractive to 75.0 per cent of tourists, but especially those from Spain, Italy and the USA;

- castles attracted 65.7 per cent of tourists, particularly those from Russia, Spain and Italy;
- nature and landscape was of interest to 63.8 per cent, particularly the Dutch, Italians and Americans;
- the discovery of a different culture was of interest to 62.4 per cent of tourists, particularly Italians, French and Americans.

The other major tourist interests were entertainment, culture, low-cost restaurants and cheap accommodation for transit travellers. These data suggest that the Czech and Slovak Republics have different tourist images. While foreign tourists associated the Czech Republic with Prague, castles, rural landscapes and a distinctive and valued culture, Slovakia was seen as an arena for outdoor tourist activities.

This tourist image of the Czech Republic was reflected in the regional distribution of foreign tourists. The most visited counties were Western Bohemia (34 per cent) and Prague (18 per cent), followed by Southern Moravia and Southern Bohemia. However, the distributions of visitors and overnights were different. Whereas Western Bohemia was the leading destination for the former because of the presence of large numbers of German excursionists, Prague dominated the regional distribution of overnights.

The differences between the principal travel *motivations* of foreign tourists (Table 3.5) were far smaller than the differences in the tourism *interests* of foreign visitors to the Czech and Slovak Republics. In the 1993 survey, approximately one half of foreign visitors to the Czech Republic stated that individual recreation travel was their principal travel motivation; 20 per cent were in transit, 20 per cent were on shopping trips, 18 per cent were visiting friends and relatives, 9 per cent had come to eat out (especially in border regions) and 7 per cent were on business trips. By 1996, the shares of recreation (55 per cent), VFR (21 per cent), and business (21 per cent) had all increased while the shares of shopping (9 per cent) and transit tourism (15 per cent) had fallen. The Czech Republic generated more VFR-related travel and spa travel than Slovakia, which can be explained by large numbers of Slovaks visiting friends and families in the Czech Republic, and the strong international reputation of the Czech spas. The Czech Republic had a lower share of transit travellers, while the shares of shopping and business were similar in both Republics.

The Czech tourism industry has a very high level of market loyalty: 88 per cent of visitors were repeat visitors (compared to 71.5 per cent in Slovakia) in 1996, and 50 per cent were on at least their sixth visit. The exceptionally high level of repeat visitors is consistent with the large proportion (87 per cent) who reported that they were fully satisfied with their visits (in Slovakia the proportion was only 50–70 per cent). Moreover, 87 per cent of visitors stated that they would like to return on a future occasion. In terms of negative impressions, there was a surprisingly high level of fear of crime, complaints about transport (the quality of road surfaces and of rail travel), and dissatisfaction with the lack of sports facilities and tourist information (GfK 1997).

Most trips by foreign visitors to the Czech Republic were of very short duration. In 1993, approximately one half were day visitors and 20 per cent spent only one night in the Czech Republic. The average length of stay was three days in 1993, and by 1996 this had slipped further to 2.8 days, when day trips accounted for 50–60 per cent of all trips by foreign visitors (GfK 1997). Transit travellers accounted for about 10–15 per cent, and tourists for about 35–40 per cent of all visitors. In addition, the proportion of lower social status visitors increased whilst total international tourist receipts decreased in 1997 (Hospodářské noviny daily 1998; GfK 1998). This may have been an erratic effect caused by the spring/summer 1997 floods in Central Europe. Similar changes in the structure of demand and receipts were registered in the same period in Slovakia.

3.4 THE ECONOMIC IMPACT OF INTERNATIONAL TOURISM

In terms of the role of tourism in the transition societies, the main interest in the international flows described in this chapter are the resulting economic impacts. We consider the limited evidence available for the two countries separately.

3.4.1 Slovakia

Official data provided by National Bank of Slovakia reports are comparable with corresponding data from most OECD countries. They are calculated using standard methods for computing international tourism income and include the foreign currency exchanged for national currency by foreign tourists in commercial banks and tourism agencies. Originally, all the currency exchanges by foreign travellers were counted as international tourism receipts. However, some foreign 'tourists' exchanged foreign currency for business purposes, related to cross-border trade, as part of the 'bazaar capitalism' economy; it was therefore difficult to distinguish between visits generated by tourists, and by such traders, whether operating legally or illegally. On the other hand, some tourist receipts were not transacted through either commercial bank outlets or travel agencies. These included payments in foreign exchange to small hotels and restaurants, and for various form of entertainment including prostitution. Such payments later emerged in the foreign currency accounts of domestic residents in commercial banks. The National Bank of Slovakia has been using an International Monetary Fund model, since 1993, to adjust estimates of international tourism receipts so as to take into account personal foreign currency receipts (see Table 5.1). Their accuracy, however, is questionable. Surveys by the Tour-

TABLE 3.8   *Tourist expenditure in Slovakia and the Czech Republic, 1994–6: by type of expenditure and travel*

Type of expenditure	Slovakia 1994	Slovakia 1996	Czech Rep. 1996	Type of travel	Slovakia 1996	Czech Rep. 1996
Total (US$ mil): of which (%)	1,275	1,808	10,650	Total	1,808	10,650
Accommodation	28.3	18.1	29.4	transit	4.9	5.5
Gastronomy	13.6	16.8	17.9	1 day trips	13.7	18.2
Transport	14.7	16.1	15.3	2–3 days	35.0	x
Shopping	33.4	43.6	28.9	4+ days	46.5	x
Services	10.0	5.4	8.5	all tourists[1]	81.5	76.4
Total	100.0	100.0	100.0	Total	100.0	100.0

Sources: Ústav turizmu (1997), GfK (1997) and authors' own computations. The 1994 and 1996 data were computed as averages of the seasonal data.

Note: 1 = excludes transit visitors and excursionists.

ism Institute (Ústav turizmu 1995–1998), based on personal interviews with 3477 visitors, estimate that the average daily foreign tourist expenditure in 1996 (including visitors with zero expenditure) was US$ 34.1 per visitor, and this represented an increase of US$ 6.1 compared to 1994. The total volume of international tourism receipts computed in this way was US$ 1808 million (Table 3.8). Even if the lowest variant of these estimates is used, decreasing calculated volume by 20 per cent to allow for sampling error, the volume was still 2.5 times greater than the official receipts recorded by the National Bank.

The average expenditure of US$ 34.1 has a seasonal dispersion ranging from US$ 21.9 in summer to US$ 34.4 in winter, and US$ 39.9 in autumn and spring. This is consistent with the higher social status of tourists in the winter and the shoulder seasons. One of the most marked changes over time has been an increase in shopping expenditure, the share of which increased from 33.4 per cent in 1994 to 43.6 per cent in 1996. Austrians, Germans and Ukrainians were the highest spenders. The latter were usually purchasing goods that were to be recycled in Ukrainian markets, so that tourism and retailing were linked to international trade via 'bazaar capitalism' in this instance. International tourist flows motivated by a mixture of shopping, smuggling and petty trade objectives date back to at least the 1970s, and were not a product of the transition (Böröcz 1996, p 184). But the transition made travel easier for a broader set of countries, and for the Ukraine and Russia in particular. There was also an increase in visitor expenditure in restaurants, which is consistent with visitors' comments about improvements in Slovak gastronomy, noted earlier (Table 3.7). Expenditure for accommodation and other tourist services decreased. This was not confirmed in the official hotel statistics on nights spent and prices charged in hotels, but Czechs, and particularly Ukrainians, frequently stayed with friends and relatives.

One question asked in the Tourism Institute surveys concerned the amount that tourists were willing to spend on a one-week half-board trip in Slovakia? The answers to this hypothetical question ranged between US$ 245.8 and US$ 252.0 depending on the season, which is remarkably close to the actual expenditure recorded by the same survey – US$ 34.1 per capita per day, multiplied by 7 days. This provides further confirmation of the accuracy of the data provided in these surveys which, in turn, indicates that a significant proportion of the tourism industry operates within the shadow economy.

3.4.2 Czech Republic

Average tourist expenditure increased from US$ 25–30 per visitor per day in 1993 to US$ 31–43 in 1996 (Ekonom weekly 1994; GfK 1997; Table 3.8). The average of US$ 35.4 per visitor per day in 1996 was seasonally dispersed, being US$ 32.7 in May, US$ 30.5 in August, and US$ 43.1 in October. The lower levels of summer expenditure are explained by higher shares of transit tourism and low-income travellers in these seasons. Both the average expenditures and their seasonal distributions were surprisingly similar in the Czech and Slovak Republics. In terms of the structure of expenditure, the share accounted for by the accommodation sector was higher in the Czech Republic (29.4 per cent) than in Slovakia (18.1 per cent) in 1996, reflecting the higher quality and prices of Czech hotels. The broad structures of other types of expenditure were similar for the two Republics (Table 3.8) (GfK 1998).

If the average spending by various categories of foreign visitors is multiplied by the numbers of days spent in the Czech Republic, then total international tourism receipts are estimated at US$ 10.65 billion in 1996 (compared to US$ 13.29 billion in 1997). The 1996 survey estimate was 2.5 times higher than the international tourism receipts recorded by the Czech National Bank in the same year. Almost exactly the same ratio of reported and actual receipts was reported in Slovakia. The shadow economy seems to operate with the same degree of efficiency in both Republics. Furthermore, these findings are broadly comparable to Böröcz's (1996, p 172) estimate that some 55–75 per cent of international tourist receipts were unreported in Hungary in 1981–3. If these estimates are reliable, then the scale of the 'informal' tourism industry in state socialist Hungary was similar to those in the Czech and Slovak Republics during transition. It can be speculated that the time lag is explained by the earlier introduction of market reforms in Hungary.

81

3.5 CONCLUSIONS: THE ROLE OF INTERNATIONALIZATION

1989 was a milestone in tourist flows to and from the Czech and Slovak Republics, and the ensuing transformation has seen a significant re-internationalization of their inbound and outbound markets. There was a degree of continuity and path dependency for the main generating countries and destinations generally remained the same before and after 1989 (Germany, Poland, Hungary, Austria). However, the scale of international tourism changed fundamentally: the numbers of incoming tourists increased four-fold and outgoing tourists eight-fold. This was reflected in rapid growth of international tourism receipts and expenditure. The main increases were in the period 1990–4, and the scale of visitor flows has subsequently stabilized.

The analysis of the international tourism statistics has identified some common but also some different trends in tourist flows to the two Republics:

- There were significant increases in business and VFR-related travel. While the former was linked to the transformation to market economies, the latter was partly enhanced by the 'velvet divorce' of 1993, when many friendship and family networks were divided by the new Czech-Slovak border. The increases in business and VFR-related travel were also stimulated by the boom in the CEFTA economies after 1993 (see Chapter 2) and improved living standards in Central Europe in the second part of the transition (see Williams and Baláž 1999). Shopping tourism, resulting from price differences in the Czech and Slovak Republics on the one hand, and Germany and Austria on the other, has also been an important component of the re-internationalization of tourism since 1989. In contrast, transit travel has decreased in relative importance, especially in the Czech Republic, as other forms of tourism have expanded more rapidly.
- While the general motives for incoming travel differed little in the two Republics (in terms of the importance of recreation, business, shopping, and VFR), their tourist images were very different. In the Czech Republic the 'tourist gaze' (Urry 1990) was organized around the attractions of Prague, pleasant rural landscapes and a lively culture, while Slovakia was considered a tourism arena for outdoor activities. The stronger tourism image of the Czech Republic has allowed it to attract more foreign visitors from more distant European, American and Asian markets than has Slovakia.
- The Czech and Slovak tourism marketing agencies seem to have had limited effectiveness. Most tourists continued to source their travel information from friends and relatives, or from brochures and articles, and advertisements by tour companies and travel agents. Few foreign tourists were directly engaged by the agencies' marketing activities.

- There was a trend of diminished seasonal variation in tourist inflows and outflows in both Republics in the 1993–7 period. In Slovakia, the summer remains the leading season but its share has decreased, while there have been substantial increases in winter travel, along with a strong component of autumn travel, particularly for business, shopping and VFR. There was also a moderate relative increase in winter tourism outflows and moderate decreases in summer tourist outflows. Different tourist images generated slightly different seasonal distributions of visitor flows in the two countries. The summer peak was sharper in Slovakia than in the Czech Republic, partly due to the greater concentration on outdoor activities and transit travel in this season. Czech incoming tourism relied more on the attractions of its historical cities so that there were relatively smaller seasonal differences.

- Most foreign visitors were from adjoining border regions and their visits were of short duration. Excursionists were the most frequent category of visitors. This reinforces the path-dependent element of tourism flows, as well as the importance of location as a contingency factor.

- There was a high level of repeat visits amongst foreign tourists, as well as a desire to return in future. The general level of satisfaction was higher in the Czech Republic, but the respective surveys do not provide sufficient information to explain this. Most complaints concentrated on the quality of tourism services (including transport) and the availability of tourism information.

- Average per capita per diem visitor expenditure, as established by border surveys, was very similar in both Republics, and was generally low. This was due to the high shares of excursionists and transit travellers in both countries. As for the structure of expenditure, the Czech Republic enjoyed higher receipts from accommodation, while shopping expenditure was more important in Slovakia. This divergence was related to price and quality differences in Czech and Slovak tourism services and general price level differences.

The above summary confirms that Czech and Slovak patterns of international travel had distinctive features. On the one hand, these countries accounted for large numbers of foreign visitors: 108 million in the Czech Republic and 32 million in Slovakia in 1997. The Czech numbers, for example, were higher than those for Italy (51.8 million), the UK (21.0) million and Spain (61.4 million) which were all far more populous countries. If countries of a similar size are taken into account, then the numbers of foreign visitors to the Czech and Slovak Republics significantly outnumbered those in Portugal (21.7 million) and Greece (11.3 million) in the mid-1990s. This rapid growth both in inbound and outbound travel started in 1989, immediately after the fall of the Iron Curtain (Figure 3.1). In

Czechoslovakia, for example, the number of foreign visitors rose from 29.6 million to 46.6 million and the number of outbound trips increased from 8.6 million to 20.6 million in 1989–90. There were similar tendencies elsewhere in Central Europe. For example, the number of inbound visitors in Poland rose from 8.2 to 18.2 million and outbound trips from 19.3 to 22.1 million in the same period (WTO 1994). However, as noted by Pearce (1995, p 34) 'countries such as Hungary and the former Czechoslovakia received large numbers of visitors who appear to spend relatively small amounts'. The pattern of 'high volumes of visitors with low per visitor spending' did not change significantly during the transition. On the contrary, the numbers of visitors increased significantly while spending per visitor remained relatively low.

The previous discussion has noted a number of distinctive but changing features of international tourism in the Czech and Slovak Republics. This leads us to consider how they compare to models of international tourism elsewhere in Europe. Concentration ratios (market share taken by the leading source countries) provide an useful device for international comparisons. In the Czech Republic, the concentration ratio remained the same for the top five and top ten countries during 1993–6. In Slovakia, the concentration ratio increased for both the top five and top ten countries in the same period. The Czech market was more diversified with 62.1 per cent of foreign overnights accounted for by the five main generating countries and 79.6 per cent being accounted for by the ten leading countries in 1996. The respective values for Slovakia were far higher at 73.4 and 86.1 per cent (Figure 3.6). How does international travel from/to the Czech and Slovak Republics compare to other countries with similar populations, such as Austria, Portugal, the Netherlands and Belgium? The Czech market was much more diversified than Portugal's (where 74.1 and 87.1 percent of nights spent were by tourists from the leading five and ten generating countries), Spain's (79.6 and 89.8 percent), Belgium's (76.4 and 85.9 percent), the Netherlands' (79.6 and 88.3 percent) and Austria's (85.4 and 94.0 percent). Slovakia's market structure resembled these countries in 1994 (Figure 3.7). There were also low concentration ratios in Hungary (61.6 and 77.9 per cent). This indicates a lesser degree of dependence on a limited number of generating countries in the Czech Republic and Hungary than in Slovakia.

The main markets of the Czech and Slovak Republics were their neighbouring countries. The ratios of short-haul travel to total travel (42.8 and 59.3 percent respectively), as expressed in terms of the proportions of foreign overnights spent by tourists from neighbouring countries, resembled those in the Netherlands (69.5), Belgium (62.9) and Austria (73.9). In all these countries, short-term travel, generated mainly by business, VFR and short breaks, was of major importance. In contrast, Spain (8.0), Portugal (9.6) and Hungary (16.7), were far more dependent on long-haul travel,

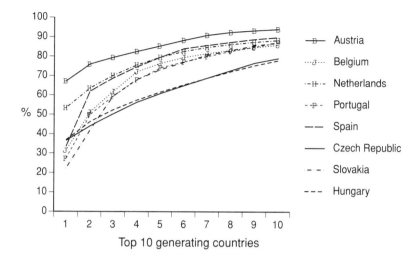

Top 10 generating countries

Fig. 3.6 Concentration ratios for nights spent by foreign tourists in selected OECD countries and the Czech and Slovak Republics in 1996: top ten generating countries.
Source: OECD (1996), Štatistický úrad Slovenskej republiky (1991–1998a), Český statistický úřad (1989–1998b).

and especially on the German and UK markets. The Czech Republic had a relatively higher ratio of long-haul travel (57.2) than either Slovakia or Belgium, indicating its greater geographical market range as a tourist attraction, with at least some structural similarities to Southern European destinations.

The patterns of international tourism have already changed significantly since 1989, but what are the likely future trends? Business and VFR-related travel have been the most rapidly growing market segments since 1990, and these tend to be concentrated on neighbouring countries. Therefore, Czech–Slovak, Czech–Polish, Czech–German, Slovak–Ukraine and Slovak–Austria flows are likely to remain of major importance. The Czech and Slovak Republics are unlikely to follow the Spanish and Portuguese patterns of holiday travel and become dependent on longer-haul intra-European travel. As such, the Czech and Slovak markets will remain more similar to those in the Netherlands and Belgium than those in Spain and Portugal. On the other hand, the Czech Republic has attracted growing numbers of foreign tourists from more distant markets, such as the UK, USA, Israel and Japan (Baláž and Mitsutake 1998), and shows a limited shift towards the Southern European model of international tourist flows. In terms of outbound tourism, there has been a clear shift in Czech and

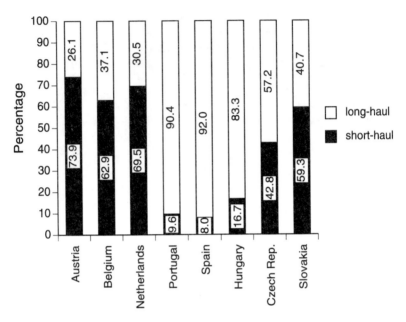

Fig. 3.7 Ratio of short-haul to long-haul travel in selected OECD countries and the Czech and Slovak Republics in 1996.
Notes: short haul travel: nights spent by tourists from neighbouring countries
long-haul travel: nights spent by tourists from other countries.
Source: OECD (1996), Štatistický úrad Slovenskej republiky (1991–1998a), Český statistický úřad (1989–1998b).

Slovak interests to the 'sun and sea' destinations, notably Italy, Spain. Greece and Croatia. These destinations replaced the Black Sea coastal regions in Bulgaria, Romania and the former USSR as the destinations of holiday tourism. As indicated by surveys reported in Chapter 7, there have been sharp contrasts between interests and preferences, and the reality of foreign travel. The economic difficulties of the early stages of the trans-formation were reflected in increased travel to neighbouring transition countries, due to cost constraints, especially given the preponderance of VFR tourism. 'Sun and sea' destinations, however, were of increasing importance for the Czech and Slovak middle classes, which burgeoned in the second part of the transformation. With living standards improving, the 'sun and sea' destinations are likely to increase in importance and Czech and Slovak patterns of outbound travel may become similar to those of Austria, Germany, Netherlands, Belgium and other 'non-sun' European countries. There has also been an increase in travel to long-haul destinations outside Europe (mostly related to business), but their market shares are limited. Holiday trips to Caribbean or Asian destinations remained the preserve of a relatively narrow group of new rich.

Finally, we return to the question of path dependency and path creation. There was inevitably a considerable degree of path dependency, if only because the location of the Czech and Slovak Republics in the geographical heart of Europe could be expected to generate large volumes of transit tourism, almost irrespective of political and economic regimes. Secondly, there is good accessibility between Leipzig, Vienna, Prague, Budapest, Krakow and Bratislava (or the Tatra mountains), facilitating interchanges between these major centres of population. If price differences (which existed under state socialism as well as being integral to the uneven transformation), together with the family ties resulting from the multicultural environment in Central Europe (VFR travel) are taken into account, then it is not difficult to understand the high levels of short-haul and short-break tourism. They are determined by geography, economic conditions and historical ties. The same motives for short-term travel (VFR, shopping, petty trade and smuggling) have also been observed in Hungary in the 1980s (see Böröcz 1996, pp 144, 153–73).

Path dependency can also be seen in the concentration ratios. Most of the international travel in the GDR, Czechoslovakia, Poland and Hungary before 1989 was concentrated amongst these five states. There were a number of reasons for this. Russians, Bulgarians and Romanians were not allowed to travel freely to the rest of the Eastern block, let alone the West, whilst there was at least relatively free travel amongst the other five nations. In addition, travel was dominated by economic objectives. Czechs, Slovaks, Poles and Germans travelled to Hungary as consumers and traders, because the Hungarian government was importing consumer goods from the West on a relatively large scale. Eastern tourists travelled in order to obtain profits (or reduce their losses) resulting from different structures and performance levels in their national economies – and this remained as true after 1989 as it had been in the 1980s.

There was also evidence of path shaping after 1989. With the establishment of market economies and the removal of barriers to foreign consumer imports and travel, the economic objectives of travel (shopping/trade/smuggling) and the VFR function did not disappear. On the contrary, these gained in importance but also expanded into new geographical and economic areas. Large Russian and Ukraine travel markets opened up, and Ukrainians and Russians now travel in order to exploit differences in their national economies and life styles. They buy and sell tobacco products, alcohol and other items on which it is possible to make a profit in Poland, Slovakia and Hungary. Much of the travel also relates to job seeking, and this is facilitated by the fact that Ukrainians and Russians do not need visas in Hungary, Poland and the Czech and Slovak Republics. In turn, Czechs,

Slovaks, Poles and Hungarians travel to Austria and Germany, and elsewhere in Western Europe, for the same purposes. The nationals of CEE countries have long been used to scanning and exploiting the opportunities resulting from differences in national tax and price levels, and sometimes absolute supplies, but the transformation has produced new possibilities. Similarly, Böröcz (1996, p 192) found 'international tourism a major driving force behind the creation of a large-scale informal economy in Hungary' in the state-socialist period. This characterizes most of the transformation economies, because such international mobility helps erase differences between the transformation economies themselves, and between the transition and market economies.

Perhaps the key to understanding short-haul international travel in Central Europe is that it is multi-functional. A typical example is a Slovak student working illegally for two weeks on a farm in Austria, making a one-week trip to the Alps, then buying a new jacket in Vienna, buying/smuggling a computer for himself/herself and buying/smuggling/selling a snowboard in Slovakia. Of course, such multi-purpose trips also occur in the West (see Urry 1990 on the notions of post-modernist tourism), but mostly at a reduced level.

Elements of path creation can also be seen in the longer-haul holiday tourism markets, both at the intra-European and the intra-continental scales. With the lowering of administrative and legal barriers to foreign travel, new forms of holiday packages have evolved, focused mainly on Southern Europe. Whilst modelled on Western European inclusive tours in many respects (and sometimes organized by Western European tour companies – see Chapter 4), indigenous capital has also been innovative in developing holiday packages within the market constraints emanating from the highly polarized distribution of incomes in Central Europe. There are many indicators that, in future, the patterns of holiday tourism from Central Europe will converge more on these Western (more precisely, Northern) European models.

4 THE PRIVATIZATION AND DEVELOPMENT OF THE PRIVATE SECTOR

4.1 PRIVATIZATION: NEO-LIBERALISM AND 'POLITICAL CAPITALISM'

Privatization is one of the key components of the transformation in Central Europe (Nielsen *et al* 1995). It plays a number of roles in the sharp shock neo-liberal model of economic transformation, but especially in improving enterprise efficiency, and facilitating the creation of markets. Individual property rights are integral to the linking of enterprise performance, and the returns to individual owners, managers and workers. Privatization was mainly presented as an economic issue in the early stages of transformation in Czechoslovakia. The transformation from central planning to a market economy required a strong private sector but – in a country, where the average salary was only US$ 110 per month – this presented an enormous challenge. The creation of a private sector through 'normal' market processes of capital accumulation, even if this had been possible, would have taken several decades. Instead, the privatization of state-owned enterprises offered a shortcut for creating a private sector within three to five years. This strategy, however, had major shortcomings; not least, a general lack of capital in Central Europe meant that privatization was mainly implemented as a form of property re-distribution, which generated little new capital.

The neo-liberal perspective on privatization set out above is over-simplistic, for the economic transformation can not be viewed as rational process of designing economic institutions, but instead involves '... rebuilding organizations and institutions not on the ruins but with the ruins of communism' (Stark 1996, p 995). In other words, the institutional legacies of state-socialism significantly shaped privatization in Central Europe in the 1990s. This chapter examines the redistribution of property rights after 1989, which has followed distinctive phases, focusing on the divergent experiences of the Czech and Slovak Republics after 1993. There were different strategies for controlling and distributing property rights in the two Republics, and these need to be understood in terms of the coincidence of interest groups and firm networks. The strategic decisions about privatization were determined less by technical issues than by political and social interests (Cox 1994, p 406), which perceived that privatization provided a one-off opportunity to accumulate wealth. To some extent this approximates to Staniszkis's (1991) notion of the emergence of political capitalism, whereby a new relationship is forged between political power and the control of capital; privileged access to political power has been used to accumulate power and wealth (Williams and Baláž 1999), especially in the absence of effective regulatory frameworks for privatization. The last point is critical, for the creation of markets has been highly uneven with far more attention being given to property rights than to institutions and regulation.

The first part of this chapter reviews the general topic of the Czech and Slovak privatizations between 1990 and 1997, while the second part is concerned with privatization in the tourism sector. Given that tourism has often been at the leading edge of privatization, the sector has been surprisingly neglected in research on this topic (but see Johnson 1997 on the Hungarian hotel industry and Hall 1995 for a general overview). The key issues are the privatization of the main state-owned tourism enterprises, the volume of property privatized, the privatization timetable and the methods and processes of establishing a class of new owners. Case studies are presented to illustrate the process of establishing the private sector in the different branches of tourism, and data is also drawn from in-depth interviews with a sample of firms.

4.2 PRIVATIZATION PATHWAYS

Privatization is a loose term which signifies the expansion of privately owned property, and it can be deconstructed into two main forms (Dallago 1995): distributive privatization, involving the redistribution of property rights relative to existing assets, and creative privatization, based on the creation of new privately owned assets. Here we focus principally on distributive privatization, in respect of which Estrin (1994) identifies ten possible approaches:

1. sale by public offering of shares;
2. sale by private treaty (closed or limited tender);
3. sale by public auction;
4 leasing assets or firms;
5. management and/or worker buyouts;

6. free (or almost free) distribution of shares/vouchers to the population at large;
7. free or subsidized distribution of shares to the workforce/management;
8. free distribution of shares to social institutions;
9. restitution of property to former owners;
10. privatization via liquidation or bankruptcy;

That list omits one important form of privatization, the transfer of state property to municipalities. The latter accounted for a significant part of the total volume of the property privatized both in the Czech and the Slovak Republics.

Most of these different privatization mechanisms have been used in the Central and Eastern European countries, with the precise mix reflecting differences in political organization and inherited economic structures. While there have been important national differences in the privatization programmes, there have also been broad similarities in their sequencing if not in their speed. In every country, there were two basic stages of privatization: small-scale and large-scale. The Small Privatization began almost immediately after the fall of the communist regimes in 1989 or, in Poland, even earlier. Auction was the dominant method of privatization. Retail units, restaurants and small service and manufacturing firms were sold to domestic investors, backed in some instances by foreign capital. Sale prices were close to book or market values, and investors were paid by cash or via loan allowances. This stage lasted a limited time period, of some two to three years, in all of the Visegrád Four Central European countries.

Large-scale privatization commenced later and was usually based on tenders and direct sales of medium and large State-owned enterprises (SOEs). Both domestic and foreign investors participated. The former usually relied on bank loans and the large discounts from market value that were available to management-led employee collectives, while the latter had the resources to pay the full market price. In the period 1991–6 this phase overlapped with the mass privatization programmes implemented in the Czech and Slovak Republics, and in Poland. These programmes converted SOEs into joint-stock companies and distributed their shares free of charge amongst the population as a whole. Finally, there are indications that a third phase of privatization has taken place, implemented not by the state but by powerful industrial and finance interests groups. These lobbies assembled diluted shareholdings from the mass privatization programmes in the Czech and Slovak Republics, and used the leverage effect of majority stakes in investment funds to secure control of much larger capital in the underlying companies (see Williams and Baláž 1999). One of the positive outcomes of the Large Privatization was creation of capital markets. Although these were illiquid and flawed by corruption, they significantly helped to advance the process of investment allocation and re-allocation (Baláž 1996a).

The process of privatization in the Czechoslovak federation originated within a single legal and economic framework but, after the independent republics were created in 1993, the programmes diverged to some extent.

4.2.1 The Czech Republic

The Small Privatization programme was based on Act 427/1990 ('the Small Privatization Act'). This project mainly applied during 1990–93 to operational units of state enterprises active in retailing, travel and catering services. The process was managed by regional privatization commissions and included sales and auctions. In total, 22,212 units, with a total opening bid value of Kč 21,028 million (US$ 725 million), were sold for an aggregate price of Kč 31,234 million (US$ 1077 billion), equivalent to 3.4 per cent of GDP in current market prices in 1993. Foreign investors were officially excluded from bidding, but given the shortage of domestic capital are believed to have backed many domestic bidders. While the clandestine nature of these links precludes definitive evidence of foreign involvement, the fact that the average wage was US$ 100 and that the price of even a medium sized hotel with 50 beds was US$ 500–700,000, makes it difficult to believe that they were not widespread.

The Large Privatization programme was based on the 'Large Privatization Act' 91/1991. SOEs, or parts of these, were transformed into joint-stock companies (JSCs), transferred to the National Property Fund (NPF), and, finally, privatized. By 1991, total assets of Kč 1514–1614 billion (US$ 54–58 billion, equivalent to some 125–133 per cent of the 1995 GDP in current market prices), had been earmarked for denationalization. 78 per cent of these assets had been entered into the privatization process by the end of 1994 (Češka 1995). This involved the following steps:

1) compilation, by the relevant 'parent' ministry, of a potential list of enterprises to be privatized, which required state approval;
2) submission of privatization projects by interested parties;
3) reviews of the projects by the relevant ministries and the Ministry of Privatization;
4) approval of the projects by the Government or National Property Fund.

A number of different methods were used in the Large Privatization: public auction, public tender, capital market sales, direct sales, transfer free of charge (mainly to municipalities and restitution) and contributions to the property of joint-stock companies (including coupon privatization). A limited number of companies were sold directly to foreign investors, but this was far more common in Hungary than elsewhere in Central Europe. However, foreign investors were later able to buy all, or significant portions, of the privatized property from their new owners. Some SOEs,

TABLE 4.1   *The Large Privatization in the Czech Republic from 1991 to 31 December 1995: disaggregated by privatization methods*

Method	Total units earmarked for privatization	Property value in US$ mil.	Units privatized by 31.12.1995	Property value in US$ mil.[3]
1. Property sales and restitution				
Auctions	911	0.3	762	0.3
Public bids	1,030	1,102.9	528	684.4
Direct sales	4,600	2,251.1	3,459	2,006.3
Free-of-charge transfers	3,427	1,557.3	2,939	1,076.0
Restitution[1]	467	19.8	409	16.0
Restitution with sales[2]	256	149.0	239	135.2
Total	10,751	5,351.3	8,336	4,171.6
2. Transfers from state-owned enterprises (SOE) to joint-stock companies (JSC) and between joint stock companies				
From SOE to JSC	1,415	20,161.6	1,398	20,121.1
From JSC to JSC	309	8,080.5	306	8,185.7
Total	1,724	28,242.4	1,704	28,194.4
1. + 2. Total	12,475	33,593.8	10,040	32,366.1

Source: ČNPF, Český fond národního majetku (The Czech National Property Fund), in: Ekonom 19/1996, pp 31–5.
Notes: 1 = restitution free of charge; 2 = restitution free of charge plus payments for additional privatized property; 3 = The exchange rate was 1 US$ = 26.602 Kč, on 31.12.1995.

or large shareholdings in such companies, have not been privatized and represent strategic state holdings by the NPF. Table 4.1 summarizes the extent of the Large Privatization programme as of December 1995.

Not all SOEs were sold to new, individual owners. The transfers of state property to municipalities and restitution were expected eventually to account for Kč 450 billion of capital assets. There was also the process of mass privatization. In the First and Second Wave of Coupon Privatization, the shares of 1688 companies with a total nominal value of Kč 300 billion (US$ 11 billion) were distributed. All citizens aged over 18 were authorized to buy a book of coupons, entitling them to 1000 coupon points, for a total cost of Kč 1,035 (US$ 35). The coupons could only be exchanged for shares in the privatization of particular companies (Dlouhý and Mládek 1994).

In 1995, the so–called 'Third Wave' took place: large financial and industrial lobbies campaigned aggressively to persuade minor shareholders to sell their shares to the new majority group. These lobbies initially obtained minority stakes in the main investment privatization funds and, via lever-

TABLE 4.2.   *The ownership structure of Czech joint-stock companies: percentage shares of the main interest groups.*

Owner	1994	1995
Individual investors	25	18
Investment funds	39	32
Domestic (strategic) investors	9	10
Foreign investors	3	8
Managers	1	4
Municipalities	2	4
State	13	14
Others	8	10
Total	100	100

Source: Ekonom weekly, p. 16, 27/1996.
Note: 'Others' includes the Restitution Fund, employees and other owners.

age, effectively came to control a considerable part of the Czech economy (Williams and Baláž 1999).

Privatization created a new social class structure. Ownership rights over a significant proportion of national property have been transferred to a limited circle who, in consequence, became 'the new rich'. A Coopers and Lybrand survey (Klvačová 1996) identified the following trends in a sample of 70 joint-stock companies in the period 1994–5:

a) Rapid changes in ownership structure, as individual investors and investment funds sold large stakes to both domestic (strategic) and foreign investors (Table 4.2).

b) A decrease in the proportion of investment fund representatives in the higher levels of corporate governance from 30 to 20 per cent. This was matched by an increase in the share of domestic (strategic) and foreign investors from 8 to 15 per cent. Managers own some 4 per cent of these companies' shares, but occupy 35 per cent of higher levels (i.e. boards) of corporate governance. The managers are the most active and powerful group of owners, and their importance has increased. In contrast, individual investors and NPF representatives tend to be the most passive members of corporate governance bodies.

c) Corporate governance bodies have become more interested in business development, in response to changes in the remuneration systems, which have tended to become more performance-related. The proportion of corporate governance bodies whose remuneration is dependent on profitability increased from 16 per cent in 1994 to 54 per cent in 1995.

Managers remain the most influential class in post-communist societies, indicating the importance of path dependency. Their ascendancy started in the 1970s, when educated technocrats were fully incorporated into the communist party bureaucracy. In the 1980s, the managers – through their central position in national economic organization – constructed a strong position in the state-socialist societies. Since at least 1982, and the death of Brezhnev, the communist parties of Central Europe have become significantly more reliant on technocrats. Most of the Central Committee members were directors of major enterprises, economic ministers, or directors of government agencies. This class effectively ruled the country. The managers became highly dominant within individual enterprises because of their accumulated knowledge. They were able to exploit this advantage in the transformation, and secured property rights and direct or indirect control of many of the enterprises privatized in the 1990s.

In the early 1990s, coupon or mass privatization temporarily favoured the financial lobby (banks and investment funds) which, in many cases, were backed by foreign capital. However, the Investment Companies Act (the 248/1992 Act) limited the single stake of a single investment company in any enterprise to 20 per cent. Subsequently, many financial institutions, unable to obtain strategic holdings, sold their minority stakes to managers and domestic (strategic) and foreign investors. This creation of a new ownership structure has ironically been entitled 'the Third Wave of Privatization'. In the Slovak Republic, where the Second Wave of Coupon Privatization was replaced by direct sales to managers, the managerial class became even more influential.

By 1995, the private sector nominally accounted for about 70 per cent of GDP, and the Large Privatization programme was essentially completed. In general, private companies outperformed SOEs, but the results varied according to the form of privatization (Williams and Baláž 1999), and by sector. In addition, the results for the state sector are skewed by the fact that many basic processing industries, some of which have faced severe financial problems, have not been privatized.

Privatization in the Czech Republic brought ambiguous results, as elsewhere in Central and Eastern Europe (Pohl *et al* 1997). On the one hand, it helped to create the private sector and some of its key institutions, especially capital markets. On the other hand, it sharpened social cleavages and opened the way for fraud, corruption and market failures. The method of privatization was of particular importance. While the preferred strategy of coupon privatization enabled the transfer of property rights over large tracts of state property, its hasty implementation had negative consequences for the Czech economy and society. Share companies, in which investment funds were major shareholders, usually had relatively weak economic performances. The investment funds themselves became an arena for questionable and, or even criminal practices. Many were 'hollowed out', meaning that their assets were transferred quietly or clandestinely to limited companies owned by enterprise manages. In this way, their capital and the property rights of hundreds of thousands of minor shareholders were effectively removed, and sometimes were stolen. The most notorious example is the Czech Republic's best-known entrepreneur, Viktor Kožený (McIntyre *et al*, 1994), who has been enjoying life in the Bahamas while being accused of stealing the assets of minor shareholders; he probably represents widespread current practice rather than being an exception (Baláž 1996b).

The Czech Ministry of Finance's report on the functioning of the capital market (reported in Ekonom weekly No.45/1997, pp 78–9) provided a rare, welcome, but belated, outburst of self-criticism, stating that 'The investment funds made the process of finding the real owners of companies difficult. They obstructed the restructuring and revitalization of the Czech economy and prevented progress in increasing labour productivity and restarting economic growth.' The report also cited numerous examples of fraud and the questionable conduct of investment funds managers, which had damaged the interests of minor shareholders. It stated that 'Privatization created space for those people who were interested in personal profits, at any price. Those who organized the privatization process did not take into account the advice given by lawyers and international experts with respect to supervising the property re-distribution. By now, we (the public sector) are lagging behind the aggressive class of new owners, who do not respect any of the rules commonly applied in the modern world' (Ekonom weekly 1997). This provides graphic support for the argument that the redistribution of property rights was not matched by the creation of new institutions in the process of establishing a market economy.

In autumn 1997, it transpired in the press that the ruling Civil Democracy Party had received millions of dollars from 'unknown sponsors' (located in Hungary and Mauritius) to support its electoral campaigns. Police inquiries established that the 'unknown sponsors' were not altruistic donors but powerful interest groups involved in some of the largest privatization projects. The election contributions were effectively bribes to pave the way for the acquisition of lucrative enterprises. This scandal led to the resignation of the Klaus government and to new elections. Not only the ruling parties were involved in privatization scandals, for in March 1998 the Czech Parliament commenced an investigation into the activities of the main opposition party, the Social Democrats. The party leaders were forced to admit their presence at a secret meeting in Switzerland in 1995, at which a group of Czech–Swiss entrepreneurs had offered substantial sponsorship to the party; if the party was successful in the next election, these entrepreneurs would be appointed to government and thus secure privileged access to privatized companies. Such widespread corruption, which found fertile soil in the course of privatization, had a devastating effect on popular faith in democratic values. This was reflected in a 1998 opinion poll, which revealed that a majority of Czechs considered they had been more satisfied with life under state-socialism than under democracy (*Financial Times* special supplement on the Czech Republic, 14 May 1998).

4.2.2 Slovakia

The legislative and institutional background of privatization was the same for both the Czech and Slovak Republics in 1990–92, with the essential legal framework being provided by Acts 427/1990 and 91/1991 (discussed in the previous section).

In the Small Privatization, 9757 units with a value of Kč 12.7 billion (US$ 454 million) had been sold in the Slovak Republic (equivalent to 3.5 per cent of 1993 GDP) by the end of 1993. This mainly involved the wholesale and retail trades, and the hotel and restaurant sectors – which we return to later in this chapter.

The Large Privatization coupon scheme in Slovakia originally involved 503 major enterprises with coupon-privatized stocks valued at Kč 79,720 million (US$ 2.7 billion), equivalent to 22 per cent of 1993 GDP, in current market prices. The total property allocated in the First Wave (including NPF holdings, restitution and transfer to municipalities) had a nominal value of Sk 169.1 billion (US$ 5.1 billion), some 46 per cent of the 1993 GDP at current market prices. In the Second Wave, the property originally designated for the coupon privatization of Sk 70 billion was reduced to Sk 40 billion. Then, in 1994, the Slovak Government replaced the coupon scheme by an NPF-guaranteed Sk 10,000 bond scheme, redeemable by the year 2000. With some 3.3 million applicants, the scheme should have had a total nominal value Sk 33 billion (US$ 1.1 billion), representing 7.3 per cent of 1995 GDP in current market prices (Baláž 1996b). However, it was postponed several times and was only implemented on a limited scale at the end of 1996. The state was unable to redeem all the bonds, and it permitted the shares of a limited number of companies to be exchanged for bonds. Bond owners had to bid for these at 75 per cent of their nominal prices. The NPF promised to redeem all the bonds by the end of 2000 for the nominal price plus the discount rate. It is questionable whether it will be able to do so. The bond scheme was very generous to the new owners of privatized enterprises, who purchased individual bonds for Sk 7500 or less from the population at large. Later, they used the bonds to repay their privatization debts at the full nominal price of the Sk 10,000 bonds.

The most significant policy shift in privatization has been that, since November 1994, the state has commenced a large-scale direct sale of privatized enterprises; this subsequently became the dominant method of Slovakian privatization. In 1995 for example, the NPF issued 376 privatization decisions with purchase prices totalling Sk 36.7 billion (US$ 1.2 billion), equivalent to 8.2 per cent of the 1995 GDP in current prices (SFNM

TABLE 4.3 *The Large Privatization in the Slovak Republic, 1991–96, disaggregated by privatization method*

| Method | Property privatized, in US$ million | | | |
	1st Wave	2nd Wave	Total (Abs)	Total (%)
Sale of property[1]	477	2,767	3,245	34.6
Free-of-charge transfers[2]	63	88	151	1.6
Restitution[3]	115	68	183	2.0
Coupon privatization	2,402	0	2,402	25.6
Shares in the NPF portfolio	1,438	951	2,388	25.5
Allocation to various funds	598	414	1,012	10.8
Total	5,093	4,289	9,382	100.0

Source: Ministry of Administration and Privatization of National Property of the Slovac Republic (1996).
Notes: the exchange rate was 1 US$ = Sk 33.202 in 1993 (1st Wave) and 1 US$ = Sk 31.895 in 1996 (2nd Wave); 1=includes the government bond scheme; 2=includes transfers to municipalities; 3=includes allocations to the Restitution Fund.

1996a). 'Government-friendly' enterprise managers were the main beneficiaries. In 1995, the average purchase price was only 10–25 per cent of the nominal enterprise price. In an extreme case, a 39 per cent NPF holding worth Sk 6423 million (US$ 217.3 million) in Slovnaft, a leading Slovak oil company, was sold in 1995 to a group of 16 'government friendly' managers for Sk 100 million, which was equal to only 1.6 per cent of its nominal value (SFNM 1996a). In 1996, a further 250 state-owned companies with a total value of Sk 42 billion (US$ 1.4 billion) were scheduled to be privatized, accounting for 8.4 per cent of estimated GDP in that year, at current prices. During the Second Wave of the Large Privatization in Slovakia, a total of 610 enterprises with property of Sk 136.8 billion (U$ 4.2 billion) were privatized and 1366 new private enterprises were created. The increased number of establishments was due to the divestment or fragmentation of many units; for example, the Interhotel chain was sold in batches of 5 or 7 establishments (Table 4.3).

Slovak privatization, like that in the Czech Republic, had ambiguous outcomes. Rapid development of the private sector would not have been possible without rapid privatization. Inequitable, and sometimes illegal, practices, in the Second Wave of privatization in particular, deeply divided Slovak society into 'haves' and 'have nots', in terms of property rights. While large volumes of privatized property were subject to fraud and misconduct in the Czech Republic, property privatized in Slovakia in the Second Wave was passed directly to selected groups usually constituted of 'government-friendly' managers, ruling party officials and their spouses.

This property redistribution created a new economic and social framework in Slovakia in a very short time span.

4.2.3 Reflections on privatization

Smith (1997, p 335) contends that 'New forms of capital accumulation emerge unevenly and bring with them new class relations, but these represent the contingent implementation of capitalist and pseudo-capitalist practices and social relations rather than the creation of 'shimmering landscapes of capitalism'.' This clearly applies to the experiences of privatization, which has been a path-dependent path-creating process (Nielsen *et al* 1995, Williams and Baláž 1999). Path dependency was inevitable given the initial lack of capital and entrepreneurship, and the institutional legacy, which was evident in spontaneous or *nomenklatura* privatization, as well as in social practices. But the combination of the First and Second Waves of privatization, with the weak and uneven emergence of regulation and corporate governance, created dynamic conditions where less-intended outcomes became possible, as in the 'Third Wave' of privatization. The First and Second Wave created a property redistribution, which was inherently unstable, and generated conditions for further dynamic shifts in the control of property rights.

Privatization has had profound social implications. A one-off redistribution of property rights has contributed to the replacement of state-socialist society, characterized by constrained social inequalities, by a sharply polarized social structure. This, in turn, has had implications not only for the control of production and wealth, but also for domestic tourism markets (see Chapter 7). Arguably, the free distribution of shares via mass voucher schemes could have effected income redistribution from rich to poor (Ash *et al* 1994, p 223), but such effects have been muted by the lack of information available to individual voucher holders, and by the manipulation of property rights by managers and financial institutions in the 'Third wave'. Privatization, which was supposed to create a strong and entrepreneurial middle class, has instead significantly deepened social divisions.

By 1998 both the Czech and Slovak NPF were on the verge of insolvency, despite billions of dollars of property having been privatized. The investment privatization funds had been almost completely 'hollowed out', and the same was true for many companies privatized via Coupon Privatization. With different methods being used in the Second Wave of privatization in the Czech and Slovak Republics, the results were surprisingly similar: a thriving private sector coexisted with large sections of society feeling they had been cheated or robbed of their property rights and, ultimately, of means of consumption.

4.3 TOURISM AT THE LEADING EDGE OF PRIVATIZATION

4.3.1 Background to tourism privatization

Pre-1989 Czechoslovakia was a pseudo-federation of the Czech and Slovak Socialist Republics, within which tourism development was regulated at the national level (Table 4.4). Tourism structures, therefore, were almost identical in the two Republics. Most commercial tourism establishments were controlled by national Ministries for Trade and Tourism, including the Čedok Travel Agency and the main hotel chains (six Interhotel chains in the Czech Socialist Republic and three Interhotel chains in the Slovak Republic). District councils controlled the Restaurace, district networks of restaurants, pubs and hotels. The Jednota, national consumer co-operatives/associations, were another important player in the tourism sector. They had, and still have, shops in every municipality, as well as networks of restaurants and hotels in tourism areas in both the Czech and Slovak Republics.

There was a parallel network of non-commercial tourist establishments, of which there were three main types: spas and similar establishments controlled by the national Ministries of Health; trade union-owned hotel chains; and tourism units established by almost every enterprise and state organization. The non-commercial tourism sector was designed to provide services for 'insiders' – trade union members, employees or, in the case of the spas, individuals nominated by the health service. It is important to stress the scale of the non-commercial tourism sector. The numbers of beds in this sector matched those in the commercial one (Table 4.5), and the quality of the establishments varied from five-star hotels in Karlovy Vary spa or the High Tatras to wooden mountain chalets. Although the non-commercial sector was fundamentally designed for domestic tourism, the trade unions had exchange schemes with their partners in state-socialist countries. Most of the major Czechoslovak enterprises also had their own tourism units on the shores of Lake Balaton in Hungary, or the Black Sea coast in Bulgaria and Romania. For example, the Martin tank factory had a holiday camp on the shores of Lake Balaton, whilst the Karvina coal mines had facilities in Bulgarian and alongside Lake Balaton.

The tourism industry in Czechoslovakia was typical of Central Europe, it that it handled large volumes of visitors and generated low income. In 1990, for example, the 46.6 million visitors generated only US\$ 365.9 million of income in the accommodation sector, an average of only US\$ 7.9 per visitor including expenditures in non-convertible currency. The prices of accommodation and other services were centrally planned and there was neither the need nor scope for competition. The quality of service was generally poor and the huge tourism potential of the country was under-utilized in terms of tourism receipts.

After 1989, the new governments considered that tourism offered major

TABLE 4.4   *The tourism system in the Czechoslovak Socialist Republic*

Funding body	Tourist enterprises in:	
	Czech Socialist Republic	Slovak Socialist Republic
Ministry of Trade and Tourism	Čedok, Travel Agency Čedok Interhotel (Praha, Karlovy Vary, Liberec, Brno, Ostrava, Krkonoše, Bratislava, Rušomberok, Tatry), hotels	*Javorina*, (Liptovský Mikuláš), hotels, cable cars and travel agency
Ministry of Health[1]	*Balnea*, Czechoslovak State Spas and Springs (Prague), spa, travel agency	*Slovakoterma*, Czechoslovak State Spas and Springs (Bratislava), spa, travel agency
Other ministries and central bodies[1]	Tourism units of the state-owned enterprises and organizations	Tourism units of the state-owned enterprises and organizations
District councils	*Restaurace*, hotels and restaurants District Tourist Enterprises, hotels, cable cars, information	*Reštaurácie*, hotels and restaurants District Tourist Enterprises, hotels, cable cars, information
National Sports Associations	*Sport-turist*, travel agency	*Slovakoturist*, travel agency
National Agriculture Co-operatives' Associations[1]	*Recreation Office*, hotels	*Recreation Office*, hotels
National Consumer Co-operatives' Associations	*Rekrea*, travel agency (Prague) *Jednota*, shops and restaurants	*Tatratour*, travel agency (Bratislava) *Jednota*, shops and restaurants
	Federal bodies	
Socialist Youth Association	CKM, travel agency	
Trade-Union Committee[1]	Central Office for Recreation, trade union-owned hotels	
SVAZARM ('Army friends')	Autotourist, travel agency	

Source: Kopšo (1985).
Notes: 1 non-commercial bodies providing services for their members or within the health insurance framework.

development opportunities but that privatization was a basic precondition for increasing the sector's efficiency. Before 1989 many hotels and restaurants had operating deficits, and the new regime was neither willing nor able to continue subsidizing them. Private ownership was expected to improve profitability in the tourism sector and generate international currency

TABLE 4.5   *Capacities and performance in the Czechoslovak tourism industry in 1989*

	Number of establishments	Beds	Visitors	Occupancy rates, %
Czech Republic[1]				
Commercial sector	2,863	158,288	7,434,371	50.5
Spas	n.a.	34,781	459,593	88.7
Trade-union hotels	75	10,621	519,818	84.7
Tourism units of non-tourism bodies	10,625	264,539	2,833,750	21.9
Slovak Republic[2]				
Commercial sector	988	66,118	3,849,204	47.3
Spas	n.a.	10,989	153,216	93.5
Trade-union hotels	22	3,988	198,251	86.7
Tourism units of non-tourism bodies	3,147	61,792	592,031	17.6

Sources: 1 = Federální statistický úřad (1986–1993a), 2 = Ministerstvo obchodu a cestovného ruchu Slovenskej republiky (1990).
Notes: figures for the commercial sector, spas and trade-union hotels are for 1989; figures for non-tourist bodies are for 1985.

receipts which were a national economic priority. In addition, income from privatization would strengthen the state budget. There were also strategic reasons for tourism privatization: to promote a private sector and to create a new entrepreneur class. The tourism industry was ideal for this purpose, because of potentially strong demand conditions in that sector, and the relatively low prices of the units to be privatized.

4.3.2 Privatization and tourism: timetable and methods

A standardized privatization approach to the sector was not possible, given the variety of ownership forms involved. For example, the *Jednota* – the consumer co-operative chains of restaurants and hotels – was recognized as a private sector body, exempted from privatization, and remained in co-operative ownership. The trade-unions also rejected attempts to privatize their hotels, which included some of the largest and best-organized hotel chains in the two Republics. Non-profit associations (Socialist Youth and Agriculture Co-operatives) have been transformed but still retain most of their original property. However, the remainder of the tourism sector was earmarked for privatization, but different sub-sectors were privatized at different times and by different methods.

- Enterprises controlled by the national Ministries of Trade and Tourism were transformed into state enterprises and, later, into state-owned, joint-stock companies. The removal of central planning was seen as the first step in their privatization. The Čedok Interhotel enterprise was divided into six Czech and three Slovak independent Interhotel enterprises, which were further sub-divided to the level of individual hotels. During 1991–4 the hotels were included in the coupon privatization (mostly in the Czech Republic) and/or sold via direct sales (mostly in Slovakia). The property of the Čedok Travel Agency, one of the largest travel agencies in Eastern Europe, was divided between the Czech and Slovak Republic. The Czech component was given the rights to the original trade mark, while the new Slovak organization emerged as Satur, plc. Both enterprises were sold via public offer.
- The *Restaurace* and *Reštaurácie* chains and the District Tourist Enterprises were mostly allocated to the Small Privatization programme during 1991–2, but many units were transferred to the municipalities.
- Privatization of spas was closely linked to the privatization of health care, which was too challenging a project for the early stage of the transition. The first privatization commenced after 1994, and direct sales were the vehicle for this in both republics.
- The transformation of the tourism units of the non-tourism enterprises had to wait for the privatization of the parent companies. Coupon privatization was used in the case of large industrial firms. The approaches of the new owners to the tourism units they had acquired along with their industrial units were diverse. Some divested and sold the tourist facilities, while others incorporated these into the new business structures. Unfortunately, there are no reliable statistics available on these units. However, most seem to have been transformed into commercial firms. The tourism units of the non-profit organizations in the public sector were also transformed into commercial units, but they still maintained the function of providing cheap holidays for 'insiders', even if their markets were increasingly commercialized. Finally, a few tourism units remained closed to 'outsiders', such as Smolenice castle which is owned by the Slovak Academy of Science.

Most tourism establishments were privatized within the Small Privatization and the Large Privatization programmes. Each programme had advantages and shortcomings.

TABLE 4.6   *The Small Privatization programme and the Slovak tourism industry at the end of 1992*

Sub-industry	Units sold		Selling prices	
	Numbers	Percentage of total units scheduled for small privatization	Kč million	Percentage of total units scheduled for small privatization
Restaurants	1,276	13.2	1,648	11.3
Hotels	128	1.3	881	6.1
Other tourism units	71	0.7	56	0.4

Source: Slovak Statistical Office (1993).

Small Privatization Programme

In Slovakia the program included the privatization of 128 hotels and 1276 restaurants, representing 73.4 per cent of all the tourism units scheduled for privatization (Table 4.6) Hotels and restaurants were the most comprehensively privatized sector in the Slovak economy. The main method was public auction, with the outcome being determined almost solely by bid prices. The Small Privatization was a rapid means for effecting the transition from central planning to a market economy in the tourism industry.

In general, the results of the Small Privatization programme were positive. Without doubt, the thousands of new owners significantly helped to boost tourism development in the Czech and Slovak Republics. They were particularly flexible in responding to the increased demand from incoming tourism after 1989. However, there were also shortcomings in the process. Many bidders had little or no experience of the market economy. They took out large privatization loans, pledged against the privatized property, and sometimes paid inflated prices for these assets. Not surprisingly, they rapidly slid into bankruptcy and the properties were acquired by the banks. The banks tried to resell these at their original valuation prices because rigid accountancy rules did not permit discounting to their real market values. As a result, many bank-owned tourism establishments remained closed for several years, during which time they were often vandalized or deteriorated through neglect. These inflexible accountancy rules provide another example of the incomplete process of creating markets: the redistribution of property rights was not accompanied by sufficient institutional change.

Another negative aspect of the Small Privatization was the over-hasty privatization of the District Tourist Enterprises. These units had been established and supported by district governments, during the 1970s, as part of a concerted attempt to build up local and regional tourism infrastructures, including hotels, restaurants, cable cars and information centres.

The quality of service provided by the District Tourist Enterprises was variable, but the Enterprises had created the first effective territorial tourism structures. They were managed by the district councils and tourism development was incorporated into territorial development plans. After 1990, most of the Enterprises' property was divested to individual entrepreneurs via public auctions, and only a minor part of their property was transferred to the municipalities. This meant that the means was lost for co-ordinating tourism development within the overall territorial development framework. The lack of self-governing regions in Slovakia and the Czech Republic after 1989 further complicated regional tourism development.

Large Privatization Programme

In the Czech Republic, 11 large hotels were included in the First Wave of coupon privatization, which offered stakes ranging from 40–90 per cent of their estimated capital value. In 1994 the remaining stakes in six of these hotels were offered in the second wave of coupon privatization. The banks and the major privatization funds became major shareholders, but the state still retains important stakes in some instances.

The coupon privatization did result in some investment in Czech hotels. The basic capital in the five-star Prague Intercontinental Hotel, for example, was only Kč 646 million, but it received investment of Kč 1500 million in the course of 1995. One half of this was provided by its major shareholder, the Prague Investment and Postal Bank. The new capital funded the almost complete reconstruction of the hotel. These investments considerably improved profits, so that, in 1997, hotel sales (less VAT) were Kč 722 million (Kč 114 million higher than in 1996) and gross profit was Kč 230 million. Most of its clients come from abroad, the average occupancy rate was 73 per cent in 1997, and the average income per room/per night was Kč 6584. In another example, the four-star Prague Forum Hotel received an investment of Kč 110 million whilst its basic capital was valued at Kč 1000 million. These and similar investments were motivated by fierce competition in the sector, and the need to upgrade facilities to match Western tourists' expectations. The situation was similar outside Prague. In the Interhotel Palace hotel in the well-known Western Bohemian spa of Mariánske Lázně, for example, the originally low base capital of Kč 3.6 million was increased to Kč 95 million. Elsewhere, the Černigov hotel in Hradec Králové increased its basic capital of Kč 64 million by Kč 40 million as facilities were upgraded in order to retain its three-star rating (Vechter 1995).

One of the effects of privatization was to create a relatively low concentration of ownership of Czech hotels. The coupon privatization diluted the hotels' shares amongst investment funds, banks and minor shareholders.

Except for the banks, most shareholders were unable to generate investment funds. On the other hand, the smaller stakes are being transferred by a step-by-step process to the major domestic and foreign investors. For example, the powerful CKD Blansko group became the major shareholder in the Interhotel Palace hotel in Mariánské Lázně spa (Vechter 1995). Only the major shareholders were able to raise the funds urgently required for reconstruction, so that the redistribution of property rights via privatization was of vital economic importance.

The fragmentation of the Czech hotel industry retarded the establishment of hotel chains. The financial group Top Spirit (related via personal ties and financial holdings to the above-mentioned Investment and Postal Bank), for example, prepared ambitious plans for establishing a major chain of ten hotels with 1500 beds, travel agencies, spas and transport companies. The holding company, City Hotels Group, was expected to have a 20 per cent share of total Czech tourist income. The Top Spirit group tried to assemble the chain from the property which was directly and indirectly owned by its parent bank. This property, however, was of variable quality and types, so that the luxury Prague Forum and Panorama hotels were placed in the same group as eco-farms and rural inns. After a period of mismanagement, the City Hotels Group was sold to Malta-based Corinthia Hotels International in 1996 (Zeman 1998b). This transaction attracted unexpected controversy when, in March 1998, the US embassy announced that Corinthia Hotels International was controlled by the Libyan government. Given that American law embargoed business with Libya, it was illegal for American citizens to stay in any of the group's properties. This was a devastating blow for the group's Prague hotels which were heavily reliant on the high income American market. This quirky anecdote illustrates how, even after several years after privatization, the process of identifying the real owners of property was incomplete, and that the Czech authorities had little control over this.

In many ways, spas were 'the jewels in the crown' of Czech tourism. Most spas were privatized via the coupon method in 1992, but some units were sold through direct sales or scheduled for restitution. Selected health establishments specializing in health care for children and the treatment of particular diseases, such as arthritis, were retained in state ownership for social reasons. Other spas which were scheduled by the Czech National Property Fund (CNPF) for future public tender were subject to the dubious privilege of being placed under state management in the meantime. Many spa managers, appointed by the Ministry of Health, became adept at 'hollowing out' the capital of their own enterprises. The Southern Bohemian Třeboň spa, for example, was programmed for public tender in 1993, but this could not be realized because – due to mismanagement – it had accumulated debts of Kč 200 million (US$ 7 million). These debts had been purchased, at a discounted rate, by a private entrepreneur, Petrík. In order to effect the privatization tender, CNPF had to repurchase these Kč 200 million debts from Petrík. After several delays, the tender finally took place in November 1997, and Lavana plc's bid was successful. However, Lavana was unable to obtain control of the spa, because meanwhile its new management had made further dubious agreements with Petrík, generating new debts of Kč 111 million. Petrík's claim, which relied on a court judgement concerning the spa's insolvency, had priority over the privatization tender. An inquiry by CNPF established that both the old and new spa management group and Petrík had belonged to the same interest group and had deliberately signed unreasonable agreements (Hospodárske noviny daily, 11 March 1998). These followed the classic pattern of contracting some minor works with a firm (in this case Petrík) which were then charged for at a grossly exaggerated rate. This form of 'hollowing out' was common amongst the managers of SOE, not least because dishonest managers did not risk prosecution for – under Czech law – there is no penalty for mismanagement of SOE.

Not all spa managers were corrupt or incompetent, and privatization was not always impeded. In 1997, there were 34 spas in the Czech Republic and, after rapid privatization, most passed into the ownership of various plc and limited companies. The Czech Spa Inspection Office, a unit of the Ministry of Health, was responsible for supervising quality standards. The spas operated under very different conditions to the free care provided under the previous state-socialist system. Since 1993 the National Insurance System has only paid full costs for small numbers of patients. Instead, the state has paid only the health care fees of most patients, with the individuals having to bear the costs of accommodation, food, etc. In contrast to the previous system, the patients have had a degree of consumer choice in being able to choose from amongst the different spas and/or facilities, which has resulted in intense competition. This has helped to improve the quality of service provided .

There are both similarities and differences in the experiences of privatization in the Slovak Republic. Two large enterprises were privatized via coupon privatization – the Kyjev hotel in Bratislava and a complex of the former Javorina enterprise in the Demänovská valley (Liptovský Mikuláš district). The latter emerged as Ski Jasná plc, which was one of the most efficient tourism enterprises in Slovakia. It was, for example, the only tourism enterprise that issued bonds on the Slovak capital market.

After the Mečiar government came to power in November 1994, direct sales became the main method of privatization, and this became subject to corruption and clientelism. There was strong political intervention in the selection of successful purchasers, and parliamentary supervision of the process was denied. The identities of the real buyers were usually concealed behind anonymous plc or limited companies which secured 51 per cent of their shares from the National Property Fund at highly discounted prices.

TABLE 4.7 *Slovak tourism enterprises privatized via direct sales during 1995-7*

Property and date of sale	Book value of stake sold (Sk million)	Stake as %	Purchaser(s)	Sale price (Sk million)	First payment (Sk million)	Investment required (Sk million)
Štrbské Pleso Spas, 15.06.95	50.190	51	Vzájomná životná poisťovňa (health insurance company)	99.5	59.5	40.0
Lučivná Spas, 20.07.95	5.378	51	Spoločnosť pre rozvoj klimatickej liečby Ltd	30.0	15.0	15.0
Turčianske Teplice Spas, 20.07.95	46.918	51	Vzájomná životná poisťovňa (health insurance company)	170.0	50.0	120.0
Vyšné Ružbachy Spas, 20.07.95	76.605	51	Travertín Vyšné Ružbachy, Ltd	23.8	4.8	11.9
Lučky Spas, 20.07.95	32.218	51	Vzájomná životná poisťovňa (health insurance company)	124.5	40.5	84.0
Satur travel agency, 17.08.95	98.181	100	Merk-Tour plc	100.0	20.0	49.5
Bojnice Spas, 17.08.95	45.17	51	Terramis Ltd	50.0	10.0	20.0
11.12.96	14.171	16	Slovenská Sporiteľna plc (Slovak Saving Bank)	8.9	8.9	0
Trenčianske Teplice Spas, 24.08.95 and 23.05.1996	191.602	51	Slovbad Ltd	192.5	38.5	148.0
Nový Smokovec Spas, 7.09.95	19.013	51	Liku Ltd	46.0	23.0	23.0
Korytnica Spas, 5.10.95	23.361	54	Balnea-Korytnica Ltd	51.4	7.0	23.7
Rajecké Teplice Spas, 5.10.95	25.874	51	Mr. Miškolci	70.0	14.0	35.0
Sliač and Kováčová Spas, 5.10.95	127.137	51	Corvas Ltd	151.6	30.3	75.8
Číž Nature Spas, 5.10.95	22.328	51	Mineralia Gemer Ltd	29.0	5.8	14.5
20.11.96	7.005	16	Slovenská Sporiteľna plc (Slovak Saving Bank)	2.3	2.3	0.0
Sklenné Teplice Spas, 19.10.95	4.302	54	BKM Ltd	8.0	2.0	4.0

TABLE 4.7—*continued*

Property and date of sale	Book value of stake sold (Sk milion)	Stake as %	Purchaser(s)	Sale price (Sk million)	First payment (Sk million)	Investment required (Sk million)
Honttherma (Dudince Spas), 29.02.06	67.242	67	Spa-Novum plc	78.9	15.8	28.0
Interhotel Bratislava, Devin Hotel, 29.02.06	30.369	100	Yield Ltd	66.0	20.0	32.0
Piešťany Spas	769.854	51	Spoločnosť zamestnancov piešťanských kúpeľov plc (management-led employee company) + Vadium Group plc	302.4	120.0	300.0
23.05.96 24.07.97	256.618	17		50.0	18.0	0.0
Brusno Spas, 27.08.96	56.800	51	Hepar Ltd	30.0	11.6	28.5
Hotel Bratislava, 30.10.96	95.303	67	Co invest Ltd	63.0	30.0	20.0
2.10.97	42.672	30	Agency Establishment Ltd	10.0	10.0	0.0
Štos Spas, 30.10.96	16.800	51	Frobad Ltd	9.5	3.8	9.5
Bardejovské kúpele Spas, 30.10.96	170.084	58	Prameň Ltd	115.0	20.0	85.0
Nimnica Spas						
20.11.1996	23.819	22	Zdravie plc.	2.5	0.5	4.0
20.11.1996	23.819	22	Hemamedik Ltd	2.5	0.5	4.0
20.11.1996	28.151	26	Balnea ML Ltd	3.0	0.6	4.0
Interhotel Bratislava, Magnolia Hotel, 20.11.06	38.084	100	Panorama plc	19.4	7.6	18.7

Source: TREND weekly *(1998c)*
Notes: exchange rate, 1 US$ = Sk 29.569 in 1995, 1 US$ = Sk 31.895 in 1996 and 1 US$ = Sk 34.782 in 1997 (end of period).

The buyers were only required to pay the first instalment and, in return for investment pledges, were exempted from the remaining payments. The other shares remained in the NPF portfolio and, or were transferred to municipalities and employees. 'Government-friendly' buyers were preferred, and were usually expected to contribute to the finances of the governing parties.

This kind of opaque and often corrupt privatization was widespread in all the transformation countries of Central Europe. As noted earlier, in the Czech Republic, privatization bribes caused the downfall of the Klaus government. In Slovakia, however, this form of privatization was openly promoted as a means of creating a strong domestic capitalist class. This desired class was of course limited to a narrow group of the 'new rich'. In the period 1995–7 there were 889 direct sales. Property privatized in this way had a book value of Sk 103 billion (compared to Sk 80 billion of property privatized via coupon privatization in 1992–3). The total sale prices were Sk 48.8 billion, representing some 84 per cent of the book value of their assets. The total value of the first instalments paid by the new owners was only Sk 11.1 billion, just 23 per cent of the sale price and only 11 per cent of the book value. Moreover, the investments promised by the new owners accounted for only Sk 50 billion, or 49.5 per cent of their total book value.

During 1995–7, there were 29 direct sales related to the tourism sector and, excepting three hotels and the Satur Travel Agency, they were all in the spas (Table 4.7). Some hotels divested from the former Interhotel enterprise, such as the Carlton Hotel, were sold via public and non-public tenders. The total book value of the property privatized was Sk 2,419 million, and the sale price of Sk 1746.38 million represented 74.3 per cent of this. The first payments accounted for 25.1 per cent of the book value and the total investment promised represented a further 50.9 per cent. In general, there were smaller discounts on the sales of tourism enterprises than for other industries, while the ratio of book value to pledged investment was similar. The lower discounts provided in the privatization of tourism, compared to other sectors, can be explained in two ways. First, most tourism enterprises were supposed to be more competitive than manufacturing ones. Second, higher discounts were provided for the sales of very large enterprises (usually in manufacturing), where the potential new owners only had limited opportunities to secure from domestic banks the substantial down payments and privatization loans which were required to effect the purchases.

Except for Vzájomná životná poist'ovňa, a health insurance company, most purchasers were managers, or management-led employee collectives. Foreign capital was excluded from the sales. After 1995, insurance companies were also excluded from bidding, and the tourism enterprises were sold exclusively to domestic plc and limited companies. The limited companies obtained much larger discounts than had been available for the public health insurance company, but the Slovak NPF did not publish any explanation for this. This point was picked up by the Commission of the EU which criticized the Slovak government for lack of transparency in its privatization rules (Commission of the European Communities 1997). In most cases, the new owners were backed by political parties in the ruling government. Different aspects of privatization via direct sales are discussed in case studies of the Piešťany spas, Dudince spas and the Devín Hotel. These and other case studies are discussed below.

4.4 CASE STUDIES OF TOURISM PRIVATIZATION

The privatized firms have encountered many difficulties. To a large degree, these have depended on the privatization method, changes in tourism demand and the professional skills of the enterprise management. The lack of published statistics precludes a systematic study of the processes of tourism privatization and outcomes at the level of individual capitals, which is necessary given the complexities involved. Instead, we explore these issues through case studies. These are based on two data sources. The first is a series of in-depth interviews that were undertaken with the managers (sometimes coincident with the owners) of a total of 51 tourism firms in the two countries. These were selected to represent both 'core' and 'non-core' tourism regions, and the interviews were limited to the accommodation sector. The samples were stratified to include a number of different ownership/privatization forms. Anonymity constraints preclude the identification of these firms by name, and given the difficulties of concealing identities in relatively small economies, we have only been able to present these results in the most depersonalized form. We have therefore also taken the opportunity to complement these surveys with case studies of individual firms drawn from published sources, particularly from the financial, professional and mainstream newspapers and journals. All the individually named case studies are drawn from these latter sources.

4.4.1 Slovakia

Twenty-six firms were included in our survey in Slovakia. These were undertaken in three different types of areas. First, in some of the strongest tourism areas: Poprad (the High Tatra mountains), Bratislava City, Trnava (which has the Piešťany spa, Western Slovakia) and Žilina (a county capital in Central Slovakia). Second, several interviews were carried out in the district of Prievidza, which is of medium tourist importance and wealth. Third, interviews were also carried out in two relatively poor and remote districts (Vranov – far Eastern Slovakia, Dolný Kubín – far Northern Slovakia). The survey ranged across all the major types of tourist accommodation from four-star hotels to hostels, and from metropolitan hotels to small country inns. The survey also tried to encompass all the main categories of ownership. These were establishments which had been created by: public auction in the small privatization; public or other tender; coupon privatization; transfer to municipality or other body; direct sale to domestic investor; sale to foreign investor; and other methods (especially new establishments). The distribution of types broadly reflects the actual structure of ownership types in the tourism economy. Given that many hotels had experienced a succession of owners and managers since 1989, the present incumbents were not always able to provide detailed histories of the management of their establishments. Many owners and managers were also suspicious of the survey and were very guarded in the information they provided. In general, the managers of the smaller hotels were more open in the interviews. A brief summary of the findings is presented in Table 4.8.

Changes in number of employees, and occupancy rates. There were decreases in the average numbers of the hotel employees after 1989. These were mostly related to privatization and ensuing rationalization. However, it should be noted that the total hotel workforce in Slovakia increased in this period, due to the investment in large numbers of new facilities after 1989. Occupancy rates also fell after 1989, mainly due to declining domestic demand. A decline in demand was the problem identified most frequently in firms' self-assessments of their operations. Therefore, the survey data confirm the difficulties faced by many firms even as late as 1997, and the profound restructuring pressures in the tourism economy.

Managerial competencies. Managers reported that their range of competence expanded considerably after 1989, especially in respect of being able to choose suppliers. The actual increase in the choice of supplier was probably far greater than was reported in the survey; whereas 14 managers claimed to have this right in 1989, they did not necessarily have the means to do so in a centrally planned economy. In contrast, increased numbers of competing producers after 1989 provided a far greater choice of suppliers. The real increase in control over the use of profits was also greater than reported; while 10 out of 21 managers claimed to have competence in profit allocation in 1989, they referred to that part of the surplus income left to the facility after compulsory transfers to the state. These transfers accounted for 70–95 per cent of surpluses. Different ownership categories had different levels of competence. Municipally owned hotels, for example, were mostly leased by 1997 and the leaseholders had virtually complete autonomy from the owners. The managers of hotels privatized via direct sales by domestic and foreign investor had the lowest level of competence,

TABLE 4.8 *Characteristics of tourism firms by ownership/privatization type in Slovakia in 1997*

Method of privatization or establishment	Tender, Small Privat- isation	New firms	Transfer of muni- cipality	Direct sale, domestic investor	Sale to foreign investor	No change	Total
Number of firms	5	5	3	8	3	3	27
Since 1989, number of employees:							
increased	2	x	1	1	2	2	8
decreased	3	x	2	6	1	0	12
did not change	0	x	0	1	0	1	2
Since 1989, occupancy rates:							
increased	2	x	1	2	3	0	8
decreased	1	x	2	4	0	2	9
did not change	2	x	0	2	0	1	5
The management has competence in the selection of supplier:							
1989 yes (no)	1(4)	x	2(1)	7(1)	2(0)	2(1)	14(7)
1997 yes (no)	4(1)	5(0)	3(0)	7(1)	3(0)	3(0)	25(2)
The management has competence in the recruitment of employees:							
1989 yes (no)	4(1)	x	3(0)	7(1)	2(0)	2(1)	18(3)
1997 yes (no)	5(0)	5(0)	3(0)	6(2)	3(0)	3(0)	25(2)
The management has competence in the targeting of markets:							
1989 yes (no)	4(1)	x	3(0)	4(4)	1(1)	2(1)	14(7)
1997 yes (no)	3(2)	5(0)	3(0)	5(3)	2(1)	3(0)	21(6)
The management has competence in the use of operating surplus:							
1989 yes (no)	5(0)	x	2(1)	4(4)	0(2)	0(3)	11(10)
1997 yes (no)	2(3)	4(1)	3(0)	4(4)	3(0)	1(2)	17(10)
The main source of capital in privatization/setting up the firm was:							
financial institution %	60	28.0	x	48.8	6.7	x	40.5
other company %	28	0	x	17.3	6.7	x	14.2
personal money %	10	72.0	x	30.3	10.0	x	32.5
foreign investor %	0	0	x	0	73.3	x	10.5
other %	2	0	x	3.8	3.3	x	2.4
The hotel is:							
a member of a hotel or TA chain	2	3	0	2	3	2	11
owned by non-tourist firm	2	0	0	2	0	0	4
owned by public sector body	0	0	0	0	0	1	1
fully independent	1	12	2	3	1	0	9
other kinds of links (inc. leased)	0	0	1	1	0	0	2

TABLE 4.8 —*continued*

Method of privatization or establishment	Tender, Small Privat- isation	New firms	Transfer of muni- cipality	Direct sale, domestic investor	Sale to foreign investor	No change	Total
The hotel uses the following marketing methods (multiple answers possible):							
own activities	4	5	3	6	3	1	22
travel agencies	3	4	2	6	2	2	19
visitors are supplied by holding company	1	0	0	1	0	2	4
relies on passing trade	3	1	3	4	0	x	0
After 1989 the hotel:							
added a new facility	1	1	0	6	2	0	10
carried out a significant reconstruction of accommodation	3	2	0	7	2	0	14
The main problems faced by the firm are (multiple answers):							
lack of capital	4	1	3	2	0	2	12
lack of professional staff	2	3	1	1	1	0	8
staff behaviour	2	3	0	0	2	0	7
declining demand	4	3	1	5	1	3	17
increasing competition	3	1	1	2	0	0	7
technical problems	4	1	3	5	1	1	14
ecological problems	1	0	0	0	1	0	2
others	0	0	0	0	0	0	0

Source: authors' survey.

especially with respect to profit allocation. These hotels mostly were large units privatized by plc and limited companies.

Capital sources used to establish firms. Different owners used different capital sources for establishing/privatizing hotels. Investors buying hotels via the Small Privatization programme and/or tender mostly relied on financial institutions (60 per cent of the capital, on average) and capital provided by other firms (28 per cent) usually owned by the same investors. During the Small Privatization in 1990–1992, special privatization loans were provided by Slovak financial institutions. Newly established firms were financed from personal capital (72 per cent) and from loans provided by financial institutions (28 per cent). The relatively low share of the financial institutions was explained by the general capital shortage in Slovakia, difficulties in securing long-term loans and high interest rates (over 20–30 per cent per annum at a time when inflation was only 8–10 per cent; see Chapter 2). Personal capital was usually provided by individuals (sometimes earned abroad) and their families. Medium- and large-scale hotels were mostly privatized by direct sales to domestic investors. Financial institutions (48.8 per cent) and personal capital (30.3 per cent) were the main capital sources. Most hotels privatized via direct methods were 'sold' at major discounts to 'government-friendly' managers and lobbies. Despite these discounts, the payments were too large to be covered from personal sources alone, so that financial institutions provide most of their capital. Hotels sold via direct sales to domestic and foreign investors attracted some of the wealthiest individual owners. They were usually better placed to invest in new facilities and/or reconstruct their existing ones. Those hotels which remained in the public sector usually lacked the funds for such investments. The same applies to the municipally owned hotels. They were on short-term leases which, of course, also discouraged major investments.

Affiliation and marketing. Eleven of the 27 hotels claimed to be members of a hotel and/or travel agency chain and nine to be fully independent. Only four firms reported that they were owned by a non-tourist firm. In terms of marketing, the hotels mainly relied on their own activities (advertisements on the Internet and in the press), collaboration with travel agencies and passing trade. Some establishments owned by the public sector obtained most of their visitors from their parent holding companies, which effectively represent a continuation of social tourism practices.

Challenges and constraints. The hotel managers were mostly (17 responses) concerned with declining demand. There had been an overall decrease compared to 1989 levels, although there had been a partial recovery since 1994. Technical problems were reported in 14 cases, followed by lack of capital (12 cases). There also were problems of shortages of professional staff (eight) and inappropriate staff behaviour (seven cases), including unfriendly and inefficient service provision.

The above summary serves to highlight the complexity of the sector. New forms of ownership have emerged, although some of these still have links to pre-1989 structures. The firms have experienced considerable restructuring in the face not only of ownership changes, but also of a collapse in demand. To some extent, increased managerial competence since 1989 has provided greater scope for individual establishments to respond to these changing conditions, but their ability to do so remains constrained by shortages of capital (both external and self-generated) and of professional staff. These aspects and the considerable variety evident at the level of individual firms is explored further in the following case studies which are drawn from secondary sources.

The Piešt'any spas: political capitalism in action

This case study, which draws on Leško (1997), provides insights into the privatization methods used in the Slovak spas. The starting point for this is to note that since 1995, Mrs Martinková, wife of the general director of the Devín Bank, is known to have become a close friend of Prime Minister Mečiar. In June 1997, her husband, Mr. Martinka, was forced to resign from his post, and the new general director of the Devín bank asked the police to investigate his predecessor's activities. However, Mr. Martinka and Mrs. Martinková were well protected by the ruling party, which was hardly surprising given that Mrs. Martinková had become deputy chair of the HZDS (government party) election committee and had personal links with the prime minister. On 23 May 1996, the NPF sold the Piešťany spas – the largest, most modern and most profitable in Slovakia – to a management-led employee company Spoločnosť zamestnancov Piešťanských kúpel'ov (The Piešt'any Spa Employees Company). The spas, with a market value of Sk 1.6 billion (US$ 53 million), were sold for a symbolic price of Sk 302.5 million (US$ 10 million). This transaction was subjected to several public inquiries, but these were all terminated without issuing reports. At the end of 1996, the Central Securities Register announced that 51 per cent of the shares had passed to Vadium Group plc, founded by Mr. Martinka. The Vadium Group also acquired a further 16 percent of the shares directly from the NPF. Mr. Martinka established several spin-off companies and transferred much of the spa's profits and assets to these (an example of 'tunnelling', transfer pricing). After the fall of the Mečiar government, the police and Slovak NPF launched a new round of inquiries. In spring 1999, the spa's top managers were captured on the Austro-Slovakian borders, when they tried to smuggle out documents related to the spa's privatization. Mr. Martinka, however, escaped to Austria.

The Devín Hotel: successful privatization via direct sale

The five star Devín Hotel (central Bratislava), constructed in 1954 and designed by Emil Belluš, a renowned Slovak architect, was conceived as the most luxurious establishment in Slovakia at that time. Its interiors were richly embellished by period paintings, glass sculptures and furniture. Between 1954 and 1996 the hotel was part of Interhotel Bratislava, a state-owned chain of hotels and restaurants, which provided services for prominent state and other visitors to Slovakia. During the late 1980s, the quality of service deteriorated, mostly because of a lack of investment. Then in July 1996, Yield Ltd. privatized the hotel (Janků 1996a) for Sk 60 millions (US$ 2 million), an exceptionally low price in view of its location on the Danube and its reputation. The new owners aimed to renew the Devín's reputation as the most prestigious hotel in Slovakia, and prepared a comprehensive reconstruction plan for 1997–2000, at a total cost of Sk 70 million (US$ 2.3 million). In practice, Yield Ltd has tried to preserve the hotel's original architecture and interiors, in consultation with the Historical Architecture Office. The hotel was refurbished with replicas of 1950s English furniture and hand-made Turkish carpets. Two conference halls and a foreign exchange office were rehabilitated immediately after privatization, in July–December 1996, at a cost of Sk 7 million (US$ 230,000), and there was a 30 per cent increase in income in the same period. The renewal of its bedrooms is the focus of the next stage, while the opening of a high-profile French restaurant should help to re-establish the hotel's top position in Slovakia. The Devín Hotel represents a positive example of privatization by domestic investors via direct sale. While the privatization price was low, this enabled Yield Ltd to press ahead with the hotel's renewal, unencumbered by large bank loans.

The Dudince spas: modernization by a domestic owner

These spas, in southern Slovakia, were established in 1951 to provide treatment for arthritis and rheumatism. There were major investments in 1966 and 1978 in two spa hotels, the Rubín and Smaragd, which were equipped for balneo-therapy. After 1991 this SOE was transformed into Honttherma plc (owned by the NPF), and it was privatized in February 1996 (Józsa 1998). SpaNovum plc obtained a majority ownership stake of 67 per cent. The price was set at Sk 78.9 million and the company (with equity of Sk 100 million) paid a first instalment of Sk 15.8 million and pledged Sk 32 million of future investment. At the time, the Honttherma director stated that he did not know the identity of the new SpaNovum owners. Later, several Slovak newspapers published the information that two government ministers and several parliamentary members of the ruling party were major shareholders. Privatization to 'government-friendly' owners is not uncommon in Slovakia, but their identity often tends to be concealed behind the facades of anonymous plc and limited companies. A further 20 per cent stake was owned by Všeobecná životná poisťovňa, the largest Slovak health insurance company, whilst 10 per cent was owned by the town of Dudince, and 3 per cent by the Restitution Investment Fund.

Immediately after privatization, SpaNovum initiated extensive reconstruction of the spas. One third of the 350 rooms were refurbished with a view to attracting foreign clients. Investments of Sk 9.8 million and Sk 16 million were undertaken in 1996 and 1997, respectively, while a further Sk 14 million was scheduled for 1998. According to the company director, no loans had been required as the investments had been funded from their own resources. The spas seemed to be profitable, recording profits of Sk 24.2 million and (an estimated) Sk 23 million in 1996 and 1997.

In 1997 the spas had 8706 clients, 85 per cent of who were provided by the National Social Insurance System, 8–10 per cent by the Všeobecná životná poist'ovňa, and the remainder by other health insurance companies. In future, the company aims to increase the share of recreational and entertainment activities in its turnover, and to build golf and tennis facilities, and cafés. A 15 per cent increase in the numbers of foreign clients (paying higher prices) was predicted for 1997–2000. Honttherma also aims to increase the share of domestic *commercial* clients and plans to collaborate more closely with travel agents in its marketing activities. The higher prices paid by foreign clients and domestic self-financed customers should yield higher profits and increased resources for further investment. The company has also had to resolve staff shortcomings. In particular, a lack of foreign language proficiency has been tackled in partnership with the Hotel Academy in Brezno. The Honttherma case demonstrates how new owners can secure a profitable firm at an extremely low price, and fund the pledged investments from their profits, without having to raise additional capital loans. Despite concerns about transparency and equity, it can be argued that this privatization method helped Honttherma to avoid crippling debts, and the new owners were broadly competent.

Terchová village: problems of municipal management

The village of Terchová, in Northern Slovakia, is favourably located in the Malá Fatra National Park, some 20 km from Žilina and about 120 km from a number of major industrial cities in the Czech Republic and Poland. Since the 1950s, the village has been renowned for its folklore traditions, its scenery, and the opportunities it provides for skiing and walking. Numerous hotels and camping sites in the village mostly attracted tourists from Eastern Germany and the Czech Republic in the state-socialist period. About 30–40 per cent of the village's economically active population were employed in the tourism sector.

In the early 1990s, the situation changed dramatically (Janků 1996b). Most of the hotels were privatized in 1991 as part of the Small Privatization programme via auctions. Two major hotels Pod Sokolím (300 beds) and Jánošík (40 beds) were bought by entrepreneurs from southern Slovakia. Both entrepreneurs had little experience of mountain hotel management, had unrealistic expectations of future income and paid relatively high prices. Moreover, they both required bank loans on which they paid very high interest rates (20–25 per cent per annum). In addition, these hotels had a legacy of typical state-socialist tourism architecture, with huge expanses of energy-inefficient windows. While this had been of little consequence in a centrally planned economy with low energy costs, rapidly increasing prices after 1989 were a problem. There were a number of changes in the owners of the hotels, but none were able to eliminate the hotels' deficits. Eventually they passed to the banks, which had provided the initial privatization loans, but they were unable to find buyers given their high operating costs. After 1992, both hotels were closed and were badly vandalized.

The lack of accommodation reduced the competitiveness of the village, at the same time as the (East) German and Czech tourist markets were discovering new destinations. Both employment in and income from tourism decreased in 1992–5; for example, the female unemployment rate reached 70 per cent in 1996. The municipality intervened with a local development strategy, and initiated a programme of infrastructure reconstruction to enhance the appearance of the village. Local residents were encouraged to adapt their houses to provide tourism accommodation, and received subsidies from the TDP for this purpose. About 1000 new beds were generated in this way, and the provision of modern tourism facilities in traditional timber houses has been particularly popular with foreign tourists. In addition, several recreation units, which had previously operated as components of industrial enterprises, have been privatized or leased, and these have been converted into inns and guest houses. One local tourism firm has also invested in snow cannon, thereby extending the winter season to 120 days. The municipality obtained a return for its initiative in the form of Sk 1.5 million (US$ 50 thousands) in taxes on tourist activities in 1996, and there were plans to invest this in infrastructure as part of a green tourism programme.

The village of Terchová provides an example of how an inappropriate privatization method, combined with changes in tourism flows, can devastate a local economy. Municipal intervention has improved the position and helped to recapture, at least a part of the former market. However, the re-development of tourism in the village still faces a number of challenges. Local government and local entrepreneurs have tried to buy the two semi-derelict hotels, in order to rehabilitate them and broaden the supply of tourism services. The banks, however, have been bound by rigid accountancy rules, and have been unable to sell the hotels at realistic prices. The village council has also had problems in persuading local residents to declare their receipts, and pay the due tourist taxes; according to a special law, every tourist pays Sk 10 per night as part of the accommodation price.

The Borová Sihot' hotel: re-privatization by a domestic entrepreneur

The Borová Sihot' hotel and camping site (in the Liptovský Mikuláš district) was included in the Small Privatization programme in 1992. The 40,000 m^2 property was estimated to be worth Sk 70 million (US$ 2.3 million) but, as this proved to be beyond the reach of domestic investors, the original bid price of Sk 19 million was lowered to Sk 9 million (Šporer 1997). The new owners took a bank loan of Sk 41 million, but had little interest in the management of the hotel. Rather they stripped it of all its movable assets and made a 'midnight flight', for which they were later imprisoned. The hotel passed to the bank, which sought to sell it at a price, which recouped the original loan. This was unrealistic and, for five years, the hotel was abandoned and vandalized, and its value plummeted. Finally, in April 1995 the bank sold the hotel by public auction for Sk 5 million to a local entrepreneur, Mr. Kováč.

The new owner invested Sk 10 million to repair the most serious damage to the hotel. As no bank would lend him the entire sum, he had to strip capital from his copy-machine business and pledge his family house as a guarantee. The bank loan was only used to cover a small part of the investment because of the high interest rates (about 20 per cent per annum at a time when inflation was only 6 per cent; see Chapter 2). The hotel was transformed into a family business and, after major reconstruction, was re-opened in July 1996. This case study illustrates the difficulty of finding the 'right owner' for property privatized via the Small Privatization programme. In general, many of the original buyers were either unable to manage their properties, or were only interested in short-term exploitation. Most of the wilder transactions in the tourism sector occurred in the period 1991–4. Subsequently, via market mechanisms, most property has passed to a second generation of owners, who usually had previous business experience in other sectors. Most relied on personal capital and family labour, in the face of a general capital shortage and high interest rates.

The Carlton hotel: a difficult privatization by an international investor

The city-centre location and architecture of Bratislava's nineteenth-century Carlton hotel made it one of the most prestigious establishments in pre-1989 Slovakia. But it had declined through long neglect during the state socialist period. In 1990 the hotel closed and new owners willing to undertake the necessary investment were sought. The sheer scale of the task excluded most potential domestic investors, and in 1992 BESIX, a Belgian company, was duly selected via international tender (Hajko 1996). BESIX, however, did not secure control of the hotel, for it transpired that it had bribed the privatization commission. There were then a number of bids by foreign and domestic investors, but conflict amongst the various interest groups involved politicized the hotel's privatization. Eventually the privatization was halted and the Carlton declined further. Finally, the NPF made the hotel subject to a new international tender in 1995. The tender rules gave preference to 'preserving the hotel's historic architecture and atmosphere' over narrow price considerations. Seven original potential foreign investors were reduced to two, and in November 1995, Clinvest, the French auditors who managed the tender, selected a Belgian firm TEI. The successful tender offered a price of Sk 30 million (US$ 1 million) and guaranteed additional investment of Sk 1500 million (US$ 50 million). TEI also guaranteed that Slovak firms would obtain at least 53 per cent of the reconstruction project, which prioritized preservation of the building's intrinsic architectural value. TEI was selected partly on the basis of its previous successful involvement in the construction of a new hospital in Bratislava, and also political considerations, for Belgium was a strong supporter of Slovakia in negotiations over EU membership. This case study illustrates how corruption and interests group conflict can delay privatization, but also the persistent attraction of prime tourism assets to foreign investors.

Holiday Inn: greenfield investment in an up-market hotel

In 1983, *Jednota*, the hotel and restaurant co-operative, proposed developing an international hotel. *Jednota*'s founder, the Slovak Consumer Co-operative Association (SZSD), would provide land, while capital would be supplied by *Jednota* itself. Work started in the state-socialist period, but lack of capital and rising construction costs after 1989 delayed the project (Sme daily 1997). In 1993, new investment loans were provided, by an Austrian partner, and subsequently the hotel has been owned by Slovkarpatia plc. Over 50 per cent of the shares in Slovkarpatia, Plc were owned by Slovenská Poisťovňa plc, a major state-owned Slovak insurance company; the remainder were held by *Jednota* and SZSD. All the shareholders were Slovak, but 80 per cent of their capital was provided by a foreign investor and the hotel was, effectively, in foreign ownership which had ultimate control over major management decisions. The foreign partners also provided the hotel's name and it became a member of the international chain, Holiday Inn Inc. Construction was completed in August 1996 and involved investment of Sk 270 million (US$ 9 million).

The three-star hotel has 165 air conditioned rooms, two restaurants, a brasserie, a winter garden, fitness centre, sauna, swimming pool and congress centre. Despite its unattractive designs (which originated in the state-socialist period), the interior and the quality of service match Western European standards and attract high-income national and international clients. The hotel was mainly designed for business tourism, and has been used as a conference and meeting centre by major companies and international organisations. Despite its strong client base, the hotel encountered financial difficulties, and in the first four operating months (September–December 1996) had losses of Sk 58.87 million, followed by further losses of Sk 43.48 million in 1997. According to Mrs. Bakkaiová, Slovakarpatia's principal economist, the loss was due to the high level of loan repayments and interest charges, which accounted for 30 per cent of total operating costs. The hotel covered the loss via a new share issue of Sk 150 million, an unusual strategy in the Slovak hotel industry, which has tended to rely mostly on bank loans, retained income and debt securities. This is an example of how foreign investment can operate effectively in tourism in

Slovakia. The capital was provided by Austrians, the project was located in Bratislava and relied on wealthy Western clients and the domestic elite. Above all, this demonstrates how foreign capital tends to be invested in border regions, in an attractive industry where there is the prospect of early returns.

4.4.2 The Czech Republic

The survey in the Czech Republic was based on an identical methodology to that used in Slovakia. Most of the interviews were carried out in Prague, and the Karlovy Vary spas in the Western Bohemia. These districts are the strongest tourism regions in the Czech Republic. Several interviews were carried out in Brno, the capital of Southern Moravia, which is medium ranked in terms of tourism. Interviews were also carried out in two relatively poor and remote districts (Vyškov in far South Eastern Moravia, and Krnov in far North Eastern Moravia). A total of 27 facilities were included in the survey, and as in Slovakia it encompassed most forms of ownership, quality and type of facility: from five-star hotels to hostels, from metropolitan hotels to small country inns, and from spa facilities to mountain and winter sports centres.

Compared to Slovakia, several differences in ownership can be noted. Newly built hotels, hotels sold via direct sale to a domestic investor, and foreign investment were more important in the Czech Republic. The structure of ownership had changed more rapidly since 1989 in the Czech Republic than in Slovakia. In one case study, there had been six owners since 1989. This meant that, of the 20 hotels established before 1989, comparative information was missing for the earlier period in eight cases. The interview results are summarized in Table 4.9.

Changes in the number of employees, and occupancy rates. The hotel industry in the Czech Republic had expected a real boom after 1989. Most of the individual hotels interviewed actually reported a decrease in their staff, visitor numbers and occupancy rates, but this was counterbalanced by a major increase in the total number of hotels and other forms of accommodation. Decreased occupancy rates were also partly offset by the increased prices paid by foreign visitors. The decline in employees was caused by two main factors: owners of privatized and/or newly built hotels increased labour productivity, while the boom in the tourism industry was reflected in an increased demand for professional staff, which could not be satisfied from existing labour markets. Not surprisingly, a lack of professional staff was the most frequently stated problem by managers in their assessment of operating conditions. The Czech tourism industry generally enjoyed more positive conditions than the Slovak one and had for less dramatic decreases in occupancy rates after 1989. The Czech hotels also tended to have more

TABLE 4.9 *Characteristics of tourism firms by ownership/privatization type in the Czech Republic in 1997*

Method of privatization or establishment	Tender, Small Privat- isation	New firms	Transfer of muni- cipality	Direct sale, domestic investor	Sale to foreign investor	No change	Total
Number of firms	3	5	3	8	5	3	27
Since 1989, number of employees:							
increased	0	x	0	0	2	1	3
decreased	2	x	1	1	1	0	5
did not change	0	x	0	0	2	0	2
Since 1989, the occupancy rates:							
increased	0	x	0	1	0	0	1
decreased	2	x	0	1	1	0	4
did not change	0	x	1	2	0	1	4
The management has competence in the choice of supplier:							
1989 yes (no)	2(0)	x	1(0)	5(1)	2(0)	1(1)	11(2)
1997 yes (no)	3(0)	5(0)	2(1)	7(1)	5(0)	1(2)	23(4)
The management has competence in the recruitment of employees:							
1989 yes (no)	2(0)	x	1(0)	5(1)	2(0)	1(1)	11(2)
1997 yes (no)	3(0)	5(0)	2(1)	7(1)	5(0)	1(2)	23(4)
The management has competence in the targeting of markets:							
1989 yes (no)	2(0)	x	0(1)	4(2)	2(0)	1(1)	9(4)
1997 yes (no)	3(0)	5(0)	1(2)	7(1)	5(0)	1(2)	22(5)
The management has competence in the use of operating surplus:							
1989 yes (no)	1(1)	x	0(1)	2(4)	1(1)	1(1)	5(8)
1997 yes (no)	1(2)	5(0)	0(3)	5(3)	4(1)	1(2)	16(11)
The main source of capital in privatization/setting up the firm was:							
Financial institution %	50.0	20.0	x	33.8	0	x	23.5
Other company %	50.0	0	x	13.8	0	x	10.5
Personal money %	0	80.0	x	27.5	0	x	31.0
Foreign investor %	0	0	x	0	100.0	x	25.0
other %	0	0	x	25.9	0	x	10.0
The hotel is:							
member of a hotel or TA chain	0	0	0	2	4	1	7
owned by non-tourist firm	1	0	0	3	0	1	5
owned by public sector body	0	0	3	0	0	1	4
fully independent	1	5	0	3	1	0	10
other kinds of links (inc. leased)	1	0	0	0	0	0	1

123

TABLE 4.9 —*continued*

Method of privatization or establishment	Tender, Small Privat- ization	New firms	Transfer of muni- cipality	Direct sale, domestic investor	Sale to foreign investor	No change	Total
The hotel uses the following marketing methods (multiple answers possible):							
own activities	2	3	1	8	4	2	20
travel agencies	3	3	0	7	2	1	16
visitors are supplied by holding company	0	0	2	1	3	2	8
relies on passing trade	0	2	1	1	0	0	4
After 1989 the hotel:							
added a new facility	0(3)	3(2)	0(3)	7(1)	0(5)	0(3)	10(17)
carried out a significant reconstruction of accommodation	2(1)	3(2)	1(2)	7(1)	2(3)	2(1)	17(10)
The main problems faced by the firm are (multiple answers):							
Lack of capital	2	2	0	4	0	1	9
lack of professional staff	0	1	1	4	4	0	10
staff behaviour	2	1	0	1	1	0	5
declining demand	1	0	0	2	0	1	4
increasing competition	0	1	0	2	0	2	5
technical problems	0	1	1	3	0	2	7
ecological problems	0	0	0	0	0	0	0
others	0	1	1	1	1	0	4

Source: authors' survey

active strategies than their Slovak equivalents for raising quality. Of the 27 hotels, 10 added new facilities and 17 significantly improved their accommodation facilities after 1989. In addition, 12 hotels were newly built after 1989.

Managerial competences. There was an overall increase in the range of competencies delegated to hotel managers in 1989–7. By 1997, almost all the managers were able to choose their suppliers, employees and visitors. As for the use of operating surpluses, 16 of 27 managers had virtual autonomy in this. Managers with little or no competence in profit allocation were mostly in the private sector and in large hotels owned by non-tourist firms. The overall pattern of competencies was very similar both in the Czech and Slovak Republics.

Capital sources used in establishing firms. There was a larger number of hotels privatized/built by foreign investors in the Czech Republic than in Slovakia. This is reflected in some differences between the capital sources used by hotels in each Republic. In the Czech hotels surveyed, foreign capital played a more important role than in Slovakia and accounted for 25 per cent of total capital sources. The basic structures, however, were quite similar in the Czech and Slovak Republics, both in aggregate terms and in each ownership category. In the Czech Republic, hotels bought within the Small Privatization programme were paid for from a combination of loans from financial institutions (50 per cent) and personal capital (50 per cent). Owners of newly built hotels used loans from financial institution (20 per cent) and personal capital (80 per cent). The domestic owners in the direct sales programme used the same combination of a loan from a financial institution (33.8 per cent) and personal funds (27.5 per cent).

Affiliation. Of the 27 hotels, 10 claimed to be fully independent and 7 to be a member of a hotel/travel agency chain, while 5 were owned by a non-tourist firm. This resembles the structure in Slovakia.

Challenges and constraints. Czech managers complained less about capital shortage than their Slovak counterparts (9 compared to 12 cases). Since 1989, the Czech Republic has enjoyed a better international reputation than Slovakia and this was reflected in a large influx of foreign capital. The number of complaints about technical problems was also less in the Czech Republic (7 compared to 14 cases), which can partly be explained by the better availability of capital to overcome such difficulties in the Czech Republic. Problems of a decline in demand were quoted less frequently than in Slovakia (4 to 17 cases), due to the strong foreign demand and the less deep recession in domestic markets. The Czech managers seemed to be less concerned with business problems than Slovak ones (44 to 67 complaints).

In the remainder of this section we explore some of these general issues further, through a number of individual case studies drawn from secondary sources.

Fischer Reisen: the making of the leading travel agency in the Czech Republic

Václav Fischer entered college in 1969, one year after the abrupt end of the Prague Spring, and graduated from the Economic University in 1978 at what he later described as 'one of the deepest points in the country's political darkness' (Syrovátka 1997). On the very day that he graduated, he illegally crossed the border into West Germany. His only capital was intellectual – a knowledge of three foreign languages and a basic under-standing of the tourism business. Thereafter, good fortune and his personal qualities helped him secure a job in a travel agency, and several years later he established his own firm. By 1989, Fischer Reisen was the fourth largest travel agency in Germany, which probably represented a unique success for an outsider from the Eastern block.

After 1989 Fischer extended his activities to his country of origin, and in 1990 he established subsidiaries in the Czech Republic and Slovakia. These agencies quickly became the second largest tour operators, after the state-owned monopoly Čedok (Satur). While Čedok (Satur) relied on an established network of regional branches, Fischer Reisen relied on its German capital and experience and built new branch networks. From the very beginning, Fischer Reisen has used its own methods of marketing, management and product development. Whereas the former state-socialist travel agencies operated on the basis of assembling groups of about 150 Czech travellers, transporting them in a single aircraft, allocating them to one hotel and organizing their evening programme, Fischer offered a more flexible product; there was varied accommodation in different locations, which were comparable to those used by Western European tourists. Fischer was also sensitive to the particular preferences of Czech tourists, especially for self-catering as opposed to serviced accommodation.

In 1995, Fischer sold his German interests to Lufthansa in order to concentrate on the Czech and Slovak markets. His prices were above average but the quality and reliability of service was also higher. Fischer benefited from the crashes of several major Czech travel agencies in 1996 and 1997 and accounted for most of the major increases in business in both years. By 1997, Fischer Reisen offered a full range of travel products, had clearly branded offices, and had its own airline, Air Fischer. In 1997, it owned four 148-seat B-737-300 planes, and these were in operation 11 hours per day, which was above the European average. Despite relatively high prices, Fischer had few problems in selling its packages, because of the favourable contrast between its customer policies and the numerous frauds and bankruptcies amongst its competitors.

Hotel S.E.N.: an American dream in Bohemia

After 1989, Steve Watson, an American citizen of Czech origin, searched for tourism investment opportunities in the Czech Republic. Eventually, he decided to build a luxurious hotel, located in a peaceful rural setting, but within a maximum distance of 30 km from the centre of Prague. The search for a site took several years but, in 1994, he finally found the ideal location in Senohraby, 28 km from Prague (Procházka, 1997). His idea was to construct a modern hotel in the form of a gothic castle. The project was undertaken by a Czech firm Watimex in 24 months and, unusually, the construction and suppliers were directly managed by the owner. His main problem had been finding firms which specialized in unusual architectural features, and he also considered that Czech architects had little understanding of his concept of the hotel design.

The hotel S.E.N ('dream' in Czech) was opened in 1997. Its customers mostly originate from the banks, industry and trade companies, and it offers conference facilities, the largest of which accommodates 210 participants. The hotel has a French restaurant, several night clubs, bars and cafés, a dance floor, fitness centre and sports centre. The new owner has tried to establish good relationships with the local community: many employees are local, and the community has been given access to the hotel's water purifying facility.

The S.E.N. hotel is a good example of an entrepreneur identifying and occupying selected market niches in a hotel industry in transition. There were few luxurious hotels in pre 1989 Czechoslovakia and they were mostly in the city centres. Moreover, the high quality of construction and the imaginative, if controversial architecture, has been attractive to business customers. Arguably, only a foreign investor had access to sufficient capital for such a project.

The Košík Hotel: from an Asian dormitory to a modern hotel

Prior to 1989 there had been a complex of dormitories with 640 rooms in the centre of Prague. The dormitory was originally designed for construction workers, but was later occupied by Vietnamese 'guest workers'. By 1989, there was no less than 2500 Vietnamese small-scale 'business-owners' occupying the dormitory and adjoining storage rooms, and they had converted the complex into the largest Asian market place in Czechoslovakia. In 1990 the complex was sold to a private owner, Vladimír Dohnal (Špelinová 1996). The new owner was faced with two main alternatives: either to continue renting the rooms to the Vietnamese, most of whom had stayed in Czechoslovakia illegally and had not previously paid rent, or to convert the building to a modern hotel. Vladimír Dohnal opted for the latter strategy.

Reconstruction took several years: the reception area was completely rebuilt, a new beer and wine cellar was added, and all the rooms were refurbished. By 1997, the hotel had 640 beds in a three-star complex, and a further 760 beds in a two-star complex. The new owner had to overcome the poor image of the complex, as a Vietnamese black market place. His marketing strategy included meetings with travel agents, and participating in tourism fairs. He also offered part of the accommodation to the Czech Police, as business accommodation. These measures had positive effect. The reconstruction was completed in March 1996 and in that year the hotel enjoyed a 50 per cent increase in visitor numbers compared to the previous year. Above all, the new owner successfully identified and catered for a market gap by providing modestly priced hotel accommodation for domestic business tourists. However, in 1997 the hotel still faced acute problems resulting from its state-socialist heritage. It could only use one quarter of its 9 ha. site, the remainder being either waster land or occupied by car parks. The new owner had earmarked these areas for the development of family housing, a supermarket, swimming pool and mini-golf, but his plans were delayed by a lack of capital. The Košík hotel shows how privatization via direct sale to a domestic investor can bring about marked improvements in a tourism facility but also how a lack of capital can frustrate further development.

4.5 CONCLUSIONS: PRIVATIZATION AS A PRECONDITION FOR MARKET RELATIONSHIPS

Privatization was the foremost precondition for establishing a market economy in a country where almost all the GDP had been generated in the public sector. In 1989 and 1990, there were discussions concerning the optimum speed of privatization. A long process threatened to undermine or, at least, retard the transition. Support for this argument was provided at a later date by the experiences of Russia, Ukraine, and Bulgaria, which opted for a slower transformation. Having adopted the rapid road to transition, the Czechoslovak government faced a major problem: how to privatise establishments in a country where the average monthly salary was just US$ 110. Czechs and Slovaks lacked the capital to buy their own property, at market or book values. As massive sales to foreign groups were politically sensitive, it became clear that a free of charge distribution to the population at large and to investors (or sales at substantial discounts) were the only realistic alternatives. However, privatized companies lacking capital were likely to face major problems.

By 1997, privatization was in its final stages in both countries. About 80 per cent of GDP was generated nominally by the private sector and private enterprises seemed to have been the driving forces behind the economic recovery after 1994. A small proportion of the property was privatized by public auction within the Small Privatization programme, but large and medium-sized enterprises were privatized via Coupon Privatization and direct sales, usually at substantial discounts.

The social implications of privatization were controversial. Most property was directly (in the First and Second Wave) or indirectly (in the so-called Third Wave) acquired by those with good connections with the old regime or with the ruling governments after 1989. Most minor investors were effectively 'robbed' of their property by the illegal or semi-legal activities of the managers of privatized companies and investment funds. The legacy of privatization was a thriving economy, but a deeply divided society.

Privatization rapidly became subject to corruption. The Slovak government openly proclaimed that 'a strong domestic capital class must be created' and distributed state property to those individuals and companies which supported the ruling party. The Czech government sought to project the image of a more transparent privatization, but also distributed state property to supporters of the ruling party and was forced to resign after an associated scandal in 1998.

Foreign investment in the hotel sector was far more common in the Czech Republic than in Slovakia, and there were two reasons for this: Prague's reputation as a tourist centre and the large volumes of international tourism receipts in the Czech Republic; and the poor reputation of Slovakia as an investment destination, mainly because of the non-democratic privatization methods of the Slovak government.

Tourism was one of the most privatized industries in both Republic. Most establishments, particularly in the restaurant sector, were sold in public auctions within the Small Privatization Programme. This privatization was transparent and fair, if hasty. However, many new owners had little experience of tourism in a market economy. They often overpaid for their hotels and restaurants, arranged expensive loans and frequently had to re-sell their property to a second generation of entrepreneurs. On the other hand, this kind of privatization did enable a form of 'natural selection' of property owners under market conditions. Large hotels and spas were privatized either via coupon privatization, particularly in the Czech Republic, or via direct sales (in Slovakia). Few sales via these methods brought direct investment to the hotel industry. Slovak privatization, in particular, tended to be inequitable and to lack clarity. On the other hand, direct sales incorporating substantial discounts did have positive impacts on enterprise efficiency. The new domestic owners of Czech hotels and Slovak spas were not burdened with privatization debts and were able to use their capital for hotel and spa reconstruction. The next chapter seeks to evaluate the economic performance of the different types of privatized tourism firms.

5 THE ECONOMIC PERORMANCE OF TOURISM BUSINESSES: OWNERSHIP AND CORPORATE GOVERNANCE

5.1 INTRODUCTION: A LEADING ECONOMIC SECTOR?

After 1989, international tourism was seen as an important source of international currency in the transition economies (Baláž 1996d). Paradoxically, the state did little to foster tourism in most of these countries and there was an assumption that the private sector would be able to utilize their natural and cultural heritage to attract foreign tourists. Amongst the transition countries, the Czech Republic probably had the greatest tourism potential. This was reflected in the fact that per capita international tourism income was greatest in the Czech Republic in 1996 (US$ 400), followed at some distance by Hungary (US$ 220). Slovakia realized only US$ 130 of international tourist receipts per inhabitant (Annex IV). The Polish per capita income statistic of US$ 195 was not comparable because different methods were used in its computation. The growing volumes of international tourism receipts were reflected in their increasing share of GDP, exports and the National Bank's currency reserves, as can be seen in the Czech and Slovak Republics.

A brief comparison of the shares of tourism in the GDP before and after 1989 provides a superficial assessment of the impact of transformation and privatization: in short, tourism businesses appear to have had more positive trajectories after 1989 (Table 5.1). The numbers of foreign visitors have grown rapidly, international tourist receipts increased at a remarkable rate of approximately 100 per cent per year, and tourism became the most rapidly growing sector in the transformation economies. The real picture was, of course, far more complex, as the case studies in Chapter 4 showed.

TABLE 5.1   *International tourist receipts in Slovakia and the Czech Republic, 1989–97*

Year	1989	1990	1991	1992	1993	1994	1995	1996	1997
				Slovakia					
Receipts									
(US$ million)[1,2]	32	70	135	213	390	568	625	673	545
Share of GDP	0.4	0.9	1.4	2.2	3.5	4.5	3.6	3.7	2.9
Share of exports	1.2	2.4	4.4	6.5	7.1	8.5	7.1	8.0	6.4
Tourism balance									
(US$ million)	n.a.	n.a.	35	58	129	284	303	190	107
Balance as a share of National Bank reserves[3]	x	x	x	x	28.6	16.3	8.9	5.5	3.2
				Czech Republic					
Receipts									
(US$ million)[1,2]	128	419	714	1126	1558	1966	2875	4075	3647
Share of GDP	0.7	2.1	2.8	4.0	5.0	5.0	5.8	7.4	7.7
Share of exports	2.8	4.4	5.1	7.4	9.0	10.1	12.3	16.0	17.7
Tourism balance									
(US$ million)	n.a.	n.a.	412	659	1048	890	1245	1122	1267
Balance as a share of National Bank reserves[3]	x	x	x	x	27.7	14.5	8.9	9.0	12.9

Sources: Národná banka Slovenska (1993–1998a); Český statistický úřad (1993–1998a).
Notes: 1 = data for the 1989 GDP are estimated, and for 1990–91 were recalculated by the National Statistical Offices from state–socialist national income – only since 1992 has GDP been directly calculated; 2 = since 1994, the recommended IMF methodology has been used for computing receipts 3 = the National Bank was established in 1993; n.a. = not available.

5.2 TOURISM IN THE NATIONAL ACCOUNTS

Numerous methodological problems are encountered in any comparison of the tourism economy before and after 1989. During the state-socialist period, the statistics were based on the Material Product System (MPS), which was rooted in the Marxist concept of 'productive and unproductive industries'. Except for food production in restaurants and international tourism receipts, all tourism services were considered to be 'non-material and unproductive' and were not taken into account in computing the Gross National Product (GNP). In addition, many tourism services were provided by the recreation units of industrial and other companies, and therefore, were not recorded in the tourism statistics. Later estimates (see notes in Table 5.1) were produced in an attempt to evaluate both the 'official' and

TABLE 5.2 *Share of the hotel and restaurant sectors in total value added and employment in Slovakia*

Year	1992	1993	1994	1995	1996	1997
Value added, Slovakia						
(Sk million)	4,395	5,141	6,848	8,396	10,463	n.a.
Value added, Czech Republic						
(Kč million)	n.a.	28,456	21,101	8,956	13,062	n.a.
Shares in total value added:						
Slovakia	1.6	1.5	1.7	1.8	1.8	n.a.
Czech Republic	n.a.	2.7	2.1	1.1	1.5	n.a.
OECD 16 average	2.8	2.5	2.3	2.1[1]	n.a.	n.a.
Number of employees, Slovakia	28,273	37,843	36,340	38,003	39,700	
Number of employees, Czech Republic	100,635	111,770	137,125	141,925	166,200	175,600
Shares in total employment:						
Slovakia	1.3	1.8	1.7	1.8	1.8	
Czech Republic	2.0	2.3	2.8	2.8	3.2	3.6
OECD 14 average	3.7	3.4	3.3	3.1[1]	n.a.	n.a.
Share of total investment, Slovakia	1.7	0.9	0.6	0.9	0.8	n.a.
Share of total investment, Czech Republic	1.5	0.8	0.7	0.6	0.5	n.a.

Sources: Štatistický úrad Slovenskej republiky (1994–1998); Český statistický úřad (1993–1998b); Český statistický úřad (1994–1998); OECD (1997).
Notes: 1=data available for France and Norway only; n.a. = not available.

the 'unofficial' tourism sectors. These estimates must be used cautiously because of fundamental differences in centrally planned and market economies. But, in general, the actual volume of tourism services was greater than the volume computed by the recalculation of the communist GNP to a GDP basis. The numbers of beds in, and the domestic tourists using, 'unofficial' tourism establishments, matched those staying in formal hotel accommodation. These holidays, however, were either non-commercial, or involved very low prices, and were not included in official statistics on the hotel and restaurant sector. A system of National Accounts was introduced in 1992 and, since then, tourism data have been broadly comparable to those used in the market economies.

The tourism sector expanded at a relatively modest rate of 0.2 per cent in terms of share of total value added, 1992–5, in Slovakia (Table 5.2). By 1996, its 1.8 per cent share was still lower than that in most OECD member states. In contrast, the share of the tourism sector both in total value added and total employment was higher in the Czech Republic than in Slovakia, and was broadly similar to the pattern in OECD states. These relatively modest changes in value added and employment do not seem to be consistent with rapid increases in international tourist receipts. The increases in receipts, however, were not only a function of the growing number of foreign tourists, but – and probably more importantly – of price increases which, nevertheless, were still affordable to Western tourists. As for tourism's share of total employment, the rate of growth exceeded the growth in valued added in both Republics. This can be explained by the large numbers of small business established after 1989, many of which were based on facilities bought in the Small Privatization, or the conversion of family homes to inns and pubs, requiring limited investment. Larger investments were anyway beyond the resources available to many small-time innkeepers while, in addition, small- and medium-scale investments were frequent in the shadow economy. The latter partly explains the declining share of total investment in tourism, despite the apparent buoyancy of the sector. Another feature to note is that, after 1993, a significant part of GDP growth was generated by fixed investments, which were undertaken by large firms (including state-owned ones) in the power supply, transport, communications, chemical and metal manufacturing industries. In both Republics, a substantial proportion of these investments was financed from bond issues and loans raised on international financial markets, and this was particularly true in the Czech Republic. Tourism entrepreneurs had to rely on domestic bank loans. These were difficult to secure and they were burdened by high interest rates of 15–25 per cent per annum by 1997.

There is also the question of the scale of the shadow economy, which was estimated at 15 per cent of GDP in aggregate, but was likely to be higher in tourism. Most payments were made in cash, especially in sex-tourism, illegal seasonal work abroad and shopping/smuggling activities, and so provided good opportunities for tax evasion, money laundering and other illegal or semi-legal activities. If the official share of the tourism industry in total value added seemed to be relatively low in 1996, the real share was probably much greater; this is evident from comparing bank receipts for international tourism receipts (Table 5.1) with data from tourist expenditure surveys (see chapter 3.8). These suggest that the real share of tourism in total value added may have been at least 4 per cent in Slovakia and 6 per cent in the Czech Republic 1996. There were also likely to be differences between reported and real levels of investment. Many local authorities turned a blind eye to the unreported conversion of family homes into small inns. Given that most small-scale private entrepreneurs relied on 'personal capital sources', many owners probably preferred avoiding having to explain how this had been acquired.

Tourism businesses in the transition economies had to overcome several major shocks in a relatively short time: a switch from a planned to a market economy, privatization, the loss of traditional markets, changes in the structure of demand, and numerous re-organizations and changes in corporate governance. Most of these changes occurred in the period 1991–3. Because of these shocks, a very differently structured tourism sector emerged after a few years of transformation. By 1998 very few of the original business units operated within the same organizational structure as before 1989, as almost all the original businesses had been privatized. Not surprisingly, these 'wild times' affected the old hotel and restaurant businesses negatively. The new owners had to face the same difficulties as other small businesses in the transition economies: lack of capital, high interest rates, incomplete and unclear regulation, mounting bureaucratic obstacles, corruption and increasing crime. Many privatized businesses accumulated debts and were bankrupted in relatively short time periods. There were rapid ownership changes in such companies, which had further negative results. On the other hand, hundreds of new tourism companies and thousands of successful personal businesses emerged in this period. In Slovakia for example, in 1996 almost one half of value added was generated in small and medium units (with up to 24 employees).

5.3 BUSINESS STRUCTURES AND ECONOMIC OUTCOMES

Hotels and restaurants account for an estimated 2.4 per cent to 8.5 per cent of all businesses in the CE transition countries in 1997 (Annex V). The importance of tourism depended on the legal form of the businesses, for its share decreased inversely with increasing capital adequacy (the minimum amounts of capital, and the capital structure required to establish a company) and was greatest in the personal business sector. The proportion of all total personal businesses which were in tourism ranged from 4.6 per cent in the Czech Republic to 10.7 per cent in Hungary. There were comparable data on personal business for Poland, where civil companies were the most commonly encountered legal form in the tourism sector; 4.1 per cent of these were in tourism. As for limited companies, the shares of tourism ranged from 1.6 per cent in Poland to 3.5 per cent in Hungary. Joint-stock companies were mostly found in manufacturing and extractive industries and although in Hungary tourism accounted for 4.6 per cent of these, this was untypical. In Poland the corresponding share was only 0.8 per cent in 1997, and in the Czech Republic it was 2.2 per cent.

Personal businesses (mostly family businesses) were the most widespread ownership form in Czech and Slovak tourism (Table 5.3), as in most market economies. These businesses were mostly in the restaurant sub-sector (pubs, inns, cafés, etc.), and their numbers increased rapidly 1990–3. Many were established under the Small Privatization programme, in which tourism had played a major role. Later, these businesses faced market saturation because of the large numbers of new (or revamped) entrants into the sector.

Privatization produced a very fragmented tourism industry. The former

TABLE 5.3   *Numbers and organizational structure of Slovak and Czech tourism businesses, 1992–7*

	1992	1993	1994	1995	1996	1997
			Slovak Republic			
Companies (plc and limited), of						
which:	565	822	956	1,101	1,157	1,324
(a) Public sector	111	140	67	69	61	49
(b) Private sector, of which:	454	682	889	1,032	1,096	1,275
Foreign	9	17	35	44	52	58
International	32	54	82	96	91	100
Domestic private	413	611	772	892	953	1,117
Personal businesses	12,060	13,788	14,301	14,204	14,004	14,521
Foreign capital, Sk million as	11.33	528.2	534.01	535.54	600.0	400
% of all total foreign capital	0.2	4.9	3.2	2.5	1.3	0.8
			Czech Republic			
Companies (plc and limited) of						
which:	1,703	2,371	3,197	4,009	4,207	4,810
(a) Public sector	n.a.	59	15	72	67	58
(b) Private sector	n.a.	2,312	3,182	3,937	4,140	4,752
Personal businesses	57,779	68,815	44,944	50,338	59,933	63,637

Sources: Štatistický úrad Slovenskej republiky (1994–1998); Český statistický úřad (1993–1998a) and (1993–1998b).
Notes: international signifies that at least one partner is Czech or Slovak, owning more than 50% of shares, whereas foreign implies that more than 50% of shares are in foreign ownership; the private sector in this table refers to establishments owned by private companies as opposed to individuals/partnerships; the private sector includes co-operatives; the exchange rate was about 1 US$ = Sk 30–32 in the period 1992–5; n.a. = not available.

state-socialist enterprises had been large firms, often comprising of 20 or more units, incorporating hotels, restaurants, cable cars and other tourism activities. In the course of the transition, these units were, first, reconstituted as separate firms, and later were either sold to various kinds of investors or transferred to municipal ownership. In Slovakia, transfers to municipalities mostly occurred in 1993 (statistically evident in an increased number of tourism firms in the public sector in that year). After 1993, the importance of juridical (i.e. non-personal and partnership) ownership increased. Large hotels were privatized in the form of plc or limited (joint-stock) companies. In 1996, most of the spas and several large hotels in the High Tatras were privatized in this way in Slovakia, with ownership usually being acquired by domestic private firms.

The *numbers* of international investors expanded rapidly in 1992–5, but the *volume* of foreign investment stagnated after 1993. The level of foreign investment accounted for a relatively larger share of output in the tourism sector than in the economy as a whole but, in general, both shares were very low (Tables 5.2 and 5.3). At first sight, this seems at odds with the rapid increase in international tourism receipts noted earlier? The explanation lies in the fact that the volume of foreign investment in Slovakia grew very slowly after 1993, mainly because of the poor reputation of the government which led to Slovakia being regarded as a higher-risk investment environment. Only the largest and most profitable firms attracted foreign investment, and these were mostly in the steel, aluminium and chemical sectors. In contrast, most tourism firms were probably too small and vulnerable to attract such investment. In 1997 there was actually a decrease in the total volume of foreign direct investment in tourism (Table 5.3), as some foreign owners of Slovak tourism businesses divested their assets to domestic investors. In the Czech Republic, more hotels and spas were privatized via coupon privatization than in Slovakia, and the market was more transparent. Transfers to municipal ownership were also frequent in the Czech Republic. Direct sales became an important privatization method, but to a more limited extent than in Slovakia.

The relative importance of different forms of ownership changed after 1989 in the Czech and Slovak Republics. As would be expected, the public sector share of total turnover decreased while that of the domestic private sector increased. The public sector, however, still played an important role in 1996, at least in Slovakia. How was this possible, given that tourism was the most privatized sector in the Slovak economy? The explanation is to be found in three factors: the particular structure of the former state-socialist tourism sector; the privatization methods used; and the statistical coverage of tourism.

In considering the performance of tourism businesses, we turn first to the output structure of the sector in Slovakia. The total volume of sales was Sk 8274.8 million (US$ 259.4 million), and this can be disaggregated by ownership type and enterprise scale (Table 5.4). Large enterprises generated 78.3 per cent of total income, and these can be sub-divided according to whether the firm is classified in the tourism sector or another sector, indicating that tourism is not its major activity.

1) Domestic private ownership is more important in the tourism-related sector than in the non-tourism sector. There was still one state-owned chain in 1996, originating from the Interhotel hotels and restaurants, but all the other tourism chains had been privatized. Individual data protection requirements make it impossible to identify this single firm, but it accounted for a large part of the public sector's 8.1 per cent share of accommodation services and 6.8 per cent share of catering. Another reason for the relatively high share of the public sector was extensive municipal ownership, for many hotels and restaurants had been 'privatized' via transfers from the state to the municipalities.

136

TABLE 5.4   *Income from accommodation and catering in Slovakia in 1996: by ownership, type and size of enterprise (percentages)*

| Ownership | Large enterprises, over 25 employees | | | | Small enterprises, up to 24 employees | | Total |
| | Tourism-related businesses | | Non-tourist businesses | | | | |
	Accommo- dation	Catering	Accommo- dation	Catering	Accommo- dation	Catering	
Foreign	0.6	4.4	0.1	0.0	0.2	0.7	6.0
International	0.5	0.8	0.3	0.8	0.4	3.0	5.7
Domestic							
private	13.8	16.0	4.2	12.1	3.5	13.2	62.7
Public	8.1	6.2	5.2	5.4	0.1	0.6	25.6
Total	22.9	27.4	9.7	18.3	4.2	17.5	100.0

Sources: Štatistický úrad Slovenskej republiky (1997a) and (1997b).
Notes: international ownership: at least one partner is foreign and at least one is Czech/ Slovaki public includes establishments owned by the state, municipalities, associations, political parties, churches etc; domestic private includes private sector companies, personal businesses and co-operatives; there are 18,724 reporting units in the small firm sector, of which 790 are hotels and 359 are travel agencies, while most of the remainder are pubs and restaurants; in the large enterprise sector, there are 636 tourism-related business and 4,810 non-tourism businesses.

2)   The situation was different amongst non-tourism firms, where the public sector accounted for a larger share than the private sector. This relates to the political construction of tourism as an important form of collective provision in the state-socialist period, whereby almost every firm or organization had its own recreation unit. The largest manufacturing and extractive enterprises owned chains of hotels, restaurants and sanatoriums for their employees. The total number of such establishments matched the provision in the 'normal commercial' tourism sector. After 1989, many firms either divested their recreation units separately or these were privatized as an integral part of their parent firms. Some major enterprises (and their recreation units), however, were assigned a 'strategic status' and remained in state ownership. The ZŤS Martin armaments producer, was one such strategic firm, which owned several hotels, ski areas and cable-car facilities even in 1998.

Small enterprises accounted for 21.7 per cent of the income from accommodation and catering, with the latter being dominant. Given a generalized shortage of capital and high interest rates, it was easier to establish a pub or restaurant than to build or lease a hotel. Privatization generated large numbers of small businesses but, subsequently, their growth was overtaken by that of their larger competitors. Whereas, in 1992, 322 small businesses (with up to 24 employees) had accounted for 28 per cent (Sk 681.6 million) of total sales, this share had declined to 21.7 per cent by 1996.

What assessment can be made of the economic performances of Slovak tourism enterprises during the transformation? This depends, of course, on the indicators selected, but some consistent variations can be identified. Table 5.5 summarizes a number of economic indicators for a sample of 138 large Slovak tourism firms, and compares these to the data for other Slovak and OECD businesses. These firms were medium- and large-scale businesses and so do not provide any insights into the performance of the small tourism firm sector. These statistics should be viewed alongside the data on the structure of the tourism sector in 1993–6 (Table 5.3).

There has been a generalized capital shortage in the transition economies, so that most enterprises have relied on their own financial sources. In Slovakia, the share of own funds was significantly higher than the OECD average and was close to the maximum OECD value (56.5 per cent in the UK). Tourism, however, was different. Their share of own funds was much lower than the Slovak average and, furthermore, it decreased during the transformation. Most tourism businesses were privatized, and the new owners had to borrow capital, initially for the privatization purchase and later to restructure their businesses. Non-tourism establishments were mostly privatized via coupon privatization or direct sales at very low prices, so that their owners had relatively smaller borrowing requirements.

The above average proportions of borrowed capital in the total funds of tourism businesses contributed to their above-average debt-servicing costs. Funds for privatization were borrowed over short time periods, and debts had to be repaid relatively quickly. The short-term nature of loans (and a falling inflation rate) meant that the amount of debt and interest decreased over time; there was also an upturn in the share of own funds towards the end of the period (Figure 5.1). The share of financial assets in the total assets of Slovak firms seems strikingly low in comparison to OECD countries, where the minimal share was 15.9 per cent (in the USA). However, this is typical of transition economies, where enterprises have critical shortages of capital and are denuded of cash reserves, often being unable to pay their suppliers. Tourism businesses are no exceptions in this respect. After 1995, the situation improved and firms were able to retain more cash reserves; both the shares of financial assets and profit ratios increased in the period 1993–6 (Figure 5.1).

The general economic situation in CE (and to some extent in Europe), and the numerous shocks in the course of the economic transformation, had a negative impact on profitability. The ratio of gross total profits to total assets is much lower in Slovakia than in the OECD, where the lowest value is 3.2 per cent (Finland). There was a significant difference between tourism and other businesses in Slovakia. While there was little variation

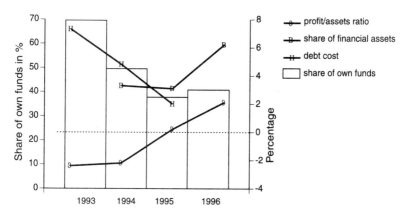

Fig. 5.1 Economic indicators for Slovak tourism businesses, 1993–6.
Source: Ministerstvo hospodárstva Slovenskej republiky (1994–1996).

in the ratio for other businesses in the period 1993-6, tourism businesses recorded losses in both 1993 and 1994, and only attained the average profit/ assets level for the economy as a whole in 1996. The purchase costs of privatized firms, and their restructuring, were the main reasons for the losses in 1993–1994, but debt servicing costs also contributed to these. But it should be noted that some managers deliberately ran their hotels and restaurants to the verge of bankruptcy, in order to depress privatization prices.

While debt costs were significant, as the case studies presented in Chapter 4 demonstrate, the recorded low level of debt-servicing costs initially seems puzzling for a transition economy. In particular, it can be asked why the servicing of debt accounts for only 2–7 per cent of costs in a country where the interest on bank loans is 15–20 per cent per annum? The answer lies in the structure of debt. Except for the initial privatization loans, tourism firms have tended to obtain relatively few other loans. Moreover, the main part of their real debt is in the form of trade credits. A special system of trade credit has developed in the course of transformation, known as 'secondary receivables' or, more simply, 'squeeze'. Enterprises, with a liquidity shortage, tend either not to pay their suppliers, or do so very late. In turn, they often do not receive payments from their customers, or these arrive belatedly. These unpaid supply bills constitute a form of trade credit with a zero interest rate. In a mature market economy, enterprises with unpaid debts are usually liquidated, but this is problematic in a transition economy, where virtually all enterprises exercise a squeeze on their customers. Czech and Slovak hotels are no exception, with unpaid trade

TABLE 5.5   *Economic indicators for Slovak tourism businesses, 1994–6*

	Share of own funds in total funds (%)	Share of financial assets in total assets (%)	Debt servicing: interest paid to borrowed capital (%)	Gross total profit to total assets (%)
Slovak hotels & restaurants	49.5	4.2	4.7	−0.6
Slovak NFEs	59.3	4.4	3.8	2.8
OECD 12 NFEs, 1990–1995	38.7	49.0	5.1	10.8

Sources: Ministerstvo hospodárstva Slovenskej republiky (1994–1996); OECD (1996).
Notes: NFE = non-financial enterprises; Slovak data are averages for the period 1993–6; the NFEs are large enterprises with more than 25 employees, including 138 reporting units in the hotel and restaurant sector; the OECD data are averages for the period 1990–5 and mostly refer to large and medium-sized enterprises.

credits being substituted for normal financial loans, which are unavailable to them on the financial markets.

A further insight into firm performance is provided by the Banking and Clearing Centre of Slovakia which, since 1993, has been computing the median values of the financial indicators of Slovak businesses (Bankové a zúčtovacie centrum Slovenska 1997). This information, originally designed for investment banking, provides a unique insight into the performances of Slovak tourism businesses. The statistics summarize information from all types and sizes of enterprises. Selected indicators for tourism businesses are shown in Table 5.6. It is important to stress that, while Table 5.5 only includes larger enterprises (which were relatively homogenous), Table 5.6 summarizes data on all types of enterprises, excepting personal businesses.

An overwhelming majority – 757 out of a total of 803 – of tourism enterprises in Slovakia had less than Sk 50 million (US$ 1.7 million) in assets in 1996. Most had basic capital of only Sk 100,000 (US$ 3000), which is the lowest capital requirement for a limited-type company. The low capital requirement explains the very low share of own funds in the total capital of most Slovak tourism businesses. Additionally, the rapidly growing number of small businesses explains the decreasing average share of own funds in the period 1993–6. In contrast, large enterprises, with assets over Sk 150 million (15 units) and turnover over Sk 100 million (4 units), mostly relied on their own capital.

In general, there is a positive relationship between the size of assets and/or turnover, and the profitability of the enterprise. The industry, in aggregate, made a net loss, mostly because of the performances of smaller enterprises. This has to be seen against the growth in the number of enterprises (compare Tables 5.3 and 5.6) and the fact that newly established firms tend to record losses initially. By 1996, however, the average (median) loss (virtually zero) had declined significantly compared to the equivalent figure for 1993. Additionally, small enterprises had to maintain relatively high levels of financial assets, in relation to their capital requirements (only Sk 100,000 for small enterprises whereas many have turnover of Sk 1–10 million) because of the increasing demands of suppliers for cash transactions and the large share of trade credits in their total capital. The average (median) share of financial assets, however, was very low.

Table 5.6 also provides an insight into the structure of the tourism industry. Most medium- and large-scale enterprises were in the hotel sub-sector. In contrast, only one restaurant chain had a turnover more than Sk 100 million (US\$ 3 million) in 1996. Profitability also differed in the hotel and restaurant sub-sectors. In the hotel sub-sector, medium-sized and large enterprises were more profitable (ratio of profits to assets) than small firms, but the inverse applied in the restaurant sub sector; the small numbers of very large firms (there were only eight hotels and three restaurant chains with assets over Sk 150 million) mean that these trends have to be treated cautiously, and it is not useful to speculate on the underlying causes. However, profitability improved in both sub-sectors during the observed period, after the initial costs of privatization had been absorbed and as tax collection became more efficient. Finally, we can note that Slovak tourism enterprises were, generally, less efficient than the remainder of the economy. This is mostly due to the establishment of large numbers of new, small tourism businesses after 1989. These had lower shares of own funds and financial assets in their total assets, and many were burdened with privatization debts. On the other hand, tourism businesses shared in the more generalized trend for the economic performance of Slovak firms to improve during the transition.

Far less detailed financial indicators for tourism businesses are available in the Czech Republic. However, it is known that their profitability was below average for the Czech economy (Table 5.7). It is difficult to compare the two countries because their data sources are compiled on different bases, not least due to the different sizes of firms covered by the statistics. However, there is broad evidence that, at least in 1996, large and medium-sized Czech and Slovakian tourism businesses had similar profitability rates. The reasons for the operating losses in the Czech tourism sector are similar to Slovakia: privatization debts, high interest rates, and the start-up costs of establishing new businesses.

While the published data provide insights into the transition process, and especially into changes over time, their reliability has to be seen in context of the operational realities of a transition economy. Most market institutions are still being created in transition economies, including the tax and statistical systems. There is a thriving shadow economy and tax evasion is known to be widespread. The tourism industry in a transformation eco-

TABLE 5.6   *Selected financial indicators for Slovak tourism business, 1993–6*

	1993	1994	1995	1996	1996					
	All enterprises				Assets, Sk million			Turnover, Sk million		
					up to 50	51– 150	over 150	up to 25	26– 100	over 100
Tourism industry (hotels, inns, camping, restaurants, pubs and bars)										
Number of enterprises	440	603	721	803	757	31	15	737	62	4
Share of own funds %	6.9	4.2	3.2	0.0	0.0	14.4	68.9	0.0	0.0	76.6
Share of financial assets %	7.4	7.4	8.3	9.3	9.1	1.4	0.7	9.1	7.7	13.3
Profits to assets %	−4.3	−5.1	−3.6	0.0	0.0	−0.9	−0.1	0.0	1.1	1.6
Profits to own funds %	−16.8	−22.6	−16.1	−2.2	−2.2	−4.3	−0.5	−2.6	−0.3	39.8
Hotels										
Number of enterprises	92	136	169	191	166	17	8	174	15	2
Share of own funds %	3.5	2.8	2.0	1.0	0.0	28.1	71.2	1.3	−0.4	idp
Share of financial assets %	4.0	5.0	5.4	5.3	5.5	3.5	0.6	5.2	5.2	idp
Profits to assets %	−2.9	−5.7	−4.9	−0.2	0.0	−1.8	−0.4	−0.5	0.1	idp
Profits to own funds %	−6.4	−16.4	−14.1	−4.2	−4.4	−4.4	−0.8	−4.1	−7.0	idp
Restaurants										
Number of enterprises	265	371	425	444	432	9	3	407	36	1
Share of own funds %	7.5	2.9	2.0	0.0	0.0	9.8	1.9	0.0	0.0	idp
Share of financial assets %	7.1	8.1	7.5	8.4	8.4	0.9	0.5	9.3	10.5	idp
Profits to assets %	−5.6	−4.5	−2.9	0.0	0.0	0.1	−2.7	0.0	1.4	idp
Profits to own funds %	−29.5	−23.2	−17.8	−1.6	−1.4	−4.7	116.5	−2.2	−0.1	idp
All Slovak industries										
Number of enterprises	18,764	24,871	29,220	33,381	8,243	1,100	749	7,761	1,558	773
Share of own funds %	11.1	10.1	7.8	6.5	6.8	44.5	45.6	6.9	19.6	35.2
Share of financial assets %	12.1	12.7	12.1	11.4	9.6	2.5	2.4	9.5	4.1	3.2
Profits to assets %	−0.6	−0.1	0.0	0.0	0.0	0.0	0.0	0.0	0.5	0.5
Profits to own funds %	−1.9	−1.3	−0.7	0.0	0.0	0.0	0.0	0.0	0.6	1.0

Source: Bankové a zúčtovacie centrum Slovenska (1997).

Notes: the data refer only to plc and limited companies and exclude personal businesses; idp = data suppressed due to individual data protection (two or less units). Share of financial assets refers to financial assets as a percentage of all assets.

TABLE 5.7   *The ratio of profits to own funds (%) in the Czech Republic, 1993–6*

	1993	1994	1995	1996
Total non-financial enterprises	6.5	5.4	6.9	3.6
Hotels and restaurants	−7.1	−6.7	−0.5	−4.8

Source: Český statistický úřad (1994–1998).
Note: the data are for businesses registered in the Business Register and these are mostly large and medium-scale.

nomy is usually characterized by large shares of cash payments, and a failure to issue receipts for payments made by foreigner visitors. These conditions favour the non-reporting of income, particularly amongst small businesses. This was underlined earlier (Chapter 3) by the difference between the US$ 672.8 million of international currency receipts reported by the National Bank of Slovakia (computed according to recommended IMF methods), and the receipts of at least US$ 1808 million indicated by a market survey. There is also the difference between the international tourism receipts of US$ 4.1 billion reported by the Czech National Bank and the US$ 10.7 billion estimated in tourism surveys. This means that the actual profitability of Czech and Slovak tourism businesses was probably far stronger than was reported in their financial statements. During 1992–6 the numbers of tourism-related companies increased two-fold in Slovakia and 2.5 times in the Czech Republic, and this is only likely to have occurred if the profits outlook was favourable.

5.4 PROPERTY RIGHTS, MANAGEMENT AND CORPORATE GOVERNANCE

5.4.1 Transition and the structure of the tourism industry in Slovakia

Changing role of the hotel sector

A key question is whether the introduction of market relationships has contributed to qualitative changes in the provision of accommodation services in Slovakia? An initial examination of Table 5.8 indicates substantial falls in occupancy rates for all types of establishments, mainly as a result of a decline in domestic tourism. In the state-socialist period, hotels and similar establishments accounted for only 44 per cent of all overnights, because Czechoslovaks favoured low-cost camping, hostels and inns. These lower quality types of accommodation were the first to be affected by a decline in living standards in the period 1990–3. Subsequent improvements in living standards and a recovery in domestic tourism did not, however,

143

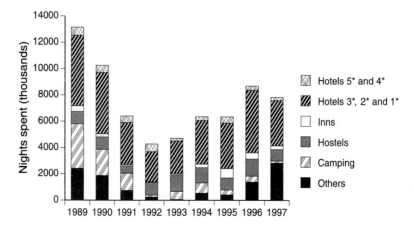

Fig. 5.2 The structure of the nights spent in Slovak accommodation by type of establishment.
Source: Štatistický úrad Slovenskej republiky (1991–1998b).
Note: the 1997 data were collected from a sample of 530 firms, while the 1993–7 samples included 700–1000 firms. The 1997 data are not fully comparable to previous years.

result in replication of the 1989 structure of nights spent. Instead, by 1996 hotels accounted for 74.1 percent of total nights spent.

Most of the construction of new accommodation was in inns and three-star hotels, while a number of older hotels were renovated to attract business tourism. The structure of the nights spent in various forms of accommodation changed substantially in 1993–6 (Figure 5.2). The share of all nights spent in hotels increased from 53 per cent to 74 per cent, while the share of hostel accommodation decreased from 27 per cent to 19 per cent. To some extent there has been a substitution of demand for inns and other means of accommodation (rented rooms, second homes, etc.) for camping and hostels. The real improvement in terms of volumes and standards of accommodation services was, however, greater than appears at first sight. The 1996 statistics included, for the first time, more than 550,000 nights spent in accommodation provided by personal businesses. This, of course, depressed the share of all nights spent in hotels. In addition, as of 26 December 1995, a new, more stringent hotel classification system was introduced which resulted in many hotels being downgraded.

The shift from camping and hostels to inns and hotels was an expression of a more general increase in demand for higher quality accommodation. While occupancy rates in camping and hostels either stagnated or declined,

TABLE 5.8   *Occupancy rates in Slovakia*

	1989	1990	1991	1992	1993	1994	1995	1996
Type of establishment								
Hotels: ★★★★ and ★★★★	61.6	53.8	41.2	39.0	28.1	35.6	38.4	43.5
Hotels: ★★★, ★★ and ★	55.5	48.9	35.4	38.0	31.5	31.5	31.5	37.6
Inns	41.5	36.0	22.2	42.6	23.8	28.3	31.8	47.0
Hostels	39.4	36.5	24.7	25.4	28.6	26.2	24.8	29.1
Camping	40.4	28.4	42.9	30.7	19.9	24.2	27.4	13.8
Others	n.a.	n.a.	n.a.	n.a.	23.6	24.8	17.6	39.3
Average	47.3	39.0	35.1	n.a.	28.3	28.7	28.2	31.9
Ownership								
Public	n.a.	n.a.	n.a.	n.a.	30.5	29.5	28.3	37.3
Domestic private	n.a.	n.a.	n.a.	n.a.	28.1	23.9	27.4	31.4
Foreign	n.a.	n.a.	n.a.	n.a.	17.4	34.7	49.1	52.1
International	n.a.	n.a.	n.a.	n.a.	29.0	25.7	25.3	27.4
Average	47.3	39.0	35.1	n.a.	28.3	28.7	28.2	31.9

Sources: Federální štatistický úřad (1986–1993); Štatistický úřad Slovenskej republiky (1991–1998b).
Notes: n.a. = not available; international = at least one partner is Czech or Slovak, owning at least 50% of shares; foreign = over 50% of shares in foreign ownership.

those for hotels and inns increased significantly 1993–6 (Table 5.8). The development of new inns was entirely within the private sector, but both the private and public sectors were involved in redevelopment of large hotels.

There was also a shift to higher quality establishments in the Czech Republic (Figure 5.3). Between 1990 and 1996, the share of camping in total overnights decreased from 24.2 per cent to 8.5 per cent, while a sharp decrease was also reported in the hostel share from 15.3 per cent to 8.6 per cent. A small decrease was recorded in the hotel share, from 49.0 per cent to 45.6 per cent, but this was mainly due to changes in the compilation of statistics. In 1996, the category of 'other facilities' was more comprehensively covered than previously, and doubled in size compared to 1995, thereby reducing the relative weight of hotels. In practice, hotels continued to become more important and the total numbers of nights spent in the Czech hotels increased from 12 to 17 million between 1990 and 1996. On the other hand, the absolute numbers of nights spent in hostels and camping in 1996 fell to just 40 per cent of their 1990 level. The reduced preference for lower quality accommodation is mainly explained by changes in the structure of foreign demand. The increasing numbers of German tourists (including visitors from the former GDR) preferred, and could afford,

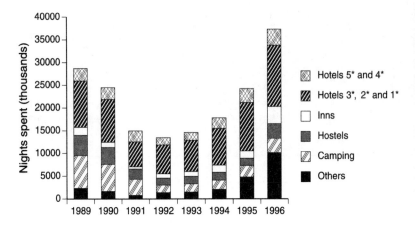

Fig. 5.3 The structure of the nights spent in Czech accommodation: by type of establishment.
Source: Český statistický úřad (1989–1998a).

higher quality facilities. The sharp fall in Czech living standards in 1990-3, also undermined domestic demand for hostels and camping in this period. When the new Czech middle class emerged in the latter part of the transition, they also preferred higher quality accommodation.

There were similar changes in occupancy rates in the two Republics (Figure 5.4). A sharp decrease after 1989 was mainly caused by declining living standards and economic recession, which depressed domestic demand. A large influx of foreign tourists was insufficient to substitute fully for the fall-off in domestic demand. The situation changed with renewed economic growth in 1994. Five- and four-star hotels, mostly designed for business tourism, accounted for the largest increases in occupancy rates. This trend was more clearly visible in Slovakia, where the supply of luxury accommodation was smaller than in the Czech Republic. However, with improvements in living standards throughout Central and Eastern Europe, inns and one to three star hotels also recorded increased occupancy rates.

Public v private sector: a question of efficiency?

A major issue concerning the transformation is the relative efficiency of the private and public sectors. This is necessarily a complex question as can be seen in the case of Slovak hotels (Table 5.4, Table 5.8 and Figure 5.5). The share of the public sector in total overnights fell from 76.5 per cent in 1993 to 65.1 per cent in 1996, whilst the private sector share increased from 21.4 per cent to 31.2 per cent (Figure 5.5). This shift represents the outcome of both

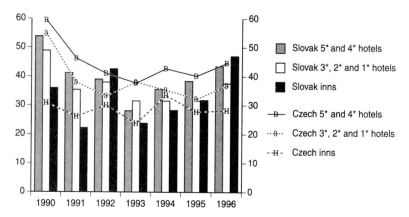

Fig. 5.4 Occupancy rates (percentages) in Czech and Slovak tourist accommodation, 1990–6.
Sources: Štatistický úrad Slovenskej republiky (1991–1998b). Český statistický úřad (1989–1998b).

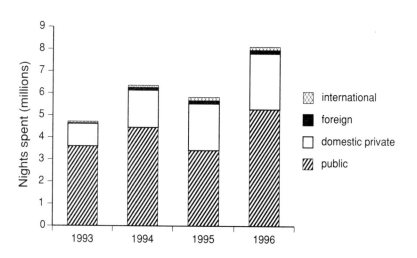

Fig. 5.5 Structure of nights spent in Slovak accommodation facilities by ownership type.
Source: Štatistický úrad Slovenskej republiky (1991–1998b).

privatization and new business starts in the private sector. In terms of occupancy rates, the public sector outperformed the private sector in every year in this period (Table 5.8). There are several explanations for this.

First, public sector hotels usually have well-established reputations with loyal clienteles. Moreover, most public sector hotels are relatively large-scale, which facilitates co-operation with domestic and foreign tour-operators. In contrast, the owners of smaller, private establishments some-times lack professional know-how. It is, however, misleading to refer to the public sector in aggregate, for this is a diverse sector. While state-owned facilities had a 41 per cent occupancy rate in 1996, this was only 14.5 per cent for municipally owned establishments. The highest occupancy rates (43 per cent) in the public sector were recorded by non-governmental organizations. Sorea plc, owned by the trade unions, for example, was the largest and best-managed hotel chain in Slovakia. Sorea had a programme of low-cost holidays for Slovak pensioners during the low season, which enhanced its occupancy rate. The programme was state sponsored within a social-tourism framework. Given the low prices, about Sk 1200–2000 (U\$ 40–65) for one week full-board in a hotel, and the favourable locations of Sorea hotels in some of the most attractive areas in Slovakia, it is hardly surprising that these were utilized around the year. Despite this impressive record, the highest occupancy rates were within the private sector, in for-eign–owned hotels which had been integrated into international hotel chains. They were able to capture a large part of the business tourism market, especially in Bratislava. Many of their staff had been trained abroad and their service levels matched those in comparable Western European establishments. However, the foreign and international sectors constituted only a minor part of the Slovak hotel industry, due to negative FDI reac-tions to Slovak government policies, especially after 1995.

A different perspective is obtained if market share and income are com-pared (Table 5.4 and Figure 5.5). While the public sector accounted for 65.1 per cent of overnights and the private sector for 31.2 per cent in 1996, their shares of total income were almost reversed: the domestic private sector accounted for almost two-thirds of total income, and the public sector for just one-quarter. There are a number of reasons for this. Prices were higher in the private sector, usually by some 25–50 per cent. Hotels in the public sector also accounted for a larger share of the domestic market, where clients usually received 30–50 per cent discounts, and there were also more social-tourism services for pensioners, students and others. Moreover, the private sector deliberately tried to target foreign visitors with greater potential spending power.

The changing role of the spas

In the state-socialist period, spa tourism was constructed as a combination of medical services and entertainment activities, with the former being more important. Spa activities were limited to designated towns, with a special legal status, and the Ministry of Health Care regulated spa establishments. The spas were one of the most competitive segments of the entire Czechoslovak economy. In the 1980s they generated 1 US$ in revenue for every US$ 0.1–0.25 of operating costs. In contrast, manufacturing produced 1 US$ for each US$ 0.5–1.0 of operating costs. In Slovakia, the spa towns of Piešt′any and Trenčianske Teplice were particularly successful in attracting wealthy clients from the Middle East and Germany, generating substantial inflows of convertible currencies. In a sense, spa tourism was considered to be part of the 'family silver' of the national economy, so that it received more policy attention than other sectors of tourism. For example, spa towns had a special status, prohibiting the development of heavy industries and establishing relatively tight controls over the urban environment.

The spas retained their special position after 1989. Article 4 of the Slovak Constitutional Law states that all mineral springs and natural resources used for medical purposes are in state ownership, while spa activities are private sector activities. The latter are subject to supervision by the Inspectorate for Spas and Mineral Springs (Health Care Law No. 277/1994). During 1995–8, the Inspectorate issued new statutes for each of the 22 Slovak spa towns. In some spa towns, for example, mountain-biking and the transport of heavy goods were prohibited for environmental reasons. An official strategy for spa tourism development was prepared in 1991 and was approved in 1993 by the Slovak Ministry of Health Care. This confirmed the leading role of medical activities in their future development, but also enabled commercialization and privatization.

The municipalities in the spa towns had hoped that, in recognition of the constraints on their economic activities, the spas would be transferred into their ownership, but these aspirations were not realized. The Mečiar government, which came to power after November 1994, transferred the so-called 'family silver' to some of its most powerful supporters. The largest and most profitable Slovak spas (at Piešt′any), for example, were privatized by Mrs. Martinková (a close friend of the Prime Minister after 1996) and her husband, while the Sliač and Kováčová spas were privatized directly by Mr. Soboňa, the Minister of Health Care. The municipalities only received minority shareholdings in the privatized spas.

By 1998, the Slovak spas had some eleven thousand beds and accounted for a significant share of Slovakia's tourism resources (non-spa hotels and motels only accounted for some 40,000 beds). The spa users were mostly domestic clients who, on average, stayed for three or four weeks, and whose costs were covered by the National Social Insurance System and health insurance companies. In 1996, for example, of the total of 107,000 clients, 45,000 were pensioners (aged 60 or more) and 53,000 were aged 40–60. Total demand was far higher, for about 260,000 domestic clients had applied to the insurance system and companies for paid visits. The allocation system was managed by special medical committees, which reviewed the competing claims mainly on medical grounds. In addition, there were some 24,000 foreign clients (mostly Russians, Germans, Czechs, Hungarians and Arabs) and large numbers of domestic commercial clients.

The more than 100,000 domestic clients whose visits were paid for by the insurance system and companies helped to sustain occupancy rates at about 80–90 per cent in most Slovak spas. On the other hand, these clients had relatively low expenditures on non-medical facilities, such as restaurants and night clubs. The privatized spa facilities therefore sought additional income sources. According to a 1998 survey, every spa enterprise wanted to increase its number of beds, improve the quality of its gastronomy and entertainment facilities, and built new commercial installations specifically designed to attract foreign clients (Kuminiaková 1998). The Bardejov spa, with 1178 beds and 16,000 clients in 1997, for example, wanted to reconstruct its major hotel, build a restaurant with 300 new dining places, and a congress hall for 350 guests. The Sliač and Kováčová spas had plans to use foreign finance to build a cardiology center. And the relatively small Rajecké Teplice spa, which had 440 beds and 5805 clients in 1997, wanted to increase the number of beds to 700 and install new balneotherapy facilities.

Travel agents

While three state and co-operative travel agencies (plus the federal Čedok) accounted for the entire turnover of this sector in Slovakia in 1989, some 1000 licences were issued subsequently and there were some 160 active travel agents in 1998. 1989 was, therefore, a watershed in the travel agency sector as in most segments of the tourism industry. The above-mentioned three agencies were state monopolies which specialized in different kinds of travel. They enjoyed a comfortable existence under state-socialism, being protected from competition and having a guaranteed clientele amongst the thousands of organized tour groups supplied by similar state-owned monopolies in other state-socialist countries.

Most of the new firms in the sector originated as family businesses, and the founder usually had some previous experience of working in a state-owned travel agency. Except for Satur plc (the Slovak part of the former Čedok) and Tatratour, almost all the domestically owned agencies suffered from a lack of capital, technical equipment and professional staff. The new firms began operating by creating simple products for the domestic market. The very first products were short bus trips to Vienna and Venice – the buses being hired from local bus networks and the offices being established in the entrepreneurs' own homes. A typical product in the 1990–5 period was a bus trip to an Italian or Spanish resort for US\$ 200 per capita per week. The 'mortality rate' amongst such firms was very high. Only a small

TABLE 5.9   *Travel agencies in Slovakia: economic performance, 1989–7*

	1989	1992	1993	1994	1995	1996	1997
			Incoming tourism				
Clients	193,533	68,709	82,889	112,846	174,595	146,019	143,558
Days	1,267,119	342,868	390,903	386,130	685,055	508,969	662,121
Sales, Sk '000	431,411	58,360	155,521	234,179	287,105	271,836	579,284
			Outgoing tourism				
Clients	144,931	187,995	159,143	213,554	217,578	318,059	403,471
Days	1,073,274	1,073,730	1,083,325	1,391,380	1,331,894	2,193,395	3,080,956
Sales, Sk '000	376,409	292,659	788,551	1,299,881	1,658,910	2,843,964	4,202,345
			Domestic tourism				
Clients	n.a.	n.a.	53,473	186,305	86,275	262,008	273,059
Days	n.a.	n.a.	310,448	620,216	478,962	918,659	1,020,991
Sales, Sk '000	n.a.	19,916	57,418	192,861	159,775	260,091	483,581

Sources: Federální štatistický úrad (1990–1993b); Štatistický úrad Slovenskej republiky (1993–1998b).

number of the 155 members of the Slovak Association of Travel Agents in 1998 could date their origins back to 1990.

There is, however, evidence that the travel agency sub–sector was becoming more sophisticated, for there was increasing involvement in outbound tourism, particularly for 'sunshine, sand and sea' holidays (Table 5.9). This was linked to improved living standards after 1994 as well as to more sophisticated product development and marketing. Many agents established working contacts with partners in the destination countries or with major European tour companies, such as Neckerman and TUI. The total numbers of clients and the volume of days sold increased three fold, 1989–97, with the most significant increases being in 1996 and 1997. There was little change in the average length of stay, which decreased from 7.4 days in 1989 to 5.7 days in 1992 (perhaps because of declining incomes) but increased to 7.6 days in 1997. There were more significant changes in quality. The market share of cheap bus trips has fallen and standard travel packages, with inclusive flights and accommodation, have become more important. In 1997, for example, air inclusive package trips accounted for 38 per cent of all packages, outstripping bus-inclusive trips (34.3 per cent), combined transport trips (4.8 per cent), and trips involving individual transport (22.7 per cent). As their potential customer base has become more solvent and selective, so the product supply of Slovak travel agencies has converged towards Western European models.

After Satur plc was privatized in 1996, the travel agency sector was entirely in the private sector. There was a high degree of concentration, and

TABLE 5.10   *The market shares of the top 10 Slovakian travel agents in 1997*

Shares in sales	All tourism	Outgoing tourism	Incoming tourism	Shares of numbers of clients
Ruefa, CS	14.6	15.7	0.8	4.8
Fischer Slovakia	12.3	13.3	0.0	2.9
Satur	12.0	11.7	14.7	24.5
Tatratour	9.8	7.4	39.8	10.5
VSŽ Ferrotour	5.7	6.1	1.0	3.4
Koala Tours	5.6	6.0	0.0	3.6
Globtour	5.5	5.2	9.1	7.9
Seneca Tours	5.3	5.7	0.0	3.5
CK FIFO	5.1	5.2	4.9	7.6
Kartago Tours	4.7	5.1	0.0	1.5
Top 30 agents	Sk 2,893.2 mil	Sk 2,673.9 mil	Sk 220.4 mil	clients: 516,390

Source: TREND weekly (1998a).

five major agencies accounted for 60 per cent of turnover and customers in outbound travel. Incoming tourism, on the other hand, was much more demanding in terms of human and financial resources, and only a few travel agents specialized in this. In 1997, incoming tourism accounted for only 10 per cent of total travel agency sales. The average length of inbound trip fell from 6.5 days in 1989 to 5 days in 1992, and to 3.4 days in 1994. This is probably due to the diminishing level of organized travel amongst the post-socialist countries, and to the decreasing quality of travel agency services in this early transition period. After 1995 the 'core' Slovakian travel agencies improved the quality of their services and developed closer collaboration with major EU tour operators, and this helped to extend the average length of stay by incoming tourists to 4.6 days in 1997.

The travel agency sector is highly competitive. The 160 agencies in existence in 1998 are the survivors of some 1000 units, which operated at some point during 1990–8. Domestic entrepreneurs have also faced strong competition from foreign firms, which established a presence in the Slovak market especially after 1995. By 1997, Satur plc was the largest travel agency in Slovakia in terms of customer numbers, with 126 thousands clients and a 24.5 per cent share of the market. Its main competitive advantage derived from a network of 53 regional and five foreign branches, which had been inherited from Čedok. Its size and long experience enabled Satur to provide its own products for 90 per cent of the packages, which it sold. The agency offered a broad range of domestic and international tourism packages designed mainly for the Slovak middle classes. However, the large share of domestic trips and economically priced 'sunshine, sand and sea' holidays meant that Satur had a smaller share of total sales (Table 5.10).

In 1991, the Austrian travel agent Ruefa established a branch in Bratislava. Drawing on its parent company's human and financial resources, it quickly became the second largest travel agency in Slovakia. By 1997 it had about 5 per cent of all clients, but accounted for 14.6 per cent of sales. The firm specialized in outbound tourism and air ticket sales, and its own products accounted for 60 per cent of its total sales. Ruefa's strong initial position has been challenged by Fischer Slovakia Ltd. The parent firm of Fischer was established in Germany in the 1980s (see pp 125–6), by a Czech emigrant, who expanded his activities to the Czech Republic after 1989, and established a branch in Slovakia in 1996. This dynamic firm soared to third place in the Slovakian market in its first year, capturing about 10 per cent of total turnover. By 1997, the agency had become the second largest in terms of sales. The fourth largest agency, in terms of sales, was Tatratour plc, established in 1969. Like Satur, Tatratour relied on an established network of 22 regional branches and provided a large proportion of inbound tourism packages. The firm maintained its good reputation for offering professional service in the markets for both inbound and outbound packages. In 1997, over 90 per cent of the packages it sold were its own products. The remainder of the market was accounted for by new firms established after 1989 (TREND weekly 1997; TREND weekly 1998a). Among these, VSŽ Ferrotour – established by the VSŽ steel mill – and the privately owned Koala Tours were of major importance.

Two conclusions can be drawn from the summary of leading travel agencies (Table 5.10). First, despite the establishment of a number of new private firms, the market was dominated by Satur and Tatratour, which had existed before 1989, and by foreign tour-operators. Only the largest firms had sufficient capital to invest in new technologies and marketing strategies. Second, incoming tourism was not considered an attractive market segment, particularly by foreign agencies. The small number of incoming packages were mostly provided by traditional suppliers, Tatratour and Satur.

In many ways, the travel agents were the most 'enlightened' entrepreneurs in the Slovakian tourism industry. The Slovak Association of Travel Agents (SATA) was the most effective self-regulation tourism body in the country and, for example, had designed its own Code of Conduct of Business Rules, was a member of UFTAA (Universal Federation of the Travel Agents Association), successfully lobbied for a reduction in VAT on incoming tourism from 25 per cent to zero, and had prepared a system of customer protection based on the EU's 314/90/EEC Travel Package Directive. There was strong geographical concentration in the sector, with the headquarters of 75 of the 158 SATA members being in Bratislava in 1998.

There were a number of spectacular failures amongst the Slovakian travel agents in the course of 1996 and 1997, but these were relatively small-scale. The major Slovakian tour companies (Satur, Fischer, Tatratour) had sufficient finance and experience to avoid such an ignominious fate.

5.4.2 Qualitative changes in tourism in the Czech Republic in the transition

Shifts in the provision of accommodation services

A 1997 survey by the Czech Statistical Office provides unique insights into the Czech accommodation sector (Novák and Zídková 1997). This shows that, in 1996, some 46 per cent of hotels had restaurants and some 30 per cent had bars or cafés. There was only limited provision of sporting facilities: 23 per cent had their own sports centre, 9 per cent a swimming pool and only 6 per cent a fitness centre. Only 7 per cent of hotels had the capacity to host conferences, but 28 per cent hotels claimed to provide rooms for seminars and similar activities. Prices ranged from Kč 70 (US$ 2.3) in camping via Kč 250 in inns and Kč 700 in three-star hotels to Kč 2300 in five-star hotels per visitor per night. Differential pricing was often applied to domestic and foreign visitors, with the difference between these being as high as four-fold. Such dual pricing is common in other transition economies, including Slovakia. The system is one logical response to the different purchasing powers of domestic and foreign visitors. Dual prices were particularly common in those areas, which attracted relatively small shares of foreign visitors.

The Czech hotel industry is heavily concentrated in Prague, particularly in terms of turnover. Of the 15 largest hotels in the Czech Republic, only four were located outside of Prague: the Termal and Grandhotel Pupp hotels in the spa city of Karlovy Vary, and the Interhotel Voronež and Interhotel International in Brno. In 1996, the Prague Hilton Atrium Hotel – with Kč 728 million of net turnover and 788 rooms – was the largest in the country. It was followed by the Hotel InterContinetal Praha (Kč 608 million and 365 rooms), the Hotel Forum Praha (Kč 518 million and 551 rooms), the Renaissance Prague Hotel (Kč 421 million and 309 rooms), the Hotel Diplomat Praha (Kč 311 million and 282 rooms) and the Prague Hotel Panorama (Kč 267 million and 427 rooms). The average annual occupancy rate ranged from around 60 per cent to 70 per cent in large, expensive city hotels to 40 per cent in small and medium size hotels (Csontosová 1998). The major challenge was how to redevelop those hotels which had originally been constructed as recreation centres for the employees of major firms in the state-socialist period. These had been designed for domestic clients with modest means, were constructed without due attention to energy costs, and had high operating costs. In addition, some of the major hotels also experienced difficulties, especially those owned by the Top Spirit group. The Panorama Hotel, for example, had losses of Kč 136 million in 1996, largely due to mismanagement.

154

Spas

Spas have had a long tradition in the Czech Republic, originating in patron-age of the West Bohemian spa towns by the European elites in the eight-eenth century. Most spa establishments were privatized during 1993–5 (see Chapter 4). Spas accounted for 4,167,700 of the total of 37.3 million nights spent in Czech tourist accommodation in 1996, with foreign visitors accounting for 21.9 per cent. In the former Czechoslovakia, spas were prim-arily designed for medical purposes rather than for leisure and entertain-ment. This was reflected in relatively long stays. Whereas the average length of stay of foreign tourists to the Czech republic was 4.1 days in 1996, that in the spas was 12.6 days. Germans accounted for 49.1 per cent of total nights spent in the spas, and had an average stay of 11.4 days. They were followed by the Russians (32.9 per cent nights and 19.7 days), Slovaks (35.1 per cent nights and 19.7 days) and the USA (2.1 per cent nights and 10.3 days). Domestic customers had the longest stays, 20.2 days, and these were mostly paid for by the National Insurance System.

Travel agencies

By 1997, there were 1087 registered travel agencies, of which some 800 were active. Amongst these, the privatized Čedok was a major player; with turnover of Kč 2 billion (US$ 70 million) and 350 thousands customers it accounted for 17 per cent of the Czech travel agency sector in 1996. Čedok was engaged in fierce competition with Fischer plc, a Czech branch of the German firm Fischer Reisen. The third and fourth places were occupied by Prog and Travela, but these were bankrupted in summer 1997, leaving thousands of Czech tourists stranded in Greece and Turkey. The Czech courts subsequently decided that these bankruptcies were criminal offences, being deliberate actions to defraud customers (Všudybyl 1997). In 1997, Čedok – which sold 220,000 package holidays – was the market leader, followed by Fischer (200,000 packages) and Globtour (90,000). Domestic (new) private firms, such as Prog and East–West, lacked the capital to compete and crashed.

1997 was a black year for travel agents in the Czech Republic. About 21 firms, 15 per cent of which had been established by foreign investors, announced bankruptcies, affecting 30,000 clients. The problem lay in the mismatch between demand and supply, and the lack of experienced travel agents. After a successful 1995 season, when record numbers of holidays were sold, many small agents tried to act as tour operators and booked charter flights. Supply considerably exceeded demand, and the agents resorted to selling the packages at what were effectively 'dumping' prices, but many flights remained half-empty. When these agents were unable to pay their foreign creditors, thousands of Czechs were stranded without return tickets at Greek and Turkish airports. In addition, several of the bankruptcies were planned frauds. The Guarantee Fund, created by several tour operators, was able to reimburse only a fraction of the clients' losses. There were even indications that several of the failed agencies had planned, even when the Fund was being established, to use it to repay their customers. These developments drew attention to the regulation of the sector, and the Czech government was forced to speed up the legislative work on the Tourism Law, which was to be compatible with the EU legal framework. Two associations operated in the travel agency sub-sector: The Association of the Travel Agencies of the Czech Republic and the Association of Czech Private Travel Agencies. Neither proved to be effective regulators in the 1996 and 1997 crises. The crashes of the Prog, Travela, East–West Travel and other tour operators generated a new situation on the Czech market, in terms of expectations and customer behaviour.

5.5 CONCLUSIONS: INTERPRETING ECONOMIC PERFORMANCE

The tourism boom after 1989 was reflected in different ways at the macroeconomic and microeconomic levels in the Czech and Slovak Republics. The boom had been generated by external changes in the general economic and political environment (especially re-internationalization and establishment of a market economy), which helped to increase the volumes of tourist inflows and international tourism receipts. These receipts increased by 21 times (in current US$ prices) in Slovakia and by 32 times in the Czech Republic in the period 1989–96. The development stimulus provided by the boom was less powerful than might be expected from these ratios. The shares of value added and investment in the tourism industry decreased in both Republics during the transition. The share of tourism employment increased, but even in the Czech Republic it only just achieved the average OECD level. In addition, there were the following trends.

- In both Republics the shares of international tourism receipts in GDP and exports were greater than the OECD average. These shares were particularly high in the Czech Republic which enjoyed the largest influx of foreign visitors amongst the transformation economies of Central Europe. International tourism balances made a major contribution to the foreign currency reserves of the Czech and Slovak Republics, especially in the early years of the transformation.
- The large dollar receipts were achieved in a period of high (hidden) revaluation of the Czech and Slovak national currencies. There was a process of adjustment of Czech and Slovak prices to Austrian and German levels. While the market exchange rate of Sk and Kč to the US$ changed little, domestic prices rose three-fold in the period, and

this reflected the costs of capital and labour in the tourism sector in the period 1989–96. Much of the international tourist expenditure was directed to shopping and was collected by non-tourism establishments (in terms of official designations).

- The shares of the tourism sector in total value added and investment were lower in both Republics than the OECD average, and these shares decreased further in 1992–6. Most investment activities in the Czech and Slovak Republics in this period were carried out by large firms especially in the power supply and manufacturing sectors. The access of small businesses (including tourism establishments) to finance was restricted by capital shortages and high interest rates. Development of the tourism sector was partly financed from personal sources accumulated by entrepreneurs via various activities (including those in the shadow economy).

- In 1989–93, several thousand personal tourism businesses were established in both Republics. Later, they faced saturated markets and increasingly competitive conditions, even if the tourism sector in aggregate continued to expand. In contrast, larger companies, mostly established in the limited form, had access to wider pools of capital and expertise, and emerged as the main players in the tourism market.

- Decreases in the nights spent by domestic tourists depressed occupancy rates between 1990 and 1993. Tourism enterprises sold via auctions were burdened with substantial privatization debts, particularly in 1991–4. These factors pushed the profit ratios of Czech and Slovak hotels, in aggregate, into the red. Most hotels faced liquidity crises and had limited capital for investment. The situation improved after 1994 with increasing numbers of overnights, the repayment of privatization debts and the higher prices being charged to foreign tourists. Many of the accommodation establishments which remained in the public sector were able to find new market niches and to compete with private sector establishments, at least in Slovakia. There was a visible shift in demand to facilities with higher standards, such as inns and hotels, in both Republics.

- The overall profitability of Slovak businesses increased over the period under review. There were some differences between the hotel and restaurant sub-sectors. While larger establishments performed better than smaller ones in the hotel sector, the reverse was true in the case of restaurants. In the tourism industry as a whole, medium-sized and larger firms were gradually increasing their market share at the expense of smaller businesses, increasing their proportion of total accommodation and catering sales between 1992 and 1996. Generally, tourism businesses seemed to be less profitable than the rest of the Slovakian economy, but the real situation may be different if unreported income is included. Czech hotels and restaurants also had lower profitability rates than the rest of economy.

- In both the Czech and Slovak Republics, the travel agency market was dominated by the privatized Satur/Čedok and the branches of foreign firms. Domestic private travel agents established after 1989 were able to capture a large part of the domestic market, but lacked the financial and personal resources to embark on sustainable, quality growth. Numerous failures amongst these agencies in 1996 and 1997 led domestic consumers to rely more on what they perceived to be the more reliable services provided by Satur/Čedok and foreign travel agents.
- After 1994 there was renewed interest amongst foreign visitors in the Czech spas. Excepting the influx of German clients, the return of traditional Russian customers to the spa city of Karlovy Vary was of major importance in this.

Perhaps the most important conclusion that we can draw in this chapter is that any attempt to assess the relative economic performance of firms needs to take into account the nature of privatization. There was not the emergence of a simple private/state divergence in property rights, but considerable diversity within each of these sectors as well as of 'recombinant property' (Stark 1996). In addition, the failure of many of the original owners of small privatized businesses meant that these were effectively renationalized as they were taken over by the financial institutions who had provided loans for their initial purchases. There was therefore no simple linear process of converting public into private property rights but, instead, there was 'an intersection of old and new pathways' (Smith and Pickles 1998, p 15).

The chapter has explored some of the economic consequences of the different forms of privatization in tourism, within the limits of the available secondary data. Two main conclusions can be drawn from this discussion. First, the uneven transformation of markets is critical to understanding the performance of individual tourism firms. Before 1989 there was a mixture of collective provision and 'commercial' provision to individual domestic and foreign tourists. Most domestic tourism was highly institutionalized through the provision made by trade unions and employers' own recreational facilities. After 1989, some forms of collective provision continued and the hotels in this market were able to secure high occupancy rates, but at very low prices generating limited income. The commercial tourism market sector was severely depressed, whilst there was a re-internationalization of markets which saw the opening up of access to potentially higher income Western tourists. It was the private sector firms which were able to position themselves most effectively in these markets which had the strongest economic performances; foreign capital performed most strongly, but some domestic capital was also able to benefit from these market changes. The second main conclusion to be emphasized is that the particular conditions of privatization had a major influence on the capital and debt structures of privatized tourism firms. The relatively unfavourable position of tourism – in respect of capital, debt and profits – compared to other industries, is in part due to the overwhelming numbers of small firms in this sector.

6 TOURISM AND UNEVEN REGIONAL DEVELOPMENT

6.1 TOURISM AND REGIONAL RESTRUCTURING

The economic transformation has had a distinctive geography; it has been partly shaped by the legacy of state-socialist regional structures, but the transformation itself has been characterized by the intersection of new and old pathways. The outcome has been to created new forms of uneven regional development in the Czech and Slovak republics. In broad terms, before 1989 there had been regional economic convergence, promoted and partly achieved by means of central planning. During the transformation, there was economic divergence. This was essentially related to the uneven re-integration of the regional economies into capitalist relationships. In turn, this reflected differences in infrastructure, and the human and capital resources of particular regions (despite the convergence tendencies of central planning) as well as comparative advantages in terms of access to changing international markets.

Tourism was no exception to this general pattern of economic change. During the transformation, the importance of some regions as tourism centres increased, while others declined. There were considerable changes in both domestic (Chapter 7) and international (Chapter 3) markets after 1989, and the mosaic of regional tourism complexes were differentially affected by these market shifts. Recession in the domestic market meant that the regions which were relative 'winners' were least reliant on this source of demand. Instead, they either had strong historical links with still buoyant international markets, and were able to exploit these in new forms, or they were well placed, by virtue of their tourism product, to develop new international markets. The relative 'losers' saw their domestic markets collapse (because of reductions in disposable income, and the ending of the protectionism provided by barriers to international travel), and were unable to develop new pathways into international markets. This was particularly marked in the case of those regions which depended on Eastern European markets or, in the case of Slovakia, on the Czech market – at least for a short period after the 'velvet divorce'. The prevalence of 'nearest neighbour' patterns in international tourism flows (Chapter 3) meant that these changes were most clearly evident in the border regions.

Regional changes in tourism were, to some extent, a product of wider regional economic changes, especially because of the impact of the latter on the level of demand for short break and day visits. However, tourism was also an important component in the overall restructuring of these economies. The contribution of tourism to regional economic change depended on the balance between regional diversification and the scale of the tourist industry. Its role was greatest where a large-scale tourism industry dominated relatively undiversified regional economies, as in parts of the High Tatras. The relationship between tourism and broader processes of regional restructuring lies not only in its direct contribution to GDP and employment, but also in the linkages between economic sectors in terms of products, services, capital flows and the transfer of entrepreneurial skills. For example, Chapter 4 presented evidence of the importance of entrepreneurial transfers into small- and medium-scale tourism enterprises; in some cases, entrepreneurs liquidated – or at least mortgaged – their non-tourism economic assets in order to invest in tourism firms. While we lack sufficient data to investigate some of these deeper relationships between tourism and the wider economy at the regional level, it is important to note that the aggregate regional tourism changes considered here are indicative of much deeper processes of regional restructuring.

This chapter is mainly concerned with the role of tourism in the shifting pattern of uneven regional development during transformation. It focuses on regional tourism flows, the pattern of relative 'winners' and 'losers' in the new map of tourism demand, and the contribution of the sector to aggregate regional economic change. It ends by considering whether tourism reinforced or modified underlying tendencies to regional divergence that were evident after 1989. In order to contextualize this discussion, the next section considers the aggregate regional economic changes after 1989.

6.2 UNEVEN DEVELOPMENT DURING TRANSITION: DE-INDUSTRIALIZATION AND DIVERGENCE

6.2.1 Slovakia

Rapid industrialization in the 1950s and 40 years of central planning transformed Slovakia from a rural to an industrial society. State-socialist regional policies in Slovakia were informed by the strategic and ideological objectives of establishing a strong industrial base in the eastern part of the Republic, and by social and economic concerns about regional disparities. In their own terms, these policies achieved considerable success. By the 1980s, there was at least one and sometimes several large industrial enterprises, with 2000 or more employees, in each Slovakian district. The locations of many production units were the outcome of arbitrary decision-making, having little regard to economic relationships.

Smith (1994, p 414) summarizes the changing industrial landscape brought about by extensive accumulation processes under state-socialism:

> ... a net of economic and political relations created the virtual single industry dominance of several regions in Slovakia by locally autarkic production complexes that were major local employers. Such regions were the product of forced industrialization under extensive accumulation arrived at by industrializing the countryside through the development of small and medium-sized towns.

Armaments was the largest of these new industries, and the former Czechoslovakia was the seventh largest international arms exporter (SIPRI Yearbook 1990). Some 73,000 workers directly, and 60,000 indirectly, were employed in the defence industries. Central and Northern Slovakia (the Martin, Považská Bystrica, Žilina, Banská Bystrica and Zvolen districts) accounted for one third of production. Three types of regional economy emerged from the process of extensive industrialization (Smith 1995, pp 763–5). The first were large specialized industrial centres, such as the armaments production of Martin and Zvolen, which 'characterized the early state socialist industrialization drive' (p 763). The second group were more diversified regional industrial economies, as in Bratislava and Banská Bystrica, which 'owed their levels of diversification to their earlier role in the capitalist industrialization of Slovakia' (p 765). The third group were more marginal industrial areas.

Despite a tendency to convergence, brought about by state-socialist industrialization, regional disparities persisted. By 1989, there were only six districts (Bratislava-City, Košice, Trnava, Žilina, Banská Bystrica and Liptovský Mikuláš), where the volume of fixed assets exceeded the Slovak average. On the other hand, there were less-developed areas, whose historic marginality to the national economy remained little changed. They received relatively little investment in infrastructure both before and after 1948, had poor transport links, and weak economic and social structures. Agriculture remained an important component of family income in these regions, which was reflected in traditional life styles and lower living standards. These regions experienced large-scale out-migration to more economically dynamic areas – both neighbouring and distant. After 1989 these areas were characterized by low levels of entrepreneurial activity, high unemployment rates and minimal foreign investment (Falt'an et al 1995). There were two major belts of more marginal regions: mountain districts in the northern

162

Slovak borders (Dolný Kubín, Čadca and Stará L'ubovňa) with unproductive agriculture, low levels of investment in manufacturing, and high rates of population growth; and districts on the south-eastern Slovak borders (Rimavská Sobota, Vel'ký Krtíš, Rožňava, Levice) with favourable agricultural conditions, but laggard industrialization, underdeveloped infrastructure, and low education levels.

Many of the industries developed after 1948 proved vulnerable in the economic and political aftermath of 1989 (Williams *et al* 1998). Changing economic and political relationships in Central Europe had dramatic consequences for uneven regional development in Slovakia. In 1988–92 armament production declined by a devastating 92.8 per cent (Sme daily, 22 January 1993). The collapse in the defence industry was followed by a decline in machinery production. Sophisticated production networks amongst the largest industrial units withered away and many smaller companies lost all their main customers. In turn, the collapse of these smaller units had disastrous consequences for many regional economies. Unemployment tended to be higher in Southern and Eastern Slovakia, dominated by agriculture and (domestic) branch-plant economies, as a result of the early impact of agricultural restructuring and the shedding of branch plants by core factories (Commission of the European Communities 1992a). This fundamentally changed the structure of regional production in Slovakia. Enterprises specializing in basic metals, metal products and chemicals were also initially affected after 1989, but after 1993 found new markets in the EU and the Czech Republic. Steel production, oil processing and the service industries all became more important. In general terms, the centre of economic activity shifted from Central and Northern Slovakia to Bratislava and Košice, and the former pattern of regional convergence was replaced by divergence.

Industrial restructuring after 1989 led to the evolution of what can be termed 'transition-related marginal' regions (see Falt'an *et al* 1995). Central planning had seen the development of mono-industrial areas, where employment was dominated by one or several enterprises. Several of these districts (Martin, Žiar nad Hronom, Považská Bystrica) had relatively high levels of infrastructure, incomes, educational levels and research bases. The collapse of their main export markets had a disastrous effect on their economies in the period 1989–3, and they seemed to be sliding towards economic marginality. However, they had considerable resources in the forms of skilled and educated labour forces, and infrastructure. Some of these districts were able to initiate revitalization and innovation programmes, funded by domestic and foreign capital. By 1998, these regions had still not regained their aggregate 1989 levels of development, but had better prospects for future development than what may be termed the 'historically marginal' regions.

The extent of the regional inequalities can be expressed in terms of the districts' shares of national GDP, total fixed investment, and foreign investment, and their relative levels of education, migration and unemployment (Annex I). In 1994, the top six areas (all metropolitan districts) accounted for 52.4 per cent of Slovak GDP (Bratislava-City, Košice-City, Trnava, Žilina, Banská Bystrica, Trenčín) and in 1996 for 51.0 per cent. On the other hand, six districts (Vranov, Košice-District, Rimavská Sobota, Vel'ký Krtíš, Svidník and Stará Ľubovňa) generated just 2.7 per cent of Slovak GDP in 1994 and 2.6 per cent in 1996. The above-mentioned top six districts also attracted 67.3 per cent of domestic and 74.1 per cent of foreign investment, while the bottom six received only 2.3 per cent and 1.6 per cent respectively in 1996. Unemployment rates ranged from 5 to 12 per cent in metropolitan areas, but from 13 to 18 per cent in the northern belt and from 20 to 26 per cent in the southern belt of marginal districts. Not surprisingly, there were also differences in migration and population growth rates. In the major metropolitan areas, there was overall population growth in the period 1994–6 (e.g. Žilina 6.6 per 1000 inhabitants), but the marginal districts had very diverse performances. While the poor rural region of Košice–District had strong growth (11.9 per 1000), the equally poor region of Vel'ký Krtíš had a decrease of 2.2 per 1000 inhabitants. Their differential performance is related to their locations; the former is the rural hinterland of Košice–City and attracted large numbers of commuters, while the latter is relatively remote from the main metropolitan areas. There was a clear trend towards in-migration to the major centres of economic growth although this process was hampered by the non-functioning housing market in Slovakia.

There were also strong differences between the northern and southern belts of marginal districts. The northern marginal districts had strong positive population growth (e.g. Dolný Kubín 16.3, and Stará Ľubovňa 15.7 per thousand), while southern districts mostly had negative rates (e.g. Vel'ký Krtíš −2.2, and Lučenec −2.0 per thousand) in 1994–6. The divergence between north and south was explained by differences in age structures, education and psychology. The younger population in the north were more flexible in their response to changes after 1989. Job losses in these regions were not reflected in permanent emigration, but in commuting to neighbouring and/or distant regions (including working abroad). In the Svidník district, for example, out of a working population of some 20,000 people, 2,000 were working in the Czech Republic and some 1,500 in the USA and UK (Krivý et al 1997, p 324). Their remittances were mostly invested in housing and, after 1989, in small businesses such as inns, pubs, restaurants and similar facilities. A national survey on domestic tourism after 1989 (Ústav turizmu 1995–1998) also confirms that the younger age groups had a higher travel propensity, and accounted for a major part of the travel generated by trade and trans-border shopping/smuggling – which was another form of response to changing economic opportunities after 1989.

While only limited GDP data are available on regional sectoral changes, these can be reviewed in terms of employment structure. De-industrialization was most rapid in the first phase of the transformation, in 1990–3, when most large enterprises lost significant export markets. The decline in employment and income had disastrous consequences for large agricultural enterprises and medium-sized local industrial firms, which were reliant on domestic consumer markets. After 1994, the pace of de-industrialization abated, and the shares of manufacturing in total employment increased. This was most marked in the metropolitan and industrial districts, in 1992–6, but was also evident in many rural districts, where some medium-sized industrial enterprises provided alternative employment for displaced agricultural workers.

The situation was different for those districts where international tourism receipts accounted for relatively large shares of GDP. There were two types of these areas. First, the districts with relatively large shares of tourism in GDP but smaller absolute numbers of overnights (Spišská Nová Ves, Bardejov) experienced rapid de-industrialization and sharp increases in service employment. It can reasonably be assumed that tourism was one of the dynamic forces in these local economies. Secondly, the districts with large absolute numbers of overnights, where tourism receipts were relatively important (Liptovský Mikuláš, Michalovce, partly Poprad), experienced increases in industrial and decreases in service employment. The tourism industries in these areas were amongst the most well-developed in Slovakia, and their local economies diversified through industrialization in this period.

An insight into the overall pattern of uneven regional development is provide by the special report prepared by the Slovak government in 1996 for the United Nations Habitat II conference (Ministerstvo životného prostredia, 1996). This identified several major tasks for regional development in Slovakia:

1) preparation of a Regional Development Law;
2) regional infrastructural development;
3) establishment of Regional Development Agencies; and
4) increasing intra-regional labour mobility.

The report established the 'gradual removal of regional disparities between urbanised and rural (marginalized) areas' as an important goal of Slovak regional policy. Following this, there was a radical territorial administrative re-organization. The existing 38 districts were replaced by eight counties and 79 districts in 1996. The districts were effectively extensions of central government and did not provide vehicles for regional self-government. In many cases, the new districts did nor reflect economic or planning realities of territorial development, but were shaped by the regional structures of the ruling party (HZDS), and the interests of its supporters and clients

(Krivý *et al* 1997, p 324). As a result, after 1996 Slovak regional policy became even more centralized, with many responsibilities (for finance and regional planning) being transferred to central government (Bútora 1997). In 1990–4, for example, the share of the central government budget in the Slovak GDP increased from 40 to 50 per cent, while the share of local government decreased from 21.6 to 5.0 per cent. Most regional development programmes became financed from central government funds. Since 1994, a clientelistic regime has emerged in Slovakia, whereby the success of particular regions in securing state funds is determined by the relationship between the regional elite and the ruling party. Some commentators have suggested parallels with the clientelistic cultures of Southern Italy (Krivý *et al*. 1997, p 165), although this is questionable.

The lack of a territorial planning framework has been a major shortcoming for tourism since the District Tourism Enterprises were abolished in 1990. These bodies, which had been managed by district governments, did at least provide basic regional tourism infrastructures and marketing. Since 1990 these activities have been undertaken by some municipalities, but in smaller territorial units. Central government has expressed an interest in elaborating Large Territorial Unit plans, but there is a problem in that the Units would be synonymous with the new counties, whose boundaries bear little relation to functioning tourism regions. Regional tourism development is financed by a combination of private and municipality sources, with discretionary subsidies from the TDP. TDP expenditures, however, are subject to approval by the Ministry of Economy and have mostly followed the goals determined by central government, rather than being responsive to local or regional priorities. Regional Tourism Marketing Agencies, established by private entrepreneurs and municipalities, have mostly functioned as forums for discussion and have had limited financial resources. Even the most successful of these, the High Tatras Tourism Development Agency (supported by the British Know-How Fund), had to cope with a lack of finance and a small number of active members. By 1998, there was still a lack of clear regional tourism development policies, and their development is dependent on the future establishment of an effective framework of regional government and governance.

6.2.2 The Czech Republic

Bohemia was the most industrialized region in the Austrian-Hungarian empire. Following the creation of Czechoslovakia in 1918, the Czech region inherited a large part of the Austro-Hungarian empire's industrial heritage. After 1918, Czech industry continued to expand, benefiting from strong demand conditions and its accumulated resources, particularly its skilled labour. By 1948 the Czech industrial base was probably the most developed and sophisticated in Central Europe. In 1950–75, state-socialist industrial policies focused on the industrialization of Slovakia, but in the late 1970s there was a shift in investment flows in favour of the Czech region. Unlike Slovakia, the industrial base in the Czech region remained diversified, both in terms of product range and within regions. There were, of course, large-scale and highly symbolic steel mills and machinery plants, and there were districts in Northern Moravia tending to mono-industrializm. However, there was also a mixture of traditional glass-making factories, textile production, and chemical and pharmaceutical establishments in many Czech districts. In general, the Czech republic inherited a far more diversified and regionally balanced economic structure than Slovakia, and had less extensive 'historically marginal' regions (Myant 1995).

The end of central planning and the loss of CMEA markets was a major shock for Czech industry (Williams *et al* 1998), but the consequences were less severe than in Slovakia for a number of reasons. First, few districts had been so overwhelmingly dependent on a single major production unit, with the attendant vulnerability associated with over-specialization. Second, the Czech Republic, with its long borders with Germany and Austria, was more locationally favoured after 1989. Czech enterprises and aspiring individual capitalists in border regions were well-placed to establish business links with German and Austrian partners. The German and Austrian border regions also attracted many legal and illegal Czech migrants, commuters and small-scale traders involved in the emerging bazaar capitalism. The enterprises in these border regions had access to low cost, skilled Czech labour as well as major product markets. These favourable conditions contributed to the Czech Republic having the lowest unemployment rates in Central Europe in the early years after 1989 (Williams and Baláž 1999). Despite a subsequent increase, the average unemployment rate was still only 5.2 per cent at the end of 1997. The key role of accessibility is indicated by the regional distribution of unemployment. While many districts in Western, Southern and Central Bohemia had rates below 4 per cent, several Moravian districts on the Slovak and Polish borders had rates in excess of 10 per cent. Unemployment rates also exceeded 12 per cent in some Northern Bohemian districts (for example, Most and Chomutov) whose economies were particularly reliant on heavy industries.

Regional GDP data are not available for the Czech republic for the transformation period, as the first attempt to provide such data was not planned until 1998. Therefore, regional economic changes have to be inferred from the unemployment data. These confirm that regional differences increased in the Czech Republic between 1989 and 1996. The increases, however, were less marked than in Slovakia. The winners in terms of low unemployment rates (and the development of new types and forms of production) were Prague, and Western and Central Bohemia. The losers were the agricultural districts of Southern Moravia and Southern Bohemia, and the coal and iron mining/processing regions in Northern Bohemia and Northern

Moravia. By 1996, the Czech Republic had the following regional production structure:

Prague. The largest Czech city with a population of 1.2 million, was also the country's administrative, cultural and economic centre. It had an important industrial base, particularly in machinery production (notably the CKD company), and was the foremost tourism attraction not only in the Czech Republic, but in the whole of Central and Eastern Europe.

Western Bohemia. After 1989, industrial and tourism development in this region was favoured by proximity to neighbouring Germany. Western Bohemia was already an industrial region, with Plzeň being a major centre of heavy industry and beer production. It also had a number of products with international reputations, such as Moser glass, Pilsner Urquell beer, and Bohemian crystal and porcelain. Karlovy Vary, Mariánske Lázně and Františkovy Lázně were the main centres of Czech spa tourism.

Northern Bohemia. As the Czech Republic's main domestic source of energy, Northern Bohemia was a major industrial region. The leading industry was engineering, especially the production of transport vehicles (at Liberec and Jablonec nad Nisou) and textile machinery (Chrástava). Metal production, chemicals, textiles and glass were also important, while North Bohemian glass-making had an international reputation. This region was significantly affected by restructuring of the Czech economy after 1989 and not surprisingly, had some of the highest unemployment rates in the Czech Republic.

Eastern Bohemia. The region's most important industries were engineering, automobiles, chemical, electrical goods and electronics. It suffered from the loss of international and domestic markets.

Central Bohemia: Central Bohemia was closely linked to Prague, providing much of the capital's labour force and food supplies. Its most important industries were engineering, electrical engineering, chemicals, petrochemicals, glass, ceramics, textiles, printing, wood and leather industries, and food processing. Industrial production was concentrated in Kladno, Slaný and Rakovník. Since 1898, Mladá Boleslav has been the centre of the Czech automobile industry, and after 1990 it became the headquarters of the Škoda-Volkswagen Company.

Southern Bohemia has diverse industrial production focused on engineering, electrical engineering, textiles and garments, wood-processing and furniture, building materials, ceramics, glass, chemicals, paper and brewing. České Budějovice is the most industrially developed sub-region. The town of Český Krumlov, which is on the UNESCO list of world heritage sites, is a major centre of tourism.

Southern Moravia is the largest and most populated region, and its economic strength lay in the concentration of industries in the Brno and Zlín areas. Brno is the Republic's second largest city, and its main industries are heavy engineering and the production of vehicles and agricultural machinery. The region's vineyards are a well-known tourist attraction.

Northern Moravia. Northern Moravia was the Czech Republic's leading region in terms of gross industrial production. Its main industries were mining, energy and metallurgy, but the chemical, rubber, pharmaceutical, engineering, and electrical industries were also important. The main industrial centres are Ostrava and Olomouc.

6.3 THE REGIONAL STRUCTURE OF TOURISM

The social construction of tourist attractions means that tourism development is necessarily uneven and, moreover, changes over time in the tourist gaze (Urry 1990) mean there is a shifting regional pattern. However, investments by the state and the private sector (during and after state-socialism) also changed the regional conditions for producing tourism services and attracting tourists. There is, therefore, a considerable degree of path dependency in the evolution of the regional structure of tourism.

6.3.1 Slovakia

Tourism is very unevenly distributed in Slovakia. Over a long period, the districts of Bratislava City and Košice–City (business and city tourism), Poprad, Liptovský Mikuláš, Banská Bystrica, Žilina (mountain tourism), Trnava and Trenčín (spa tourism) have been major centres of tourism – in terms of hotel capacity, nights spent and tourism receipts. There have also been significant variations amongst these leading districts in terms of their tourism products and markets. The share of international tourism receipts in GDP was significantly below average in the industrial cities of Bratislava and Košice, despite a strong overall tourism performance. In the semi-industrial districts of Trenčín, Žilina, Banská Bystrica and Zvolen, the contribution of tourism was relatively more important and generated between 2.6 and 4.1 per cent of GDP in 1996. The peripheral and less-developed rural districts in the east (Bardejov, Svidník and Humenné) and South (Komárno, Nové Zámky) also had relatively large shares of tourism-related GDP, although their overall tourism performance was weaker (see Annexes I and II). There were also a number of less-developed districts with weak infrastructures and weak tourism performances, particularly in the South (Veľký Krtíš, Rimavská Sobota, Rožňava). Finally, there were two groups of districts where tourism was especially well developed, 'the spa group' and 'the mountain group'. For example, international tourism generated

10.5 per cent of GDP in Trnava (a developed rural district), and this was mostly accounted for by the Piešťany spa. In Stará Ľubovňa, a peripheral, underdeveloped rural district, international spa and mountain tourism generated 6.1 per cent of GDP. In the semi-industrial Tatra mountain district of Liptovský Mikuláš, international tourism generated 14.7 per cent of GDP. However, international tourism was of greatest relative importance in Poprad in the High Tatras, accounting for 24.8 per cent of GDP in 1996 in the 'jewel' of Slovak tourism (see Annex I). These statistics are based only on international tourism, but domestic tourism (for which we lack comparable economic data) has a broadly similar distribution.

After 1989, and especially after 1993, Slovak tourism policy-makers considered two alternative regional strategies: either to promote new, previously underdeveloped tourism regions, or to concentrate investment so as to enhance the quality and quantity of facilities in more developed tourism regions. The later strategy was preferred and most of the resources allocated to the TDP were invested in Slovakia's 'core' tourism regions, the High and Low Tatras, and Bratislava. In 1996 and 1997, for example, investment in artificial snow-making facilities was a priority, and the districts of Poprad, Liptovský Mikuláš and Banská Bystrica were heavily promoted.

6.3.2 Czech Republic

Czech tourism has traditionally been identified with Prague and the Western Bohemian spas. These have featured prominently in the 'gaze' of both foreign and domestic tourists. Not surprisingly, the relative importance of tourism has varied amongst the Czech counties (Annex VI). There are major differences in the numbers of domestic and foreign tourists attracted, and in the share of tourism in regional production. Prague dominates: it generates an estimated 70–80 per cent of Czech international tourism receipts, and accounts for 41.9 per cent of foreign tourist nights, and 19.5 per cent of total employment in hotels and restaurants. In second position, but trailing behind in respect of all the tourism indicators, are Western and Eastern Bohemia. These accounted, respectively, for 12.4 and 15.4 per cent of foreign tourist nights, and 13.3 and 16.9 per cent of employment. Jobs in hotels and restaurants also accounted for a relatively large share of total regional employment in Prague, Western and Eastern Bohemia: 4.5, 5.0 and 4.2 per cent, respectively. These areas – especially Prague and Western Bohemia – also had significantly higher levels of what are officially termed 'supplementary accommodation facilities' – such as conference rooms, currency exchange desks, and sports facilities – than the remainder of the country (Annex VI). These differences in demand, and in the quality and range of facilities, are reflected in price structures. The average price of a night in Prague was Kč 1212, compared to Kč 448 in Western Bohemia, and Kč 314 to Kč 400 in the remainder of the Czech Republic.

Southern Bohemia is a less developed region where tourism is relatively important, accounting for 4.7 per cent of foreign tourist nights. While it accounted for only 10.2 per cent of total employment in Czech hotels and restaurants, this sector had a relatively large share of total regional employment (4.7 per cent). Therefore, although not comparable to Prague as a destination, tourism was important in this region. In contrast, the relative importance of tourism was limited in Central and Northern Bohemia, and in Southern and Northern Moravia, all of which had a below average share of foreign tourist nights; the hotel and restaurant sector also accounted for small proportions of their total regional employment (1.4 to 2.2 per cent).

A more detailed review of the tourism statistics at the county level reveals further regional variations in the structure of tourism supply and demand:

Prague is the centre of urban, business and cultural tourism. It has by far the highest number of foreign tourism nights.

Central Bohemia is a relatively less important tourism region. However, the district of Píbram is a significant centre of water-based recreation for nearby Prague.

Southern Bohemia is considered to have the most attractive landscapes in the Czech Republic, with a harmonious mixture of mountains, lakes, castles and historical towns. The district of Český Krumlov is the principal tourist attraction.

Western Bohemia's tourism is based on the spas in the district of Karlovy Vary, and German excursionism in Cheb district.

Northern Bohemia is the most industrial and the most environmentally devastated county in the Czech Republic. However, it is not devoid of tourist attractions and has good access to major potential markets. The mountain districts of Česká Lípa and Jablonec nad Nisou, located on the German and Polish borders, attract visits from these neighbouring countries as well from nearby Czech industrial areas.

Eastern Bohemia is a centre of mountain and skiing tourism, based on the Krkonoše mountains. The mountain districts of Trutnov and Semily had the highest volumes of nights spent by domestic tourists in the Czech Republic: 2.9 and 1.3 million in 1996.

Southern Moravia is a rural lowland landscape with numerous vineyards. The industrial cities of Zlín and Brno, and the hilly district of Žďár nad Sázovou, are major tourism attractions.

Northern Moravia is a heavily industrialized and urbanised region, which adjoins a similar regional economic region, Polish Silesia. These urban areas generate substantial demand for weekend recreation, rural excursions and skiing in the mountain districts of Frýdek-Místek, Jeseník, Šumperk and Vsetín. The Jánske Lázně and Luhačovice spas were also important for domestic visitors.

This brief review of the regional distribution of Czech tourism emphasises that the geographical pattern is far more complex than the first impression of a simple Prague-centred industry. While Prague was the main attraction for foreign visitors, most domestic tourists – and also many Germans and Poles living in adjacent border regions – were drawn to the mountains, rural landscapes and historical cities. There were some counties where tourism was of limited economic significance (especially in Northern and Southern Moravia) but, even within these, there were smaller foci of domestic and international tourism.

One of the most distinctive elements to emerge in this brief review of Czech tourism is the role of the spas. In the former Czechoslovakia, a spa was not an individual hotel but an enterprise consisting of several accommodation establishments and a number of entertainment and health facilities; the spa functioned either as an independent town or as an area of a town. In 1996 there were 61 spas in the Czech Republic, 32 of which provided hotel accommodation. Most of these spas were concentrated in just two regions (Annex VI). Western Bohemia was the leading area; Karlovy Vary has an international reputation, but there were also other major spas such as Mariánske Lázně and Františkovy Lázně. This region alone accounts for 41.5 per cent of all beds, 51.0 per cent of the labour force and 85.6 per cent of foreign overnights in the Czech spas. Northern Moravia is the other important region for spas, with Jánske Lázně and Luhačovice accounting for 26.7 per cent of beds, but only 7.2 per cent of foreign overnights in the Czech spas. These two regions also account for most (32.3 per cent and 30.7 per cent respectively) domestic nights spent in the Czech spas. No data is available for the income generated by the Czech spas, but the highly polarized distribution can be imagined given Karlovy Vary's overwhelming share of foreign tourism nights, and the fact that all seven Czech four-star spa hotels were located in Western Bohemia.

The lack of detailed statistics on the spas is part of the more general paucity of Czech sub-national tourism statistics. This is partly related to the high degree of centralization: since 1989, there have been no self-governing regions, while the districts were administered by the District Offices of central government. Not surprisingly, regional tourism policy has been weakly developed. The District Offices were allocated limited resources for tourism promotion, ranging from Kč 200,000 (US$ 7,000) to Kč 600,000 (US$ 20,000) per district in 1997. Furthermore, there was no clear relationship between the level of tourism activity in a district and the funds it received. For example, Cheb district – an important focus of German and domestic visits – received Kč 400,000, while Svitavy district – which had a relatively small number of tourist overnights – received Kč 800,000 in 1997. The available funds were mostly used for promotion and tourist information, and to participate in Regiontour (the largest Czech regional tourist fair). A survey of tourist officers reported that most had little detailed information about the effectiveness of these expenditures (Zeman 1998a), which they mostly blamed on the low quality of tourism data provided by the Czech Statistical Office.

The municipal governments also complain that they derive little income from tourism development. A Czech law enables a proportion of company taxes to be redirected from central to local government, but this is at the discretion of the company's headquarters. Many tourism companies have their headquarters in Prague or regional capitals and opt to pay their taxes there rather than where the tourist activity takes place. The municipalities therefore mainly have to rely on the tourist accommodation taxes that are paid by all tourists (ironically, this measure originated before 1989). This tax accounts for a considerable proportion of the municipal budget in the most popular tourism destinations. For example, Kč 2.9 million of the total budget of Kč 12.1 million of the spa town of Jánske Lázně was sourced from the accommodation tax in 1997. The ski resort of Špindlerov Mlýn collected a tourist tax of Kč 10 million, which was equivalent to almost one-third of its total budget (Hospodářské noviny daily 1998c).

6.4 RE-INTERNATIONALIZATION AND THE CHANGING REGIONAL STRUCTURE OF TOURISM FLOWS

6.4.1 Slovakia

Tourism in Slovakia has traditionally centred on outdoor activities, natural attractions, and the spas. Not surprisingly, the regional distribution of Slovak tourism has been closely linked to the social construction of the value of landscape and nature. The northern districts, for example, satisfied the demand for skiing and hiking while the southern ones were popular for thermal baths, swimming and spas. If the social construction of valued landscapes is invariable in respect of changes in the political system, then the regional distribution of tourism should be similar before and after 1989. Figures 6.1 and 6.2 compare the distributions of overnights in 1989 and 1996. There are changes but some of these are related to the overall decline in tourism overnights from 13.06 to 8.68 million. If this is taken into account, then – at first glance at least – the two regional distributions are broadly similar. At both dates, we can note that:

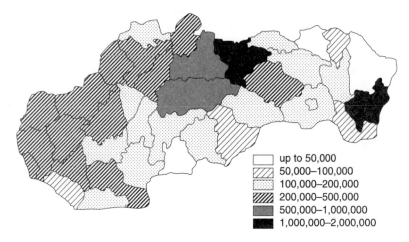

Fig. 6.1 Distribution of nights spent by domestic tourists in Slovakia in 1989.
Source: Štatistický úrad Slovenskej republiky (1991–1998b). (See fig. 1.1 p 10.)

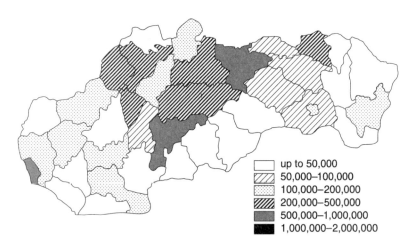

Fig. 6.2 Distribution of nights spent by domestic tourists in Slovakia in 1996.
Source: Štatistický úrad Slovenskej republiky (1991–1998b).

- there was a strong concentration of overnights in the mountain districts of Poprad, Liptovský Mikuláš and Banská Bystrica;
- a belt of tourism districts in the Váh River Valley stretched along the Czech border (Žilina, Považská Bystrica, Trenčín, Trnava);

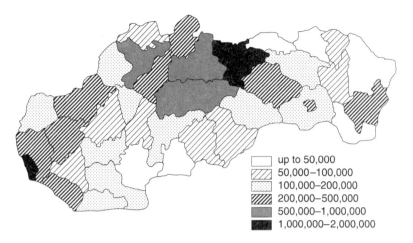

up to 50,000
50,000–100,000
100,000–200,000
200,000–500,000
500,000–1,000,000
1,000,000–2,000,000

Fig. 6.3 Distribution of nights spent by foreign tourists in Slovakia in 1989.
Source: Štatistický úrad Slovenskej republiky (1991–1998b).

- the cities of Bratislava and Košice attracted large numbers of visitors;
- the district of Michalovce was a centre of water sports;
- there were low levels of tourism activity along the Hungarian border and in north-eastern Slovakia.

The invariability of the regional distribution is even more evident in respect of the overnight distribution of foreign tourists (Figures 6.3 and 6.4), with Poprad, Liptovsky Mikuláš, Banská Bystrica, Bratislava, Košice, Trnava, Trenčín, and Žilina being important attractions.

However, in reality there were a number of shifts in the underlying distributions that are not immediately apparent in these maps. These can be summarized as relative shifts from diffusion to concentration, and then back to diffusion. In the state-socialist period, the nights spent by both domestic and foreign tourists were relatively evenly distributed amongst the 38 Slovak districts. In 1989 the five leading districts (Banská Bystrica, Bratislava City, Košice–City, Liptovsky Mikuláš and Poprad) accounted for 39.7 per cent of the nights spent by domestic tourists and 41.0 per cent of the nights spent by foreign tourists. In 1993 these ratios had increased to 61.3 and 65.2 per cent respectively, indicating a much higher level of concentration. By 1996 the ratios had fallen back to close to those of 1989, 44.7 and 64.1 per cent, indicating a more diffuse pattern, particularly for domestic tourism (Table 6.1).

What are the main reasons for the increased concentration in the first part of the transition, and the later reverse shift towards greater dif-

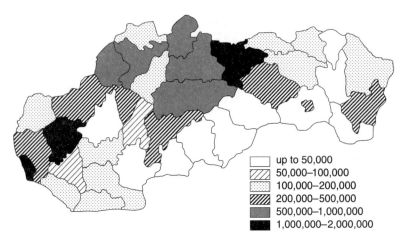

Fig. 6.4 Distribution of nights spent by foreign tourists in Slovakia in 1996.
Source: Štatistický úrad Slovenskej republiky (1991–1998b).

fusion? The answer lies in the fact that while all regions experienced an absolute decline in tourist overnights in the first phase (to 1993), the rate of decline was uneven. After 1994 some of the areas which had been most severely affected in the first phase staged a modest recovery. Given that there was only limited investment in tourism facilities during this period, the key to these differential regional shifts lies in changing demand conditions. In turn, these were determined by a number of external and internal considerations.

The two most significant internal factors were the impact of the sharp-shock macroeconomic strategy on living standards and disposable incomes, and the removal of passport and visa barriers; these had major impacts on domestic tourism, in particular.

The *sharp shock strategy* in the early phase of the economic transition (1990–93) included the liberalization of prices and of labour markets. Combined with the loss of traditional export markets in Central and Eastern Europe, this led to a 30 per cent decline in the standard of living by 1993. It is no exaggeration to state that a large part of the population was reduced to poverty. This was reflected in a dramatic fall in domestic tourism demand, the effects of which were particularly marked because, before 1989, the Slovakian tourism industry had been heavily dependent on this market segment (78.9 per cent of the total of 13.1 million overnights). By 1993 the number of nights spent by domestic tourists had collapsed from more than 10 million to just 2.9 million. Not surprisingly, the main losers in the depressed market condi-

TABLE 6.1 *Cumulative percentages of nights spent in Slovak districts by all tourists.*

Districts	1989	1993	1996
1	15.8	17.8	13.9
2	24.1	32.4	25.2
3	31.2	45.5	33.3
4	37.8	53.2	40.9
5	42.9	60.5	48.1
6	46.8	65.2	53.3
7	50.3	68.5	57.9
8	53.5	71.1	61.4
9	56.6	73.5	64.8
10	59.7	75.9	68.2
11	62.7	78.3	71.4
12	65.3	80.6	74.2
13	67.8	82.7	76.6
14	70.0	84.8	79.0
15	72.2	86.3	81.2
16	74.4	87.7	83.3
17	76.4	89.1	85.2
18	78.3	90.5	86.9
19	80.1	91.6	88.3
20	81.9	92.6	89.4
21	83.4	93.6	90.4
22	84.9	94.6	91.4
23	86.3	95.4	92.4
24	87.6	96.2	93.4
25	88.9	97.0	94.3
26	90.1	97.7	95.3
27	91.4	98.3	96.1
28	92.6	98.8	96.8
29	93.8	99.2	97.4
30	94.9	99.5	97.9
31	96.1	99.8	98.3
32	97.0	100.0	98.7
33	97.8	100.0	99.0
34	98.5	100.0	99.3
35	99.2	100.0	99.6
36	99.5	100.0	99.8
37	99.8	100.0	99.9
38	100.0	100.0	100.0

Source: Štatistický úrad Slovenskej republiky (1991–1998b).

tions were the regions which had been most dependent on domestic tourism.

The removal of passport and visa barriers opened up new destinations for outbound tourism, and revealed a strong latent demand in Slovakia for water-based recreation, and for sea, sand and sunshine holidays. Not only do the Czech and Slovak Republics lack coastlines, but they also lack major lakes (unlike Hungary). In the former Czechoslovakia, the demand for 'sun, sand and sea' recreation had been satisfied in two ways. First, a small proportion of tourists had travelled to the Bulgarian, Romanian and Russian resorts on the Black Sea, sometimes undertaking arduous car trips in order to spend their holidays in relatively low quality facilities in a heavily regulated environment. For example, the Russian authorities prescribed specific routes, including particular petrol stations, for such car-borne tourists. Second, most tourists did not have the option of holidays on the Black Sea and instead visited the Zemplín-ska Šírava dam in Michalovce (Eastern Slovakia) and the thermal baths in Southern Slovakia. After 1990 the new government signed new international agreements on bilateral tourist exchanges, and the Adriatic coastal resorts of Italy and Croatia became more attractive alternatives for many Slovak tourists. Therefore, Slovak districts which provided water-based recreational or spa tourism suffered sharp declines in their markets.

Changes in the external environment, especially in respect of the economic and political nature of the transition, also had a significant impact on the regional distribution of tourism.

Political changes in Central and Eastern Europe during the transformation, particularly the collapse of the GDR and the Soviet Union, had important consequences for tourism after 1989. Before this date, Czechoslovakia had been one of the few permitted foreign destinations for East Germans, and Slovakia – which offered opportunities for winter and summer tourism – had been a favoured location. After German reunification, a large part of that demand was redirected to competing locations in western and Southern Europe. In addition, Russians – army officers and business leaders in particular – had constituted one of the most loyal market segments for the Czechoslovakian spas, and this market also collapsed after 1989. The Yugoslav market for skiing in the Slovakian mountains also disappeared with the fragmentation and conflicts in that country.

The economic recession in the neighbouring post-state socialist states in the early stages of transformation (Williams *et al* 1998) depressed the international tourism markets of the Czech and Slovak Republics. There was a particularly sharp drop in Hungarian demand for skiing in the High Tatras, due to the severity of the economic recession in that country.

In addition to these generalized effects of transition, the 'velvet divorce' and the creation of two independent states also affected tourism in the Czech and Slovak Republics. This territorial adjustment was relatively peaceful compared to the redrawing of international boundaries in the former Yugoslavia (Carter *et al* 1995). However, there were inevitably political tensions which led to short term disruption; in 1993 the number of Czech tourists to Slovakia fell sharply. Thereafter, as political relationships were normalized, the Czech market was largely regained.

The changes in the internal and external economic environment contributed to a substantial decline in tourism demand 1990–3, the regional impact of which was highly uneven. After 1994 recession was replaced by economic boom in Central and Eastern Europe, although it should be noted that only Poland had regained pre-1989 GDP levels even as late as 1997. This stimulated growth in both domestic and international tourism. The new Slovakian middle classes had sufficient disposable income for one- or two-week holidays, utilizing commercial hotels in the Slovakian mountains, so that domestic tourism nights increased markedly. In addition, many German and Czech tourists re-discovered Slovakia as a cheaper alternative to Western Europe for their holidays. Moreover, in 1995 the political and economic environment in Russia and Ukraine began to stabilize, and their newly rich upper-middle classes increasingly travelled abroad for holidays. The High Tatras and Eastern Slovakia were favoured destinations because of their accessibility, and relatively familiar language. Business tourism also revived as the economic boom took root.

Who were the winners and the losers in the process of demand recomposition? Given the overall decline from 13.1 million overnights in 1989 to only 8.7 million in 1996, even after the partial recovery, there were few real winners; instead there were 'minor' as opposed to 'major' losers. With the exception of Bratislava City and Trnava, all districts had fewer tourist overnights in 1996 than in 1989.

The major losers were the agricultural districts of Southern Slovakia – Dunajská Streda, Galanta, Nové Zámky, Levice and Rožňava. They had supplied cheap and simple 'sun and water' holidays (based on reservoirs and small lakes) for domestic and Hungarian tourists, which effectively provided an alternative to relatively inaccessible foreign sea, sand and sun holidays. Rapid changes in income structures in Slovakia and Hungary significantly changed this market segment. While much of the population was too poor to purchase any holiday, the 'new rich' preferred the Mediterranean region. Demand for the thermal baths of Southern Slovakia also decreased sharply down to 1993 and remained subdued even in 1996. In Galanta district, for example, the number of overnights fell from 234,972 in 1989 to 44,903 in 1993 and to 37,897 in 1996. The situation was similar in Levice and Lučenec districts. Remoter districts with poor infrastructure in the south-east (Rožňava, Trebišov) and the north-east (Svidník, Vranov nad Topľou) were also losers. These regions lacked major tourism attractions and were particularly sensitive to volume changes in tourist flows. In all these districts the numbers of nights decreased by some 15–20 per cent between 1989 and 1993, and only recovered modestly thereafter.

Domestic tourism accounted for almost all the decline in the nights spent in the above-mentioned districts. This is a particular problem for the poorest districts. Given persistently high unemployment rates and their poor infrastructure, there is little prospect that a resurgence of domestic tourism will reverse their fortunes. In contrast, the total number of nights spent by foreign tourists barely changed 1989–96. The worst affected regions, however, were beyond the search spaces of many foreign tourists, especially as most were on business trips. Moreover, these regions also generally failed to attract FDI (Smith and Ferenčíková 1998). With increasing numbers of Slovakians travelling abroad, there seemed to be little prospect that these regions would be able to rebuild their traditional markets for 'sun and water' holidays. There were, however, signs of change after 1997. Economic recovery contributed to a more generalized improvement in incomes, whilst new investments were made in the spas in some of these districts. They have attracted some of the disposable income of the middle classes so that demand rose sharply in 1998, although it remains doubtful whether pre 1989 activity levels can be regained in the near future.

The minor losers or the relative winners are to be found among the mountain and hilly districts of Central and Western Slovakia, mostly in the Váh and Hron River Valleys (Liptovský Mikuláš, Žilina, Považská Bystrica, Trenčín, and Banská Bystrica, Zvolen). By 1993 the numbers of overnights in these areas had fallen to only 30–50 per cent of 1989 levels, but thereafter recovered to 50–75 per cent by 1996 (note that the poor quality of statistics in the first period means that these data have to be treated cautiously). Their shares of total overnights were, generally, the same in 1989 and 1996, but had increased significantly by 1993. These districts have relatively well-developed infrastructures and tourism facilities, are accessible, and have positive tourism images in Slovakia. They also have strong industrial economies and relatively low unemployment rates, which favour domestic tourism. The district of Banská Bystrica is a good example. Here the number of nights decreased from 672,305 in 1989 to 340,909 in 1993 and then recovered to 424,540 by 1996. Its well-known skiing centres continued to attract relatively large numbers of international tourists, while relatively low unemployment and above average incomes helped to sustain domestic tourism.

Three districts constitute a distinctive sub-group. Two of these, Liptovský Mikuláš and Poprad in the Tatra mountains, had accounted for the largest numbers of overnights before 1989. They suffered dramatic domestic tourism losses, 1989–93, and had only recaptured a relatively

Table 6.2 *Rank correlation coefficients of the regional distribution of international and domestic tourism in selected countries*

Country	Rank correlation	Country	Rank correlation
Spain (1992)	0.9141	France (1991)	0.6737
Italy (1991)	0.9083	Slovakia (1996)	0.6064
Germany (1988)	0.8909	Czech Republic (1996)	0.4279
Switzerland (1987)	0.8345	Norway (1990)	0.3316
Finland (1992)	0.7972	Netherlands (1991)	0.3273
Slovakia (1989)	0.7232	Austria (1992)	0.0833

Sources: Pearce (1995, p 102); authors' own computations.

small part of their lost markets by 1996. The position was different with respect to foreign tourism. While there had been a severe decline to 1993, when the negative effects of the 'velvet divorce' were strongest, by 1996 both districts attracted *more* foreign visitors than in 1989. Michalovce is another distinctive destination, having been the major 'sun and water' holiday resort in state-socialist Czechoslovakia. It recorded 1,087,540 overnights in 1989. Faced with competition from the Mediterranean resorts, as Slovak tourism was re-internationalized, the numbers of overnights decreased throughout the transformation, falling to 359,959 in 1993 and to only 221,074 by 1996. It did, however, benefit from increased numbers of foreign visitors, mostly from the Ukraine, a large and accessible potential market.

There were three outright tourism winners during the transition: the Cities of Bratislava and Košice, and Trnava district. Bratislava, of minor interest for holiday tourism, became the dominant business centre of Slovakia in this period. It generates over one-third of Slovakia's GDP and most visitors are on business trips. There is a broadly similar situation in Košice, which has the headquarters of the largest Slovakian firm, the VSŽ steel mill. The city also attracts business tourism from nearby Ukraine and Russia. In Trnava district, Piešťany spa is the major tourism attraction. This well-known resort attracts substantial numbers of tourists from Europe and the Middle East. Moreover, it also experienced an increase in domestic visitors during the transformation, despite sharp price increases. All three districts have well-developed infrastructures, favourable locations, strong local economic environments, and the potential for further growth in both domestic and international tourism.

Another question concerning the regional structure is whether domestic and foreign tourism produce similar or different patterns of uneven development. In Slovakia relatively high correlation coefficients between the two distributions (Table 6.2) suggest they are broadly similar (see also Figure 6.7). Moreover, international comparisons reveal that the relationship between the two spatial distributions in Slovakia was similar to those

181

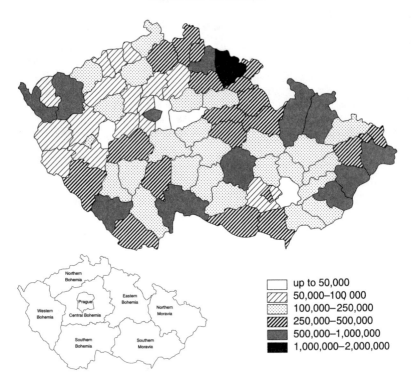

Fig. 6.5 Distribution of nights spent by domestic tourists in the Czech Republic by districts in 1996.
Source: Český statistický úřad (1989–1998b).

in Finland and France, but significantly different from Norway, the Netherlands and Austria. The situation was different in the Czech Republic, where the correlation was far lower because of the high degree of concentration of foreign tourists in Prague (see also Figure 6.8). In this, the Czech pattern resembled those in Norway and Netherlands, where foreign demand is also far more regionally polarized than domestic demand. The spatial association between foreign and domestic tourists has changed during the transformation in Slovakia, with foreign tourists becoming more regionally concentrated than domestic ones (Figures 6.3 and 6.4). In contrast, there were higher levels of concentration in the tourist distributions in the Czech Republic (Figures 6.5 and 6.6), which confirm the differences in the spatial distributions that were identified by the correlation coefficients (Table 6.2). A more spatially even distribution of domestic tourism is likely in the Czech Republic given its more developed tourism infrastruc-

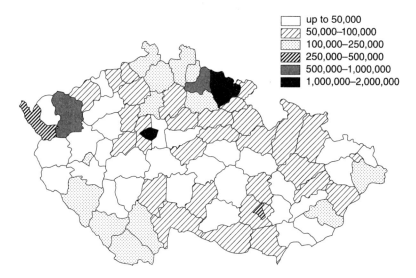

	up to 50,000
	50,000–100,000
	100,000–250,000
	250,000–500,000
	500,000–1,000,000
	1,000,000–2,000,000

Fig. 6.6 Nights spent by foreign tourists in the Czech Republic by district in 1996.
Source: Český statistický úřad (1989–1998b).

ture and a higher level of travel propensity, while the role of Prague in foreign tourism has already been noted.

Tourism and regional divergence in Slovakia

The analysis of spatial patterns of tourism development provides a starting point for analysing the role of tourism in regional economies. However, this is a complex relationship, for different types of regional economies and societies generate different kinds of tourism demand. Doering (1976), for example, in a study of the regional impacts of tourism development in the USA has suggested that as a state's population and economy increase in size, the economy becomes more diversified and less dependent on any one sector, including tourism. This conclusion is broadly valid for Slovakia.

There was generally a medium strong positive correlation (r = 0.6081) between regional GDP and the numbers of nights spent by all tourists in 1996: in other words, tourism tends to be most important in the more prosperous districts. The importance of tourism varied, however, amongst the different types of regional economies. As for the absolute numbers of nights spent, metropolitan, industrial and mixed-tourist districts accounted for the largest volumes of overnights (Figure 6.9). With the exception of the Tatra mountain districts of Poprad and Liptovský Mikuláš and the spa

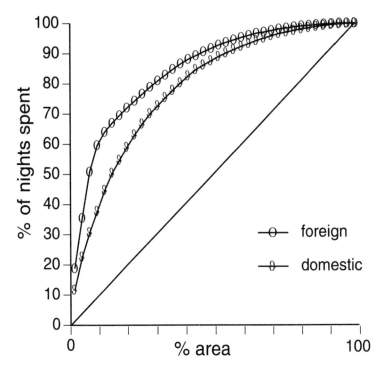

Fig. 6.7 Regional distribution of domestic and foreign tourists in Slovakia in 1996: districts.
Sources: Štatistický úrad Slovenskej republiky (1991–1998a), (1991–1998b) and authors' own computations.

town of Piešt́any (Trnava district), the major cities (Bratislava, Košice-City and Žilina) attracted the largest numbers of foreign and domestic tourists. The share of international tourism in their GDP, however, was below the Slovak average. Rural districts attracted fewer tourists, but despite the relatively small numbers of nights spent, international tourism played a relatively important role in the regional economies of some districts (Bratislava-District, Stará Ľubovňa, and Dolný Kubín). The Tatra mountain districts of Poprad and Liptovský Mikuláš and Trnava district (spa town of Piešt́any) had both large shares of international tourism in their GDPs (24.8, 14.7 and 10.5 per cent respectively) and large numbers of overnights.

The lack of data on domestic tourism receipts does not allow the impacts of national tourism on regional development to be analysed in the same

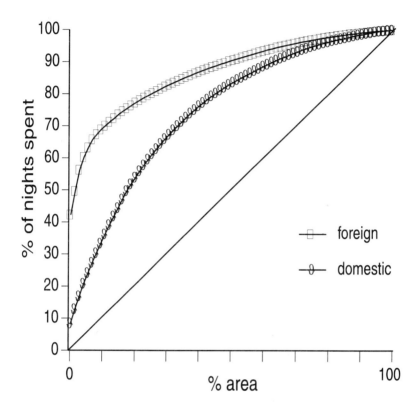

Fig. 6.8 Regional distribution of domestic and foreign tourists in the Czech Republic in 1996: districts.
Source: Český statistický úřad (1989–1998b).

way, but given the similar spatial distributions of domestic and foreign tourism, these impacts were likely to be similar.

Did international tourism significantly contribute to changes in regional GDP growth and structures? In 1994–6, some rural districts accounted for the highest rates of increase in the numbers of overnights (Figure 6.10), and this applied especially to those which also recorded some of the strongest increases in GDP per capita. Rural districts where GDP had decreased, on the other hand, tended to loose tourism markets. The same is true for some mixed-tourist districts, but industrial districts experienced higher increases in nights spent, perhaps as a result of improvements in their infrastructures (better accessibility) after 1995 and the development of business tourism. Their economic bases also became more diversified.

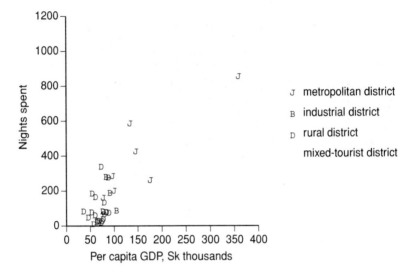

Fig. 6.9 Per capita GDP and nights spent by all tourists in Slovak districts in 1996.
Sources: Štatistický úrad Slovenskej republiky (1991–1998a), (1991–1998b), (1994–1998) and authors' own computations.
Notes: metropolitan districts = country capitals with well-developed industrial and service economies; industrial districts = strong manufacturing industrial base, large enterprises; rural districts = districts with SMEs in manufacturing and agricultural production; mixed-tourist districts = districts with relatively large shares of tourist industries in their GDP.

Tourism increased in importance in these districts. As for the metropolitan districts, these had higher rates of growth in GDP than in overnights. This can partly be explained by rapid economic growth, the development of non-tourism services and relative declines in their tourism sectors. However, there was not a strong correlation between changes in GDP per capita and the share of international tourism in GDP at the district level (r = 0.0543). There was also a weak correlation between growth in GDP and changes in numbers of nights spent by all tourists (r = 0.2447). This suggests that the changes in regional GDP were mainly generated in other economic sectors.

Some authors (Smith 1997a) suggest that the role of small and medium-sized enterprises (SMEs) in regional development was less than in the more developed regions of Western Europe, notably Northern and Central Italy. While SMEs were major sources of innovation and economic growth, large industrial enterprises remained the most important sources of growth in

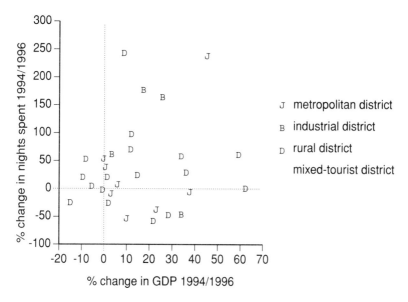

Fig. 6.10 Percentage change in per capita district GDP and nights spent by all
tourists in Slovak districts in 1994–6.
Sources: Štatiský úrad Slovenskej republiky (1991–1998a), (1991–1998b), (1994–
1998) and authors' own computations.

Slovak regions. This trend was again visible following market-reorientation
and economic recovery after 1994. The analysis of sectoral employment
provides broad confirmation of this suggestion. After a period of de-
industrialization during 1990–93, the importance of manufacturing
increased both in terms of employment and share of GDP in Slovakia.

This raises the question of why Slovak SMEs (including tourism
enterprises) appear to have been relatively less successful than the large
enterprises? A lack of capital and of skilled higher level managers and professionals appear to be the main reasons. While large enterprises secured
capital on international markets, SMEs faced domestic capital shortages
and high interest rates. Large enterprises were also significant employers
in some regions and so continued to attract state support. However, the
real importance of SMEs may have been greater than is indicated by official
sources, given the scale of the shadow and black economies. While official
international tourist receipts were US$ 672 million according to the
National Bank of Slovakia (Národná banka Slovenska 1993–1998a), actual
receipts were probably greater than US$ 1.8 billion, according to incoming
visitor surveys (Ústav turizmu 1997) in 1996.

Table 6.3   *Regional distribution of nights spent in the Czech Republic in 1996*

Region (Country)	Thousands nights spent		Distribution of nights spent by foreign tourists				
	Domestic	Foreign	Most important countries of origin (%)				
Prague	989	5,950	Ger 24.0	It 9.0	USA 6.8	UK 6.7	Sp 5.7
Central Bohemia	1,380	626	Ger 30.5	Ne 15.8	Sk 7.0	Pl 5.8	Ru 3.9
Southern Bohemia	2,854	660	Ger 40.9	At 14.0	Ne 12.2	Sk 4.2	It 3.3
Western Bohemia	2,604	1,764	Ger 58.1	Ne 8.1	Ru 6.4	Pl 4.2	At 2.5
Norther Bohemia	1,809	1,075	Ger 67.2	Ne 7.4	Sk 4.0	Ru 6.2	Dk 2.6
Eastern Bohemia	5,038	2,178	Ger 65.4	Ne 11.4	Pl 5.7	Sk 4.8	Ru 1.7
Southern Moravia	3,933	964	Ger 27.3	Pl 12.7	Sk 11.2	At 10.5	Ne 5.5
Northern Moravia	4,491	968	Ger 25.4	Pl 19.0	Sk 16.3	Ne 6.3	At 5.3
Czech Republic	23,100	14,186	Ger 36.6	Ne 6.8	It 5.5	Pl 4.7	Sk 4.0

Source: Český statistický úřad (1993–1998b).
Notes: At = Austria; Dk = Denmark; Ger = Germany; It = Italy; Ne = the Netherlands; Pl = Poland; Ru = Russia; Sk = Slovakia; Sp = Spain; UK = United Kingdom.

6.4.2 The Czech Republic

There were marked differences in the regional distribution of nights spent in the Czech Republic by domestic and foreign tourists (Table 6.3, Figures 6.5 and 6.6). In general, there were several 'core' tourism districts attracting large numbers of both foreign and domestic tourists (Cheb, Karlovy Vary, Trutnov, Semily). However, foreign tourist nights were concentrated in a relatively small number of Czech districts, while domestic tourist nights were more evenly distributed.

Prague was, by far, the leading tourist attraction in the Czech Republic. In 1996 it accounted for 41.9 per cent of all foreign tourist nights, and had a distinctive foreign market; Germans constituted the largest market segment, followed in rank order by Italians, Americans and British. This contrasts with other Czech regions where the Dutch, Poles, Italians, Slovaks and Russians were the most important national market segments, after the Germans. Western and Eastern Bohemia, with 12.4 and 15.4 per cent of foreign overnights in 1996, were other attractive tourism regions. The poles of attraction in Western Bohemia are its spas, and historical cities such as Cheb. In addition to Germans, this was a favoured destination for tourists from the Soviet Union and, later, Russia. There was a short discontinuity in Russian arrivals after 1989, but since 1994 Russian visitors have returned to the spas. Several hotels in Karlovy Vary, for example, have been bought by Russian investors. Eastern Bohemia was dependent on the former East Germany and Poland, and has a belt of heavily visited districts in its border mountain areas (Semily, Trutnov).

The distribution of foreign overnights in the Czech Republic was strongly influenced by geographical proximity, for most foreign tourists came from adjacent countries. Austrians, for example, were strongly evident in Southern Bohemia and Southern Moravia, Slovakians in Northern and Southern Moravia, and Poles in Northern Moravia and Northern Bohemia. German tourists constituted important market segments in all these regions but were particularly evident in Western, Northern and Eastern Bohemia.

In sharp contrast to foreigners, domestic tourists tended to avoid Prague which accounted for the lowest regional share of domestic nights in the Czech Republic in 1996 (4.3 per cent). Eastern Bohemia (21.8 per cent), and Northern and Southern Moravia (19.4 and 17.0 per cent) were the favoured domestic destinations.

There were some changes in the regional tourist distribution during the transformation. In 1994, for example, Prague accounted for 44.7 per cent of foreign overnights, Western Bohemia for 8.4 per cent and Eastern Bohemia for 12.1 per cent. Eastern and Western Bohemia were the major 'winners' in the process of re-internationalization, attracting new clients, particularly from Poland and Germany. Southern Moravia, on the other hand, saw its market share decline from 11.5 to 6.8 per cent. This redistribution was probably influenced by accessibility considerations and the range and quality of facilities available for tourism. Eastern and Western Bohemia had better quality infrastructures and were favourably located in respect of tourism demand from the industrial centres of Germany and Poland. Additionally, the recomposition of demand favoured some segments and types of areas: skiing, visits to mountain areas, business tourism and cross-border shopping became more important, whilst rural areas became relatively less attractive. Changes in the distribution of foreign overnights were also influenced by increasing demand for higher quality tourism facilities and services. With improvements in living standards and increasing numbers of business travellers in Central Europe (including Germany's 'new *Länder*'), foreign and domestic tourists increasingly were able and willing to pay for higher quality services. Tourism facilities in Eastern and Western Bohemia and Northern Moravia were of a markedly higher standard and provided more sophisticated tourism services than those in Southern Moravia and Southern Bohemia (Annex VI), and the regions with higher quality tourism infrastructures were the main 'winners' in this period. This trend was common to both the Czech and Slovak Republics.

6.5 CONCLUSIONS: TOURISM AND REGIONAL DIVERGENCE VERSUS CONVERGENCE

The economic and social transitions in the Czech and Slovak Republics were accompanied by increasing regional differences. In both countries, rural regions and the most heavily industrialized regions were worst

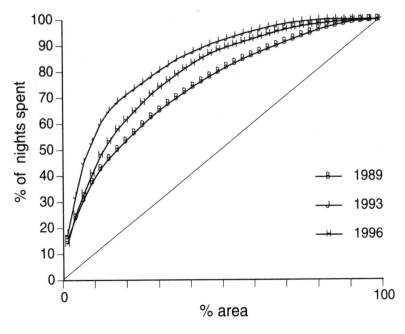

Fig. 6.11 Regional distribution of nights spent by all tourists in Slovakia in 1989, 1993 and 1996: districts.
Sources: Štatistický úrad Slovenskej republiky (1991–1998a), (1991–1998b), authors' own computations.

affected. On the other hand, Bratislava, Prague and other major cities with diversified economies gained in relative, and sometimes in absolute, importance. Whereas regional convergence had been typical in the state-socialist period, increasing regional disparities were typical in the transformation. The trend was stronger in Slovakia, where 40 years of central planning had created large dominant production complexes in many districts. These regions faced major difficulties in developing new forms of production, and in competing in the emerging market economy. These regional changes in production were, of course, reflected in living standards and tourism spending.

The regional distribution of tourism also changed after 1989 (Figure 6.11). This was only partly related to the overall pattern of regional economic divergence. A number of other changes in the external and domestic economic and political environment also informed the reshaping of the regional distribution of tourism:

- The emergence of market economies in Central Europe increased the importance of domestic and international business travel. The major cities and the main industrial regions were the main winners in this.
- Price differences between the transition economies and neighbouring Germany and Austria, and amongst the transition economies, generated large flows for shopping, trade and leisure purposes. A relatively large proportion of German and Austrian tourism expenditure was allocated to shopping, eating out, drinking and sex-tourism in the Czech and Slovak border districts. Shopping and/or smuggling were important motives for many excursionists from the transition economies.
- The 'velvet divorce' between the Czech and Slovak Republics divided families and friends by an international border. What had been previously been domestic Czech–Slovak travel now became international tourism and, statistically at least, increased the volumes of international VFR-related travel. At the same time, the removal of the Iron Curtain eased travel exchanges with Poland, Ukraine and Hungary, and increased the numbers of visits to friends and relatives. These changes mainly affected the border regions.
- Declining living standards between 1990 and 1993 had a severe impact on tourism facilities which had been designed for low-cost domestic recreation. The key to this was that increased living standards after 1994 had a very polarized social distribution. The 'new rich' and the newly established middle classes demanded higher quality facilities. The winners were those regions with more sophisticated tourism infrastructures, and a number of international destinations.
- There were significant improvements in the Czech and Slovak tourism industries, in terms of diversity and quality after 1989. These industries, however, still could not match the sophisticated tourism industries in neighbouring Austria and Germany. Most foreign visitors from the developed countries were either transit travellers or excursionists, rather than leisure tourists. This form of travel favoured the border districts, and brought them significant economic benefits, but the effects are likely to diminish as price convergence occurs between Central Europe and its Western neighbours.

In Slovakia, the brief survey of regional tourism development yields a relatively simple conclusion: with the decline in domestic tourism and the development of business tourism, the regional distribution changed significantly, 1989–96. Most districts had smaller numbers of foreign and domestic overnights in 1996 than in 1989. The losses, however, were unequally distributed. The most developed tourism regions (Bratislava, Trnava, Poprad) were most successful, maintaining high levels of domestic tourism while experiencing increasing international arrivals. The poorer regions, which relied on the demand for cheap domestic holidays, were the main losers. They lost a major part of their former clientele and lacked the resources to recapture market share. In some of these regions there has been investment in thermal baths in order to attract new clients from amongst the Slovakian middle classes, and this has had positive results.

In the Czech Republic, the regional distribution of foreign visitors was heavily dominated by Prague and some border districts in Western and Eastern Bohemia. There were, however, differences between the distributions of excursionists and tourists. Prague was the dominant tourism destination and accounted for almost one half of foreign overnights. The city accounted for above-average shares of tourists from the more distant countries of Europe and from America, reflecting its capacity to compete in globalising markets. In contrast, excursionists, especially of German and Polish origin, visited the Czech border districts. Most foreign visitors to the Czech Republic came from adjacent countries – Germany, Poland, Austria and Slovakia – but there also was also strong demand from Dutch and Italian tourists. German visitors were heavily concentrated in a few border districts in Western Bohemia (Karlovy Vary and Cheb), while those from Poland were concentrated in the border districts of Eastern Bohemia and Northern Moravia. The main motives for excursionism were shopping and VFR-related travel. The largest increases in foreign overnights were reported in Western and Eastern Bohemia and were generated by Germans from neighbouring regions. The Moravian districts bordering on Slovakia and Poland decreased in importance, mostly due to reduced demand from these countries, in consequence of the social and economic impacts of transition.

What, if any, were the impacts of these regional tourism shifts on the overall pattern of uneven development in Slovakia and the Czech Republic? In general, international tourism trends tended to widen rather than to narrow regional economic differences, especially because of the importance of Prague and Bratislava in business tourism. While it is true that international tourism, and especially excursionism, favoured border regions, they did not all benefit from trans-border movements. These flows had a number of objectives: shopping, trading and job-seeking. This means that the most positive impacts have occurred where there are prosperous consumer and labour markets in adjoining regions. Not surprisingly, these are in a limited number of trans-border regions such as Vienna–Bratislava, Leipzig–Northern Bohemia, Czech Silesia (Northern Moravia)–Polish Silesia, and Kosice–Western Ukraine. In contrast, there is a belt of poor districts in the trans-border region of Southern Slovakia–Northern Hungary, which lacks the conditions to generate cross-border economic flows. The same applies to the less populated and relatively poor south-west Bohemia and Bavaria trans-border region. In the state-socialist period, these areas enjoyed some domestic and (within the Eastern block) international low-cost rural tourism flows, but those markets have been devastated. Finally, in the case of the Tatra mountains (districts of Poprad and Liptovský Mikuláš), although tourism was important here both before and after 1989, there was also a relatively strong regional economy; the major difference after 1989 was that the decline in other sectors meant that the relative importance of tourism increased. The overall conclusion then is that tourism, both domestic and international, contributed more to regional divergence than to convergence, although there is also a need to be sensitive to the extent of regional diversity.

In Slovakia, the analysis of regional GDP and investment suggests that metropolitan districts (Bratislava–City, Košice–City, Trnava, Žilina, Banská Bystrica, Trenčín) and industrial districts (Martin, Žiar nad Hronom, Považská Bystrica) have the most favourable development potential. Their levels of existing infrastructure, population, income and education all offer comparative advantages for future tourism growth. These districts will probably continue to have above-average incomes, while an above-average part of their consumer expenditure is likely to be allocated to tourism (locally, nationally and abroad). The development of business and conference tourism is also likely to be concentrated in these districts. The regional economies of these districts, however, were diversified and tourism was a complementary rather than a leading industrial sector. As for the traditional tourist districts of Liptovský Mikuláš and Poprad, these are likely to remain of major importance in Slovak tourism in the future. Well-developed infrastructures and increasing domestic and foreign demand provide favourable conditions for tourism in these districts. As for the marginal regions, the northern and south-eastern districts have different development potentials. The south-eastern districts have unfavourable social and demographic conditions, high out-migration, large proportions of elderly peoople, lower levels of education and low levels of entrepreneurial activity. Moreover, the lowering of the Iron Curtain did not bring dramatic changes in travel flows to and from neighbouring Hungary. These regions did not share in the new opportunities generated by the transformation in respect of international trade and travel. In addition, they lost large numbers of their traditional domestic clients from the state-socialist period. The northern and north-eastern districts, on the other hand, had younger population structures, relatively high levels of births and of social mobility and of entrepreneurial activity. The removal of all barriers to travel exchanges with Poland provided an impetus for local trade and their tourism economies. Most of these movements were related to shopping and business travel, as part of the internationalization of 'bazaar capitalism', but in the Tatra mountain districts, at least, holiday travel boomed, especially after 1993. The northwest districts of Čadca and Dolný Kubín were able to utilize their locations on the Slovak–Czech–Polish borders, and access to major industrial areas in the Czech–Polish Silesia and Slovak Váh River

Valley, to profit from increased foreign trade and travel. The north-east districts of Bardejov and Staráubova exploited their tourist potential, consisting of unspoilt nature, spas and historical monuments, and experienced major increases in the nights spent by foreign tourists. These districts have the potential for further growth conditional on improvements in infrastructure. In summary, then, tourism development followed the general patterns of regional divergence during transition in Slovakia. The industry became more concentrated in selected region and this trend is likely to continue in future.

Fewer data were available for the Czech Republic. Some studies (Librová 1997) indicate that, in terms of migration, concentration tendencies still prevail over deconcentration. The transformation deepened regional inequalities, with Prague and Western and Eastern Bohemia becoming the winners due to their more developed infrastructures and greater diversification. Similarly to Slovakia, but to a lesser extent, there were regions which could be characterized as having 'historical' and, or 'transition-generated' marginality. The former were the agriculture districts of South-

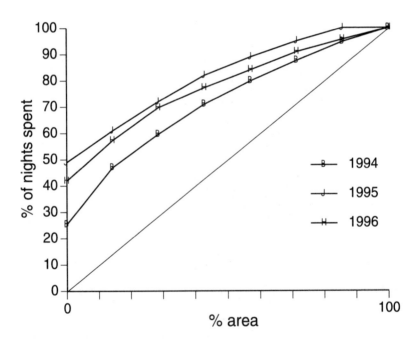

Fig. 6.12 Regional distribution of nights spent by foreign tourists in the Czech Republic in 1994, 1995 and 1996: counties.
Source: Český statistický úřad (1989–1998b); authors' own computations.

ern Moravia, the latter the coal mining and steel manufacturing regions in Northern Moravia and Northern Bohemia. The available data suggest that the spatial concentration of foreign tourists (Figure 6.12) in 1994–6 indicates increased concentration. Given the high (previous) concentration of fixed investment, and the investment made after 1989, the metropolitan and urban areas in Prague, Western and Eastern Bohemia are likely to remain the main generators of domestic tourism demand in future. These regions were also the regional tourism winners, in terms of shares of total foreign overnights in 1994–6. Analysis of the supply side and of the spatial patterns of tourist distribution suggest two main reasons for this: first, Prague and Western and Eastern Bohemia had the highest levels of tourism infrastructure, and second, districts on the Polish and German borders, in particular, were most successful in attracting both domestic and foreign tourists. They benefited from good natural conditions for outdoor activities (skiing and hiking) and proximity to heavily populated industrial regions in Bohemia, Germany and Poland. They were also able to exploit the advantages generated by the enormous increase in international travel after 1989, mostly related to shopping and informal trans-border trade/smuggling, business and leisure.

7 CONSUMPTION: COLLECTIVE PROVISION AND COMMODIFICATION

7.1 DOMESTIC TOURISM UNDER STATE-SOCIALISM

In any society, tourism participation rates are determined by a number of considerations including: disposable personal income; the availability of free time; the volume, price and quality of tourism services; cultural and social differences in tourist interests, motivations and behaviour; and political constraints on travel (Shaw and Williams 1994, Chapter Three). Domestic tourism in Central and Eastern Europe had distinctive characteristics both before and after 1989, but there were major changes in some of the prime determinants of participation rates during the transformation. We can identify three main questions relating to domestic tourist behaviour. First, the extent to which this differs from Western European model(s) of tourist behaviour (Shaw and Williams 1998). Second, whether this distinctiveness stems from differences in political regimes (and the collectivist form of tourism under state-socialism) or from different levels of social and economic development? Third, whether there are significant differences in Czech and Slovakian domestic tourism. Despite being parts of the same relatively small, territorially bounded state for 70 years, there were and are differences in cultural, religious and political values in the two countries. Czechs are popularly thought to be more liberal and West-orientated, while Slovaks are more conservative and East-orientated. This is however a contested view and, moreover, the implications for tourism behaviour need to be investigated. These questions can also be viewed within the larger framework provided by path dependency and path creation. To what extent have institutional legacies from the state-socialist period continued to constrain tourism behaviour after 1989, and to what extent have social forces mapped out new models of tourist behaviour?

There are three main aspects of domestic tourism which make it an important subject of research for those interested in the transformation in Central and Eastern Europe. First, tourism demonstrates many of the wider contradictions in the transformation from a system of consumption based on collective provision, to one based on emerging, if imperfect, market mechanisms. Second, the early years of transformation were characterized by sharp reversals in economic growth and reductions in living standards (Chapter 2), followed by a recovery in GDP per capita by the late 1990s to levels approaching those of 1989 (Williams *et al* 1998). How has domestic tourism changed in the face of depressed real incomes and consumption? Third, the transformation has created new and deeper social cleavages in terms of wealth, incomes and living standards (Williams and Baláž 1999), and this is reflected to some extent in changing access to domestic tourism.

7.1.1 Urbanization, industrialization and modernization

Before turning to a detailed consideration of domestic tourism, we first need to consider basic differences in the evolution of Czech and Slovak societies. The Czech and Slovak nations shared a common state for 70 years, and for more than 40 years experienced a tough political regime and central planning under state-socialism. While they had similar languages, the two nations had different histories and cultures, especially before 1918. State-socialism sought to eradicate this legacy of different income levels, cultures, and social practices. These experiments partly achieved their goals, at least within the period of the state-socialism, but the differential impacts of industrialization, urbanization and modernization are still visible in domestic tourism.

There were already major disparities in urban-rural population structures between the Czech and Slovak Republics as early as 1900. Bohemia was the most economically developed part of the Austro-Hungarian empire and had experienced a high level of industrialization in the nineteenth and early twentieth centuries. In Slovakia, industrialization stagnated in the first half of the twentieth century (the period of the first Czechoslovak state) and it provided labour and agricultural products for Bohemia. The most significant period of industrialization and urbanization in Slovakia only commenced in the 1950s, within the framework of state-socialism; there was rapid urbanization, development of welfare services, and investment in infrastructure. There were also substantial improvements in living standards in Slovakia (although less than in the Czech part of Czechoslovakia).

An insight into the process of modernization is provided by changes in access to leisure. By 1950, some 40.7 per cent of Czechs and 26.3 per cent of Slovaks were living in urban areas, and the share of (commercial) tourism expenditure in nominal incomes was 0.17 and 0.16 per cent, respectively. In the same year, average Slovak per capita incomes were 28 per cent lower than Czech ones. The shares of tourism in total expenditure were relatively low in both territories, because of the low degree of urbanization and the availability of collective provision in state- or trade-union-owned holiday centres. By 1960, both the urbanization rates (39.5 and 29.7 per cent respectively) and the income gap between Czechs and Slovaks (29.2 per cent) had changed little. But an overall increase in living standards and an improved supply of commercial tourist services resulted in the shares of tourism expenditure rising to 0.50 and 0.39 per cent, respectively.

The following period, the 1960s, was the most successful for central planning. The rate of urbanization increased markedly to 52.4 per cent in the Czech territory, while Slovakia lagged behind with 37.0 per cent. The high rates of economic growth did, however, lead to a significant narrowing of the income gap between the nations to 18.2 percent by 1970. Improvements in living standards generated strong growth in tourism spending, and the further narrowing of national differences: the share of tourism expenditure in nominal income increased to 0.62 and 0.50 for, respectively, the Czechs and Slovaks by 1970. However, Slovaks still lagged behind in terms of numbers of short breaks per capita in 1970. This may have been due to lower levels of urbanization and car ownership, and more traditional social practices (eschewing travel) in Slovakia. The difference, however, was not substantial. On the other hand, there were differences in travel destinations. Czechs were already beginning to travel to the 'sun and sea' destinations on the Black Sea and Lake Balaton, a phenomenon that did not emerge in Slovakia until the 1970s and 1980s. Unfortunately, after 1970 comparisons between the two nations become more difficult, as the Slovak Tourism Institute provided more detailed statistical data on domestic tourism than was available in the Czech territory (Table 7.1).

The 1970s were the most successful period in Slovak history in terms of improvements in living standards. By 1970, the level of urbanization in Slovakia finally exceeded 50 percent, and the income gap between Czechs and Slovaks shrank to 10 per cent. The shares of tourism expenditure in nominal income reflected this, increasing to 0.74 and 0.63 per cent, respectively. Education levels also converged. By 1970, some 2.7 per cent of the total population had a university degree in the Czech Republic, compared to 2.2 per cent in Slovakia; yet, by 1980 this index had risen to 3.8 per cent in both Republics. This is significant because education levels are one of the most important influences on tourism participation. In Czechoslovakia in 1974, for example, only 15.0 per cent of the population with a basic education took holidays away from home, compared to 44.9 per cent of those with university degrees. Other social cleavages in tourism were less distinct. Surveys of short breaks, for example, revealed that village and large city residents had participation rates of 53.8 per cent and 73.3 per cent respectively. Amongst socio-economic groups, the largest difference in the short break market segment was between farmers (36.6 per cent),

TABLE 7.1 *Domestic tourist trips: 1970, 1980, 1987, and 1996.*

Country	ČSSR 1970		ČSSR 1980		ČSSR 1987		Slovakia 1996
Nation:	Czechs	Slovaks	Czechs	Slovaks	Czechs	Slovaks	Slovaks
Urban population share	52.4	37.0	63.8	50.4	64.6	56.3	60.3
Income per capita, Kč	16,782	13,648	24,095	21,674	30,617	27,849	88,503
Tourism Expenditure, %	0.62	0.50	0.74	0.63	0.78	0.75	0.57
Short breaks (thousands)	79,036	32,694	95,800	48,160	103,905	52,602	71,404
Percentage of total trips	95.4	95.0	90.8	92.1	92.4	91.2	94.8
Holidays (thousands)	3,808	1,712	7,031	4,133	8,521	5,084	3,917
Percentage of total trips	4.6	5.0	9.2	7.9	7.6	8.8	5.2
Total trips	82,844	34,406	105,456	52,293	112,426	57.686	75,321
Short breaks per capita	8.06	7.22	9.28	10.49	10.03	10.55	13.29
Holidays per capita	0.39	0.38	0.68	0.82	0.82	1.02	0.73

Sources: Ústav turizmu (1995–1998), database of the Tourism Institute, for years 1970–1988 and Federální statistický úřad (1985).
Notes: Urbanization rate = share of population living in settlements over 5,000 inhabitants – the rate for 1996 is estimated; income is defined in per capita per annum terms, in Kč for ČSSR during 1970–87, and in Sk for Slovakia in 1996; the share of tourism expenditure in Slovakia refers to 1993; tourism expenditure is defined in terms of payments by domestic tourists for services provided by commercial hotels, spas, travel agencies and children's leisure facilities; holidays are defined as four or more working days spent away from the normal place of residence; short breaks include day trips and two-to-three-day trips; all these data were provided by the Tourism Institute in Bratislava. Before 1989 it was responsible for federal coverage, but after 1990 it only covered Slovakia. These surveys did not continue in the Czech Republic.

workers (64.5 per cent) and employees (77.2 per cent). As for age groups, 70.2 per cent of those aged 30–44 took short breaks, compared to only 46.8 per cent of those over 60 years (Malá 1985). Education continued to be the most significant factor influencing participation rates in the 1987 survey (Table 7.2). However, by this date, most of the other social cleavages in tourism had been greatly reduced. Territorial differences were also minimized and, indeed, by the 1980s Slovaks made more trips, per capita, than Czechs.

By the end of the period of state-socialism (the last major survey is for 1987), the income gap between the two nations had narrowed to 9 per cent and there continued to be no significant differences in participation rates in short breaks. However, Czechs were more likely to take longer holidays, and there was a 20-percentage-point gap between the two nations in this respect. This was related to differences in the overall level and form of economic and social development in the two Republics. Over several cen-

TABLE 7.2   *Tourism participation rates for selected social groups in Czechoslovakia in 1987, Slovakia in 1996 and the EU in 1985*

	Czechoslovakia 1987		EU 12, 1985	Slovakia 1996	
	Short breaks	Longer holidays	Longer holidays	Short breaks	Longer holidays
Nationality					
Czechs	75.4	40.7	x	x	x
Slovaks	74.3	20.2	x	49.8	44.4
EU 12	x	x	56.0	x	x
Age					
14–29	77.4	29.0	62.0	50.8	57.0
30–44	77.5	39.4	62.0	50.4	47.7
45–59	72.2	30.3	53.0	47.1	46.3
60+	62.7	24.2	47.0	31.0	22.1
Education					
Basic	50.3	17.3	x	34.9	26.6
Lower middle	71.8	28.2	x	43.5	44.9
Upper middle	81.3	42.6	x	58.7	59.4
University	83.8	45.5	x	63.6	77.6
Settlement size					
Up to 2,000	64.6	19.2	45.0	42.4	31.8
2,001–5,000	72.5	30.1	x	40.3	34.1
5,001–20,000	79.0	33.3	59.0	48.3	45.1
20,001–50,000	80.5	33.3	x	51.7	53.8
50,001–100,000	78.7	39.8	66.0	51.1	54.2
Over 100,000	82.3	56.2	x	56.2	67.1

Sources: Výzkumní ústav obchodu (1988); Ústav turizmu (1995–1998); Commission of the European Communities (1986).

Notes: in Czechoslovakia, the data for short trips in 1987 refer to the summer season only, whereas the 1996 data refer to all seasons; in 1987 the question asked was: are you travelling on holiday each year?, but by 1996 this had become: were you travelling on holiday in 1996?; the data on the hometown populations of those who took short breaks refer to 1987 and 1995, all the other data refer to 1987 and 1996; the corresponding age groups for the EU 12 were 15–24, 25–39, 40–55, and over 55; settlement sizes were stated as 'village', 'small town' and 'large town'.

turies, the Czechs had been more urbanized than the predominantly rural Slovaks, and this had lead to differences in tourist behaviour, with the better educated and more prosperous Czechs being more inclined to travel; they also had better transport infrastructure.

After 1948, forty years of state-socialism erased many of these economic and social contrasts, especially in terms of levels of industrialization, incomes and the provision of tourism facilities. There were, however, persistent lifestyle differences (see Guráň *et al* 1997 on rural lifestyles). While most Slovaks lived in modern cities by the 1970s and 1980s, there were enduring cultural outlooks, deeply rooted in traditional rural society (Podoba 1996, p 217). Family and friendship ties remained strong, and society was generally less open to external influences. While the family and friendship ties of first and second generation rural–urban migrants weakened in these decades, they still played an important role in social life. There were also differences in the use made of non-work time and disposable incomes: Czechs were more likely to travel to the Black Sea and Lake Balaton, while Slovaks preferred to use their 'leisure' time for building and improving houses. In the 1980s the construction boom waned as the demand for improved accommodation in Slovakia had largely been satisfied, and Slovaks became more interested in tourism. By the end of the state-socialist period, the gap between the shares of the Czech and Slovak population taking a longer holiday *each* year had narrowed to the above-mentioned 20 per cent. But if the proportion having a longer holiday *at least once in a period of several years* is considered (Table 7.2), then the participation rates were similar at about 70 per cent in each nation.

Attitudes to consumption and tourism reflect deeper cultural differences in Slovak and Czech societies, and explain some of the differences in the intersecting new and old pathways in the transformation period. In general, Slovaks attached more importance than Czechs to improvements in living standards, compared to political issues (including the imposition of barriers to freedom to travel) under state-socialism. After 1989, reductions in living standards and increases in unemployment rates were significantly greater in Slovakia than in the Czech Republic. Not surprisingly, their evaluations of the achievements of state-socialism were different. Newspaper reporting indicated that, after 1989, Czechs were more likely to refer to the 1970s and 1980s as 'lost years', while Slovaks were more likely to be nostalgic about the higher living standards they had been accustomed to (Krivý *et al* 1997, p 41). This political cleavage is confirmed in a number of social surveys (for example, Evans and Whitefield 1998).

7.1.2 Tourism, collective provision and ideology under state-socialism

Foreign travel was severely constrained under state-socialism. This has been discussed previously in Chapters 2.3 and 3.2, and here we focus on domestic tourism. However, changes in foreign outbound tourism after 1989, consequent upon liberalization of passport and visa requirements, did influence the evolution of domestic tourism after 1989. Tourism under state-socialism was also shaped by an ideological legacy, rooted in the

201

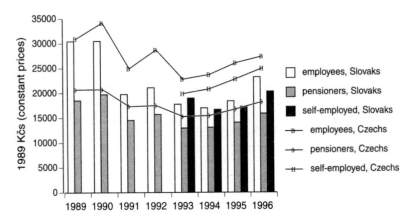

Fig. 7.1 Real gross per capita incomes of selected social groups in Slovakia and the Czech Republic, 1989–95.
Sources: Federální statistický úřad (1986–1993), Štatistický úrad Slovenskej republiky (1994–1998), Český statistický úřad (1993–1998a).

Marxist theory of production. According to this, only the production of material goods could be considered a real and, or efficient form of production. In the service sector, in contrast, only those activities directly supporting the production of goods were considered to be productive (see Hall 1984 and Burns 1998 on the experiences of, respectively, Albania and the former Soviet Union). Tourism was classified as an 'unproductive', and 'inefficient' activity, and had a low priority in central planning. During the 1950s and 1960s, the main role of tourism was conceptualized as being 'to regenerate the labour force' and 'to satisfy the demand for recreation' (Hall 1991a). This conditioned the investment in tourism, and also the balance between commercial and collective provision.

In the domestic market, expenditure on commercial tourism accommodation had a relatively high elasticity and rose significantly faster than real incomes under state-socialism (Figure 7.1). The actual consumption of tourism services, however, was greater than is indicated by the shares of tourism spending in total income/expenditure. Tourism in the state socialist countries had been characteristically non-commercial. By 1989, in what was to become the Czech Republic, there were 15,300 beds in commercial tourist facilities, but 309,900 beds in non-commercial facilities, mainly in enterprise-owned holiday centres. In Slovakia, there were 66,100 beds in commercial establishment, and 76,700 in non-commercial ones. The facilities were highly variable in the quality of service provided and had low occupation rates (21.9 per cent in the Czech Republic and 17.6 per cent in the Slovak Republic). The large scale and low cost of provision meant that cheap recreation was available for almost everyone who wanted to take advantage of this form of social tourism. This was consistent with the regime's so-called 'goulash socialism' strategy, whereby improvements in consumption (including low-cost tourism) were used to legitimize the tough political order and restrictions on human rights (including the right of free travel). If the share of tourism expenditure in nominal income seemed low (0.78 and 0.75 per cent) in the Czech and Slovak Republics compared with EU consumption levels, it would be significantly higher if non-commercial tourism services were taken into account, at their real price levels.

Domestic tourism in the state-socialist countries was essentially non-commercial in character. Only 17 per cent of the 5.1 million Slovakian holidays in 1987 (Table 7.1) were spent in commercial tourism facilities. Facilities provided by employers, trade unions and non-profit associations accounted for 24 per cent of all holidays, privately owned second homes for 24.8 per cent, and the houses of relatives and friends for 23.9 per cent. There was a similar distribution in the Czech Republic, where the share of commercial provision was only 20.8 per cent in 1987. The non-commercial character of tourism was even stronger in respect of short breaks, which were strongly family-orientated. In Slovakia in 1987, for example, only 4 per cent of travellers used commercial facilities for short breaks, but 48 per cent enjoyed the hospitality of friends and relatives and 27 per cent visited their own or a family-owned second home. The Czech distribution of short trips was, again, similar to the Slovak one. In both cases, recent urbanization tendencies contributed to these practices, for first and second generation urban residents were able to stay with family in the countryside, or in inherited properties which had become second homes. However, it should be noted that Carter (1991, p 162–3) suggests that most second homes were not acquired through direct inheritance. But their overall importance is not in doubt. Hall (1991a, p 86) comments that

> The growth of second-home ownership presented ethical problems, reflecting disparities of wealth and connections . . . The second home often acted as a safety valve for a family confined to a small rented urban apartment during the week . . . In this way the state was relieved of some of the pressure for greater investment in housing and recreation facilities.

Whatever the political motive, the growth of second homes had a major influence on the evolution of domestic tourism.

The non-commercial character of state-socialist tourism further increased in importance during the 1980s, with the construction of new facilities by employers and the acquisition of large numbers of second homes (arguably as a component of 'goulash socialism'). The distinctive distribution of longer holidays and short trips in state-socialist Czechoslovakia was, to a large extent, politically determined: there was little state investment in commercial tourist facilities, but extensive social-tourism programmes, subsidized by the state, trade unions and employers. However, as noted earlier, the pattern of tourist behaviour was also influenced by relatively strong family ties between urban and rural areas, related to relatively recent urbanization, especially in Slovakia. Further details of the size and structure of the non-commercial sector are provided in Chapter 4.

7.2 SOCIAL TOURISM VERSUS COMMODIFICATION DURING THE TRANSFORMATION

Travel patterns are influenced by a number of considerations including disposable income, leisure time, age, education, employment, culturally-informed travel habits, and settlement patterns. Income and work ties are particularly important mediators of travel. For example, a 1985 survey in the EC indicated that 44 per cent of European did not go on holiday away from home, but that only one-fifth did so by choice; the others were constrained by finances (44 per cent of the non-travellers), work ties 16 per cent), and, to a lesser extent family problems and poor health. The survey also indicated a generally positive correlation between gross domestic product per capita and travel propensity. The latter was far greater in Germany, Denmark and the Netherlands, than in Portugal, Ireland and Greece. Economic constraints were the major reason for staying home in the poorer EU members (Portugal, 67 per cent; Ireland, 61 per cent; and Greece, 55 per cent). Political conditions are also important determinants of international travel, and this clearly applied to Central and Eastern Europe before 1989. The changes in international travel during the transformation have already been discussed in previous chapters. The transition, however, has brought not only changes in political structures, but also economic and social changes. These have created new life styles, although these have been grafted onto rather than replacing deeply-ingrained patterns of leisure behaviour.

This section outlines the main changes in travel patterns in the transformation countries, and explores some of the major influences on tourism after 1989. As would be expected, changes in the axes of social differentiation have had variable importance. In broad terms, there have been few changes in either age structures or in the level or urbanization, but there have been fundamental shifts in the distribution of income, and in the intersection of working and leisure activities.

7.2.1 Social change and domestic tourism

The individualization of life projects and lifestyles is related to modernization processes in society (especially industrialization, urbanization, and secularization). An international sociological survey of 'Actors and Strategies of Transformation and Modernization' (in Slovakia, the Czech

Republic and Poland) in 1995 identified several distinctive modernization trends. These were particularly evident in the 20–24 age cohort (Macháček 1997). In Slovakia for example, the life experiences of this age group had been strongly differentiated. Their professional training and education was determined in the final years of state-socialism (1985–1990), a period of socialist modernization characterized by a high degree of social security, while their labour market experiences were in the transformation period. The transformation brought about a number of fundamental changes in life experiences: greater uncertainty in realizing individual life projects, a higher risk of unemployment, the need to retrain and to seek out alternative sources of incomes including part-time jobs, and the necessity for more frequent travel. This first post-1989 generation, in employment terms, seems to have been the most flexible age cohort in adapting to increasingly individualized life projects, and this has been common throughout Europe.

The key role of age and education in the capacity to adapt to the demands of the transformation have been confirmed by other social surveys. Gatnár (1996), for example, in a comparative study of Czechs and Slovaks, established that 'the respondents who clearly favour current societal changes have the following group attributes: they are better educated and younger than the average. All other differences are rather marginal'. The shift towards higher levels of individualization, mobility and flexibility was, to some extent, hampered by economic difficulties during the transformation. In smaller communities, with more traditional life styles, some collective values (of mutual assistance amongst family and friends) actually increased in importance (Gurán et al 1997), whereas those living in more 'modern' and more urbanized areas established economic and social networks with a broader range of individuals and institutions, as parts of their survival strategies.

7.2.2 Apparent contradictions in tourism behaviour

A lack of statistical data for the Czech Republic after 1990 means that it is impossible to examine changes in market segments in that country during the transformation. However, appropriate statistics are available for Slovakia for 1996. These show that the overall numbers of trips made by Slovaks increased during 1987–96 (Table 7.1). Within this total, both the number and the share of short breaks increased, while the number of longer 'holidays' (four or more days, see Table 7.1) decreased in terms of number and share. However, a different picture emerges if we consider the proportions of the total population who participated in longer holidays: the proportions participating in one-day trips and short breaks fell, while the proportions taking longer holidays increased (Figure 7.2).

This apparent contradiction is explained by changes in the social distribution of holidays during the transformation. In the state-socialist period,

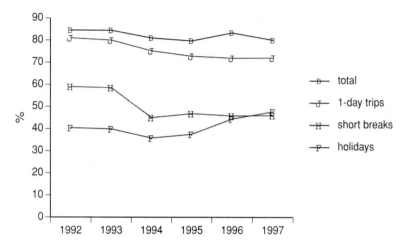

Fig. 7.2 The proportions of the population participating in selected types of tourism activities, in Slovakia in 1992–7.
Source: Ústav turizmu (1995–1998).

about three-quarters of Slovaks (and Czechs) took several short holidays each year. By 1996, one half of the Slovak population did not take any short break, but a small number took more than ten short breaks annually. The 1996 survey (Ústav turizmu 1997) shows, as would be expected, that managers, entrepreneurs and students were most likely to take several short breaks: more than 60 per cent took at least one holiday (long or short). Business constituted the main objective of their travel. In contrast, the corresponding proportions of workers, unemployed and housewives (as defined by the survey) taking any form of holiday was only 31 per cent. Therefore, the key to the apparent contradiction of a substitution of short for longer tourism trips lies in the changing function of short-break tourism. While recreation, hobbies and VFR-related travel were the main motives for short breaks before 1989, increased business activity accounted for the absolute increase in short breaks after 1989.

Whereas a large proportion of the population no longer took short breaks after 1989, increasing numbers took at least one holiday per year. Therefore, while the total number of holidays (four or more days) decreased during 1987–96, these had become more evenly socially distributed by 1996. This redistribution reflects fundamental lifestyle changes. State-socialism provided a fairly stable and regularized lifestyle with one (guaranteed) job, large numbers of free weekends and few possibilities for engaging in additional economic activities. In contrast, there were significant shifts in disposable income and free time during the transformation.

Under state-socialism, the state provided generous annual paid holidays, ranging from the three working weeks allocated to graduates to the six weeks for miners, teachers and selected other occupations. Most of the population enjoyed four to five working weeks of paid holiday, as well as seven days of national holidays. After 1989, there was little change in the right to official paid holidays. However, there were significant changes in the actual availability of free time. Under state-socialism, there had been little opportunity for taking a second job or to establish a private business. Moreover, since disposable income was sufficient to cover the costs of the available supply of goods and services, there was little pressure to seek additional work. After 1989, a decline in living standards and the transition to a market economy brought both the need and opportunities for additional jobs. Weekend travel and short breaks, in particular, were sacrificed to accommodate these social changes (Table 7.2). At the same time, there was a generalized attempt to compensate for reduced weekend leisure time after 1989 by taking at least one longer holiday per year. Hence the apparent contradiction was a logical response to changing economic circumstances.

7.2.3 Social cleavages in tourism consumption in the transformation

Income is only one of the many bases of social differentiation in access to tourism, but it does have a key role. It is, therefore, useful to consider in more detail the changes in the origin and social distribution of incomes. In Slovakia in 1989, the broad composition of income was as follows: salaries accounted for 56.9 per cent; agricultural sales for 8.6 per cent; social income for 20.5 per cent; loans, deposits and insurance for 6.3 per cent; and other sources of income (from abroad and from entrepreneurial activities for 7.7 per cent. By 1993 there had been major changes in the structure of incomes: the share of salaries had fallen to 44.6 per cent, and that of agricultural sales to 2.7 percent. The shares of social income (19.0 per cent) and of loans, deposits and insurance (6.6 per cent) were broadly the same. However, the share of 'other sources' had risen to 26.4 per cent. This is underpinned by the lifestyle changes already referred to: from secure and regular income, generated via employment or social transfers, to more dynamic income generation in the private sector or in jobs abroad. Not all social groups had equal access to alternative income sources, so income differences widened markedly. In 1989 the lowest income decile accounted for 4.6 per cent and the highest decile for 18.6 per cent of total net monetary income. By 1993, these shares were 4.6 percent and 21.3 percent. The highest income decile received 21 per cent of a nominal income of Sk 18.9 billion in the years 1985–1989, but for 25 percent of Sk 75.5 billion in the period 1989–93 (Pekník 1995).

The data presented above understate the extent of social polarization.

The real social differences would be even greater if the distribution of wealth generated via privatization was taken into account. Few members of the new elite generated their wealth via creative privatization; instead, most were beneficiaries of direct distributive privatization sales or were the managers of investment privatization funds. These income changes divided society into two groups: those who could travel (on holiday) or had to travel (on business), and those who could not travel because of financial constraints. Whereas surveys of family spending (Machonin 1994, p 341), showed that 61 per cent of families believed that they had sufficient money for a holiday in 1989, only 9 per cent stated this in 1993. Financial difficulties also remained important constraints on holidays in the latter stage of the transformation, even though the incomes of many families improved. In 1996, for example, amongst Slovaks not taking a holiday, the main reasons for this were financial (71 per cent), health (27 per cent), family problems (20 per cent), and work ties (11 per cent) (ÚVVM 1996). In this respect, there are at least superficial similarities between Slovakia in the 1990s and Portugal and Greece in the 1980s.

Changes in disposable income in Slovakia and the Czech Republic between 1989 and 1996 (Figure 7.1) show that employees and farmers experienced larger absolute losses that pensioners. However, despite these sharp relative declines, the absolute levels of disposable income of the former were still sufficient to enable participation in some forms of tourism. In contrast, the smaller relative decline in pensioner incomes had a more severe effect, bringing most of them close to the poverty line, so that their tourism expenditures fell off sharply (compare Figure 7.1 and Table 7.3). Changes in real income, together with changes in working practices and life styles, therefore had a profound impact on tourist behaviour in Slovakia and the Czech Republic during the transformation. However, the decline in real incomes was less in the Czech Republic than in Slovakia (Williams and Baláž 1999) and this is reflected in domestic tourism. There is a lack of detailed statistics on domestic tourism in the Czech Republic after 1989, but there are broad indications that the numbers of domestic overnights decreased less than in Slovakia in 1990–3. Moreover, after 1993 Czech real incomes and domestic tourism overnights grew more rapidly than in Slovakia.

Not all the increase in disposable income after 1994 was channelled into domestic tourism. Instead, improved economic conditions after 1994 were reflected in higher levels of expenditure on foreign tourism. In Slovakia, the average nominal expenditure per holiday increased from Sk 2,000 in 1993 to Sk 2,750 in 1996 for domestic holidays and from Sk 6,500 to Sk 9,900 for holidays abroad. In real terms, expenditure on domestic holidays decreased while that on holidays abroad increased. The highest income groups, managers and entrepreneurs in particular, demanded higher quality services and had the disposable income to purchase these.

TABLE 7.3 *Tourism expenditures of employee and pensioner households: Slovakia in 1992 and 1996, and the Czech Republic in 1993 and 1996*

		Slovakia			
		1992		1996	
		Employees	Pensioners	Employees	Pensioners
Total tourism expenditure, of which:	Sk	538	101	1060	160
tourism accommodation	%	6.1	0.3	6.1	3.8
domestic tourism	%	35.1	35.2	29.5	37.5
international tourism	%	58.7	64.5	64.3	58.8
Share of tourism expenditure in total net income	%	1.6	0.3	2.0	0.3
		The Czech Republic			
		1993		1996	
		Employees	Pensioners	Employees	Pensioners
Total tourisim expenditure	Kč	1,018	251	2,144	617
Share of tourism expenditure in total net income	%	2.0	0.7	2.7	1.1

Source: Štatistický úrad Slovenskej republiky: (1993–1998a):; Český statistický úřad (1993–1998a).

Notes: total income and expenditure are in Sk and Kč, per capita per household per year in current market prices; the expenditure on domestic and international tourism only includes package tours; the costs of meals and travel for individual trips were not taken into account; the exchange rate was approximately 1 Kč = 1.1 Sk in 1993–6.

There were changes in the structure of tourism expenditure in the transformation, but there are also elements of continuity. There were relative increases in international tourism expenditure, due to the rising prices of, and increased demand for, higher quality holidays. The low shares of domestic tourism expenditure reflected not only a decline in this sector but also the low prices for such services in Slovakia. Tourism expenditure in the Czech Republic has traditionally been higher than in Slovakia, and by 1996 this was a third higher, expressed as a proportion of the total expenditure of families in work (as employees). This can only partly be explained by the higher real incomes of Czech households during the transformation; there is also a need to take into account differences in life styles and cultural values. While 40 years of state-socialism, industrialization and central planing had erased most real income and educational differentials (Figure 7.1), Slovaks retained more conservative (rural in origin) values, had a greater commitment to investing in family homes, and participated less in foreign travel. To some extent this is related to the more recent urbanization of Slovakia: even in 1993, 69.6 per cent of the Czech population lived in urban areas, compared to only 57.2 per cent in Slovakia (National Statistical Offices of the V4 countries, CESTAT 1995). In the Czech Republic, the new generation of entrepreneurs was particularly interested in leisure travel, which accounted for a significant part of their expenditures. While the average, recorded nominal per capita incomes were less for the self-employed than for employees, the shares of travel in their total expenditure were, respectively, 5.0 and 2.7 per cent in 1996–7 (compare Figure 7.1 and Table 7.3).

Another perspective on changing social access to tourism is provided by Table 7.2, which compares Czechoslovakia in 1987 to Slovakia in 1996. These data have to be approached cautiously, not only because of changes in the territorial bases, but also because slightly different questions were asked in each survey. Several trends, however, can be identified:

- There were substantial increases in youth and young adult tourism, following the liberalization of border controls. Their trips were multi-purpose, usually combining leisure, exploration and work. Changing work practices, new economic openings, and life-style shifts brought new opportunities which young people, in particular, were able to exploit. In contrast, the tourism activities of older people tended to become more constrained, as a result of depressed living standards and limited access to cheap holidays.
- The basic social cleavages in tourism participation in both state-socialist Czechoslovakia and Slovakia in the transformation were broadly similar to those in Western countries. A higher propensity to travel was observed in the younger and middle age groups, those with higher education, and urban residents.
- The overall tourism participation rate decreased during the transformation, but with differential impacts on social groups and types of tourism. The main decline was in short breaks and, as explained earlier, this was due to life-style changes and growing income inequalities. The self-employed had few free weekends while many employees also gave up their leisure time to additional jobs, or to working in their homes and gardens. Table 7.4 summarizes holiday preferences in Slovakia in 1992–6, and shows the importance of various types of 'working holidays'.
- There was a positive relationship between education and tourism participation rates. The reasons for this are related to the differences in travel opportunities available in relation to income and unemployment.
- The decrease in travel propensity was relatively greater for those living in smaller towns. This was probably due to the more limited range of jobs (and income) in such communities.

Table 7.4   *The use of holiday time in Slovakia, 1992–6*

	1992	1993	1994	1995	1996
Working in home and garden	59.5	69.8	50.1	45.1	45.4
Working for relatives	35.9	44.9	36.4	30.2	31.2
Working for additional income	13.6	12.6	11.8	10.8	11.9
Working as a hobby	23.5	27.3	20.3	19.1	21.8
Recreation in home town	61.3	51.4	42.3	37.1	35.6
Recreation away from home town	52.7	48.8	40.3	34.8	37.4
Improving health	x	17.1	12.1	12.0	12.9
Others	9.6	14.3	7.0	5.0	6.1

Sources: Ústav turizmu (1995–1998).
Notes: Holidays were defined as constituting four or more paid non-working days; multiple responses were permited.

The evolution of different types of tourism (by duration) in Slovakia can be traced on an annual basis through the participation rates for 1992–7 (Figure 7.2); these data include both domestic and foreign trips. There was a 10 per cent decrease in the proportion of the population participating in one-day trips, and most of these trips were for visiting friends and relatives, shopping, and outdoor activities. Comparable data are not available before 1989, but decreasing numbers of domestic tourists in the mountains and artificial lake areas indicate the activities that experienced the major losses. There was also a 25 per cent decline in the share of the population taking short breaks of two and three days. Table 7.2 indicates that the main losers in respect of short breaks were the less-educated, older people and those living in small towns and villages, all of whom tend to have lower incomes. According to the 1996 survey, entrepreneurs and the highest income groups made 8.9 and managers made 7.3 short breaks per year, while the lowest income groups made only 1.2 such trips and pensioners only 1.5. This was the tourism sector that changed most in the transformation.

Changes in the shares of the population taking longer holidays (four or more days) present a different picture. In 1996 the total number of holidays taken by Slovaks was lower than in 1987, but the proportion who had a long holiday increased. In other words, the distribution of holidays across the population became more equitable. Participation in longer holidays declined in the early stages of the transformation, but there were no further significant decreases after 1992. The lowest participation rate occurred slightly later, being 35.8 per cent in 1994. This was a turning point in the Slovakian economy as several years of economic recession were followed by a period of growth. The participation rates in tourism closely followed the trend in disposable income and, by 1996, had increased to 44.4 per cent. This is nominally two times greater than in 1989, but the difference is partly due to methodological differences between the two surveys (see the notes in Table 7.2).

There have been a number of structural shifts within the overall trends in longer holidays. The younger age groups, living in the larger cities, with higher and university education, were the main 'winners' in the new holiday market after 1989. The 1996 average participation rate (44.4 per cent) was unequally distributed; on the one hand, managers had 90.3 per cent and entrepreneurs had 70.6 per cent participation rates, while the rates for workers and pensioners were only 40.6 and 22.9 per cent. These social class differences were similar to, but much greater, than those identified by surveys in the state-socialism period (Malá 1985). Expressed differently, 73.5 per cent of the highest income group enjoyed a longer holiday, compared to only 19 per cent of the lowest income group. In 1974, in contrast, the holiday-participation rate ranged from 46.2 per cent for the highest to 12.8 per cent for the lowest income group. Widening social inequalities during the transition were also reflected in holiday destinations; in 1996, holidays abroad were taken by 58.1 per cent of managers and 50.0 per cent of entrepreneurs, but only by 15.5 per cent of workers and 9.2 per cent of pensioners.

In 1987 there were no significant differences between the participation of Czechs and Slovaks in short breaks. However, Czechs were more likely to take longer holidays, and there was a 20-percentage-point gap between the two nationalities in this respect. The gap was related to differences in the overall level and form of economic and social development in the Czech and Slovak (Socialist) Republics. After forty years of communism and central planning, many of these economic and social contrasts had been erased.

Unfortunately, there are no detailed data available on travel intensity in the Czech population after 1989 which allow comparison with Slovakia. However, it is possible to compare the total numbers of Czech and Slovaks travelling abroad. In 1997, some 46.1 million Czechs and 22.1 million Slovaks travelled abroad for at least one day. On average, 4.5 trips abroad were made by each Czech and 4.1 trips by each Slovak. These data provide some evidence of converging travel patterns in the two countries. Most trips abroad, of course, were concerned with business and shopping and were socially selective in both countries.

7.2.4 The changing face of domestic tourism; convergence with the Western European model?

Two key questions are whether the profile of Czech and Slovak holiday-makers in the state-socialist period was different from those of Western European countries, and whether the transformation led to convergence or divergence of these profiles? Comparisons between the profiles of holiday-makers in the EU and the Czech and Slovak Republics (Table 7.2) have to be approached cautiously, because of differences in their research methodologies. However, some trends can be identified.

1) The propensity for taking longer holidays in the EU in 1985 was far greater than in Czechoslovakia in 1987 (20.2 per cent for Slovaks, 40.2 for Czechs and 56.0 for EU nationals). During transformation, the overall propensity for taking holidays increased in Slovakia to 44.4 per cent and the gap with the EU has narrowed.

2) Convergence in holiday-taking propensity was greatest for the younger age groups. On the other hand, the gap between retired people in Slovakia and the EU widened. As argued previously, this was due to the better adaptation of the younger generation to changing life styles after 1989, and their better access to complementary income sources.

3) In terms of settlement size, the convergence between the EU and Slovakia was most evident in respect of the larger towns and cities. The general holiday propensity increased for all settlement sizes in Slovakia while the relative differences between villages and larger towns were little altered during the transformation.

Another issue concerns the comparisons between Czech and Slovak families, and those in the EU, in respect of tourist expenditure. How do expenditures compare to the more (Netherlands, Denmark, France, for example) and less-developed (Greece and Spain) European countries? There were several differences in the Czech and Slovak Republics (Figures 7.3 and 7.4):

1) The average Slovak family spends very little on commercial tourist accommodation (0.12 per cent of total income compared to 1.63 per cent in Germany). Slovaks spend less on commercial accommodation than either the Greeks (0.51 per cent) or the Irish (0.28 per cent) This confirms the pattern of accommodation use, discussed earlier. Only 18.8 per cent of Slovak tourists used commercial facilities in 1996. On the other hand, the relative share of expenditure on package trips was surprisingly high (1.88 per cent) and was greater than in France (0.53). Germany (1.13) and Italy (0.48). This may be because the fixed costs in international travel packages (for flights, and accommodation abroad) make such packages relatively expensive in Slovakia compared to higher-incomes countries.

2) The pattern of tourism spending in the Czech and Slovak Republics is far more sharply differentiated that in the EU. While the change from working life to retirement did not greatly affect tourism spending in the EU (in France, for example, total tourism expenditure was higher for pensioner families than for working families), this constituted a tourism watershed in the Czech and Slovak Republics. Tourism expenditure decreased 40 and 15 per cent, respectively, compared to

213

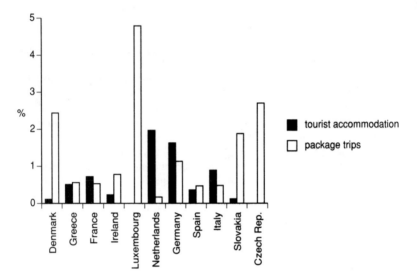

Fig. 7.3 Expenditure on tourism as a percentage of total non-manual employees'
family expenditure.
Sources: Eurostat (1992) and Štatistický úrad Slovenskej republiky (1993–1998a).
Notes: The data for EU countries are for 1988, and 1996 for the Czech and
Slovak Republics; for the Czech Republic the total expenditure is stated.

those in work. Many pensioner families lived close to the poverty line
and had little surplus income after meeting their basic needs.

Next we turn to the question of income elasticities in the state-socialist and
transformation periods. Was there convergence or divergence within the
market economies? Crouch and Shaw's (1992) review of international evidence found that, on average, a 1 per cent change in income results in a 1.76
per cent change in tourism demand. The real income of Slovak households
rose by 41.4 during 1975–88 whilst, in the same period, total real expenditure on tourism rose by 99.1 per cent; in this instance, a 1 per cent change
in income resulted in a 2.41 per cent change in tourist expenditure. The
high rate of increase may be due to the relatively low tourism participation
rates in 1975. In the period 1989–93, real income decreased by 26.2 percent,
while real expenditure on tourism fell by 67.3 per cent. A one per cent
decrease in real income caused a 2.83 per cent decrease in real tourist
expenditure. This sharp reverse in tourism spending is clearly visible after
1989 (Figure 7.5). Total tourism expenditure was not computed by the
Slovak Statistical Office after 1993 but, as indicated by family budget statistics, this started to growth again after 1993, as real incomes improved.

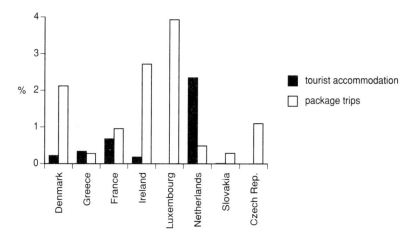

Fig. 7.4 Expenditure on tourism as a percentage of total pensioners' family expenditure.
Sources: Eurostat (1992) and Štatistický úrad Slovenskej republiky (1993–1998a).
Notes: the data for the EU is for 1988, and for the Czech and Slovak Republics 1996; for the Czech Republic the total expenditure is stated.

The income/expenditure elasticity in 1989–93 was even greater than in the period of expansion before 1989. However, there was an exceptional decline in tourism expenditure 1988–9, perhaps due to a one-off adjustment in tourist behaviour, as consumer expectations adjusted to new economic conditions. If this particular year is excluded, and the income elasticity of demand is calculated for 1990–93, a figure of 1.64 is obtained. The latter figure is similar to the estimates provided by Crouch and Shaw for the advanced market economies. In this case it could be argued that there is evidence of a convergence of income/expenditure patterns in the transition economies and the developed market economies.

In passing, we can note that the elasticity of tourism expenditure in response to changes in living standards was similar in all the transformation countries of Central Europe. The numbers of nights spent by the domestic tourists, for example, decreased from 11.4 to 5.9 million in Hungary, from 81.8 million to 39.6 million in Poland, from 17.2 to 6.9 million in the Czech Republic and from 10.3 to 3.0 million in Slovakia in 1989–1992 (WTO 1994), that is to approximately 30–50 per cent of their 1989 levels.

7.2.5 Social and national differences in the use of leisure time

While there have been relatively limited changes in travel motivations (see Chapter 7.3.1), there were more significant changes in the use made of

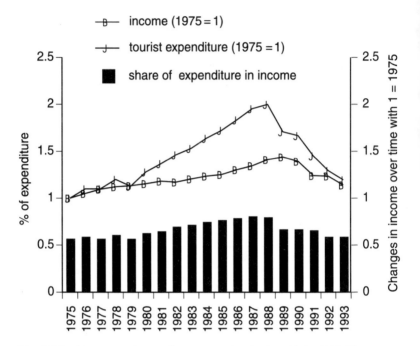

Fig. 7.5 Real income and expenditure on tourism in Slovakia in 1975–93.
Sources: Federální statistický úřad (1986–1993); Štatistický úrad Slovenskej republiky (1994–1998a).

free time. The economic transformation was accompanied by major social changes, and 1989 marked the end of the era of cheap holidays for all. Society became far more sharply divided into 'haves' and 'have nots'. This division was reflected, for example, in the types of accommodation used by domestic tourists.

In 1987, there were no significant differences in the accommodation used by Czech and Slovak tourists, except for second homes: 15.9 per cent of Czechs owned a second home and 15.0 per cent used a second home owned by family or friends, while the corresponding shares for Slovaks were 6.6 and 9.6 per cent (Table 7.5). Lower rates of second-home ownership in Slovakia were balanced by higher shares of nights spent with friends and relatives, and in rented houses. Both nations were typically highly reliant on informal tourist accommodation. The nights spent at friends and relatives, and in second homes, accounted for almost one half of total overnights. If non-business tourism facilities (spas, trade unions and enterprise hotels) are taken into account, the share of non-commercial tourism accommoda-

TABLE 7.5 *Types of accommodation used by domestic tourists in 1987 and 1996 (percentages)*

	1987		1996
	Czechs	Slovaks	Slovaks
Domestic tourism			
Hotels	15.0	10.8	10.6
Camping and hostel	8.2	8.0	12.1
Tourism units of non-tourism bodies	9.2	11.1	16.1
Trade unions and similar bodies	9.0	10.6	n.a.
Spas	1.6	3.3	n.a.
Rented houses and bed/breakfast	4.5	7.5	20.3
Second homes	20.6	14.2	9.1
Visiting friends and relatives	26.9	31.1	23.4
Others	5.0	3.3	8.3
Total	100.0	100.0	100.0
Tourism abroad			
Hotel	62.8	79.4	22.6
Camping	37.2	20.6	10.1
Others	n.a.	n.a.	77.4
Total	100.0	100.0	100.0

Sources: Výzkumní ústav obchodu (1988); Ústav turizmu (1995–1998).
Notes: n.a. = not available; in 1987 the question asked was: are you travelling on holiday each year?, but by 1996 this had become: were you travelling on holiday in 1996?.

tion was 66.7 per cent in the Czech Republic and 70.3 per cent in Slovakia.

Were there any significant changes in the types of accommodation used by domestic tourists after 1989? Again, any comparison must be qualified because slightly different accommodation categories were used in the 1989 and 1996 surveys (see the notes to Table 7.5).

In Slovakia, the following trends can be noted:

- There was a major increase in the nights spent in commercial tourism facilities, hotels, camping and rented houses, which is hardly surprising given the pace of privatization in tourism (see Chapter 4). This is compounded by the fact that, in the 1996 survey, the facilities of trade-unions and similar establishments were not included separately but instead were classified as 'hotels': this is not only a matter of reclassification, but also reflects a trend for many of these to operate, at least partly, as commercial hotels.

- While the share of all nights spent in second homes decreased, the share of nights spent in rented houses increased. These two developments were closely connected. In response to economic recession in the early 1990s, and later to the reduced leisure time available to the self-employed and those with multiple jobs, many Slovaks either sold their second homes or rented them commercially.

• The recorded increases in the nights spent in commercial tourism facilities and decreases in the nights spent in informal (non-payment) accommodation seem puzzling at first sight, given the economic difficulties of the transformation. However, both surveys covered only that part of population which did travel, and the proportion of the population participating in tourism in 1996 was lower than in 1987. In the state-socialist period, many lower income tourists had been accustomed to staying free of charge in non-commercial accommodation and/or visited friends and relatives. The transition was characterized by social polarization: the poorer segments of society travelled less, while those with higher incomes were still able pay for hotels and rented houses. There was also a middle-income group, which was not excluded from holiday-making, but was unable to pay hotel prices, and this partly accounts for the increased market shares of camping and hostels.

• Holidays and short trips spent in employer-owned facilities still accounted for a major part of all the nights spent in domestic tourism. Most of the tourism units of non-tourism enterprises were transformed into commercial establishments. However, many employers continued to provide cheap holiday for their employees, and these facilities offered substantial discounts. This remained a popular option, especially in the face of economic recession and the share of total nights spent in such facilities increased by 5 per cent compared to 1987.

• The new political and economic situation after 1989 enhanced travel abroad. In 1996, 20.7 per cent of all Slovak holidays were spent abroad. Short breaks were even more likely to be taken abroad (41.1 per cent), as were day trips (23.3 per cent).

In summary, the holiday preferences of different social groups in Slovakia had become more sharply differentiated by 1996. Seaside holidays and mountain holidays were particularly favoured by entrepreneurs, managers, younger people, those with higher levels of income and education, and urban residents. In contrast, health, and spa holidays were favoured more by those with less education and middle income groups, and pensioners. The above preferences did not reflect the actual holidays taken. In reality, free time outside of the principal employment was often devoted to various kinds of work (Table 7.4).

7.3 CHANGING PATTERNS OF DOMESTIC TOURIST PREFERENCES

7.3.1 Interests and motivations

Surveys of domestic tourists' travel preferences were restored in Slovakia in 1994 by the Tourism Institute (Ústav turizmu 1995–1998). The data for

TABLE 7.6   *Slovak tourists' preferences for main holidays in 1996 (percentages)*

Shorter visists	Domestic trips		Trips abroad	
	Day trips	Short breaks	Day trips	Short breaks
Vising friends and relatives	23.0	31.0	14.9	23.3
Shopping	13.2	4.1	40.6	13.2
Arranging personal affairs	13.0	7.8	5.2	6.7
Outdoor trips	10.2	9.7	4.2	6.1
Business trips	9.0	9.4	11.8	18.8
Visiting cultural events	4.6	4.0	5.5	4.9
Pilgrimage	4.3	2.6	1.6	1.3
Discovery travel	4.3	5.7	7.1	9.9
Working trips	4.3	6.7	1.8	2.0
Education	3.6	4.4	1.9	3.4
Visiting sporting events	3.3	1.4	2.2	3.4
Sporting (skiing)	3.2	6.6	2.3	3.8
Stays at own second home	2.3	4.4	0.3	0.3
Participation in sporting competitions	1.7	2.2	0.8	2.9

Holidays	Domestic	Abroad
Mountain tourism	31.6	9.3
Seaside holidays	x	42.6
Water-based tourism	21.6	8.4
Visiting friends and relatives	12.3	14.2
Country tourism	12.3	x
Spa tourism	10.0	1.1
Combined trips	4.4	7.8
City tourism	1.9	6.7
Circular trips	0.9	6.4
Others	4.8	3.5

Source: Ústav turizmu (1995–1998).
Notes: short breaks = 2 and 3 days; holidays = 4+ day stays (excludes holidays at home); the question asked was: how did you spend your main holiday? Only a single response was permitted to this question.

the mid-1990s do not indicate any significant changes in tourist preferences. In terms of short breaks, shopping was the main motive for day trips in 1996 (Table 7.6). Poland accounted for most of this travel, because of price differences for selected consumer goods (textiles, shoes, furniture, etc). The share of shopping trips was constant between 1994 and 1996. Day shopping trips to Poland were also popular amongst Czech tourists. In passing, we can also note that Poland was a pole of attraction for German tourists, whose shopping expenditure whilst on one-day trips accounted for one half of total Polish income from international tourism in 1995 (Polish Central Statistical Office 1995). As for short breaks abroad, VFR-related travel, business travel and shopping were the strongest motives for travel. These were also the dominant motivations for such trips in the Central and Eastern European countries. For example, Poles stated that business (28.8 per cent), shopping (24.3 per cent) and VFR (14.2 per cent) were the main motives for their travel in 1994 (Simonian 1995b). Recreation and discovery travel were less important.

In the domestic short-breaks market in Slovakia, VFR, shopping, business and 'arranging one's personal affairs' were the main motivations. In the leisure activity travel segment, mountain trips were a major interest. Business trips have become relatively less importance since 1994, but still accounted for 6.7 per cent of short breaks in 1996. Turning to the domestic longer holiday segment, the Slovak mountains and artificial lakes were the preferences of 50 per cent of holiday-makers in 1996. This share has fallen slightly since 1994, but still dominates the domestic market. The average length of domestic holidays was 9 days in 1996.

7.3.2. Destination preferences

Seaside resorts were the preferred destinations of those holidaying abroad. The liberalization of international travel after 1989 generated a new pattern of holiday destinations. While Hungary, Bulgaria, Romania and the Soviet Union had been the principal destinations during the state-socialist period, they were replaced by the Mediterranean after 1989. Slovak tourists travelled mainly to Italy (13.6 per cent), Spain (9.9 per cent) and Croatia (8.7 per cent). The Czech Republic (15.4 per cent) and Hungary (11.3 per cent) were also important destinations, with VFR being the main motivation for travel to these countries in 1996. In addition to seaside and water-related tourism, the Alps and major European cities were popular with Slovak tourists. Mediterranean coastal resorts were also the most popular destination amongst Czech tourists. In 1996, 1.5 million package trips abroad were sold by Czech travel agents: Italy, with 394,000 trips, accounted for the largest share of these, followed by Croatia (271,000), Spain (184,000) and Greece (148,000). The average length of trip was 7.3 days (TTG monthly, May 1997).

There was, however, a gap between preferences and reality amongst Slovak tourists. The proportion wishing to spend their holiday in the Mediterranean increased between 1992 and 1996, while Austria, Germany and the USA became less popular. In practice, the shares of holiday-makers going to Italy, Spain and Greece decreased in the same period. The Czech Republic, Austria and Hungary were the real winners in the Slovak market. Proximity and lower travel costs were probably the decisive factors. As for domestic holidays, Slovak preferences were stable, with the High and Low Tatras, the Váh River Valley, the Danube region and the Zemplín region being popular in the mid-1990s.

Slovaks were less comfortable about organising their holidays individually, and tended to use travel agents for holidays abroad (62.3 per cent) although not for domestic holidays (8.8 per cent). Interestingly, a smaller proportion (54.3 per cent) had used travel agencies for their foreign trips in 1994, which suggests that less accessible and less familiar destinations were being visited two years later, as foreign holidays became increasingly diverse and sophisticated.

7.4 CONCLUSIONS: NEW OR OLD PATHWAYS IN DOMESTIC TOURISM?

Forty years of central planning erased most of the social differences between the Czech and Slovak nations. This convergence was reflected in increasingly similar patterns of tourism spending and participation. Most of the convergence occurred in the 1970s and 1980s, as part of the strategy to legitimize a tough political regime through improvements in consumption. The improved access to tourism was provided through networks of non-commercial facilities, whose services were provided at very low prices. Except for differentiation related to education, access to leisure was relatively well-distributed amongst the various social groups. Despite this convergence, there were persistent differences between Czechs and Slovaks, originating in the pre-1948 legacies of the two nations. Slovak society was more rural and more traditional, while Czechs were more urbanized and more inclined to international travel. These social and behavioural differences were reflected in Slovaks lagging behind the Czechs in their spending on travel (in the period 1950–80 in particular) and in their choice of holiday destinations. There were real improvements in living standards especially in Slovakia, including the consumption of tourism services and this is one reason why Slovaks have been more cautious than Czechs about the benefits of the transformation.

The economic and social transformation generated major changes in domestic tourism. Relatively equitable access to holiday opportunities was replaced by increasingly market-determined social access to tourism and other ways of using free time. While most of the data presented here on domestic tourist behaviour referred only to Slovakia, there are good reasons to assume that there were broadly similar developments in the Czech Republic. The following trends were noted:

- The lowering of the Iron Curtain initiated a new era of outbound travel. The numbers of outbound travellers from the Czech and Slovak Republics increased eight-fold between 1989 and 1997. Limited disposable incomes and the specific economic environments in the transformation economies shaped their travel: most trips abroad were one-day excursions related to shopping and VFR, and short visits to cities.

221

As for longer holidays abroad, Mediterranean coastal resorts replaced the Black Sea coasts in the holiday preferences of Czechs and Slovaks.

- Falling living standard, 1989–93, sharply reduced domestic travel and tourism spending, but there was a partial recovery after 1993. This trend was stronger in the Czech Republic, where disposable incomes were higher than in Slovakia. There were also some differences between the travel habits of Czechs and Slovaks. Most of these disappeared during the state-socialist period, but others persisted. The fact that Czech pensioners spent 1.1 per cent of their disposable income on package trips and Slovak pensioners only 0.3 per cent in 1996, was due not only to income differentials but also to differences in tourism practices.

- In Slovakia, a widespread decline in living standards caused a major decrease in short breaks, particularly amongst elderly people, lower income groups and small towns residents. The total number of short breaks, however, increased, due to the expansion of business travel by managers and entrepreneurs.

- The changing distribution of short breaks in Slovakia was also related to life-style changes, with nominally 'free time' increasingly being spent on formal or informal work. The younger generation had access to additional income sources and new opportunities for expenditure, so that their travel increased considerably. This contributed to an absolute increase in the total number of short breaks, despite the lower numbers of participants. As for holidays (four or more days), after a strong decrease in 1992–3, the market revived. Higher income groups, in particular, preferred longer holidays (usually spent abroad) to short breaks.

Finally we argue that there has been more continuity than change in many aspects of tourism in the former Czechoslovakia. The emergence of new forms of tourism in the 1990s does not represent the simple victory of the market over collective provision. Instead, in common with other aspects of the transformation, the resulting social practices are a bricolage. Privatization has produced complex forms of ownership which coexist with both restructured and unrestructured forms of collective provision. This provides opportunities for new forms of tourism behaviour to coexist alongside a collective safety net of minimal provision for at least some of the poor. In the same way, informal provision by friends and families also represents both preferences and accommodation of the last resort; it also represents a strong element of continuity in tourism practices from the state-socialist period. Therefore, domestic tourism provides confirmation of Stark's (1996, p 995) contention that transformation involves '. . . rebuilding organizations and institutions not on the ruins but with the ruins of communism'.

8 CONCLUSIONS

8.1 REFLECTIONS ON TOURISM IN TRANSITION

This book has examined a number of aspects of tourism in the two transition economies of Slovakia and the Czech Republic. They are of particular interest as case studies because the former Czechoslovakia had the most rigid model of state-socialism in Central Europe. Moreover, the 'velvet divorce' that created the two independent Republics in 1993 provides the opportunity to trace the different evolutions of territories which had previously been subject to economic and political convergence tendencies as part of a single unified state system. These are also reasons why it is not possible to generalize from these two countries to the rest of Central Europe, let alone the rest of Eastern Europe (Hall 1995). There are differences compared to Hungary and Poland in the role of foreign investment, the nature of privatization, and the intensity and direction of international tourism flows, as well as in the overall context of the economic transformations.

The attraction of the path-dependency versus path-creation debate is that it alerts us to these differences in terms of the way that there are 'institutionalized forms of learning and struggles over pathways that emerge out of the intersection of old and new' (Smith and Pickles 1998, p 15). These institutionalized forms of learning have differed within Central Europe, both because of contrasting legacies from the period of state-socialism and also in the way that these differences were used and transformed after 1989 by particular interest groups within these societies. They help guard against the fallacy that the transition could be dictated by a neo-liberal blueprint (Gowan 1995; Stark 1994). This is explicitly recognized in the 'path-dependent path-creating' perspective advocated by Nielsen *et al* (1995, p 6), which focuses on the interaction between

223

deterministic and voluntaristic elements in institution building. While broadly in sympathy with the latter, we have argued elsewhere that this tends to a static view, and does not allow for the shifting balance between new and old pathways in the course of transition (Williams and Baláž 1999). This is particularly evident in the contrast between the periods before and after 1993, not only in that deep recession was replaced by gradual economic recovery, but also by the changes which followed the 'velvet divorce'.

The path-dependency path-creation perspective, by its very nature, does not provide a detailed guide to unravelling, let alone predicting, the ways in which old and new pathways intersect in the course of transition. Instead, there is no substitute for detailed analysis of particular territories and sectors of activities. There is of course a growing body of such studies but they have mainly been concerned with manufacturing or with the financial services (Williams and Baláž 1999). In contrast, consumer services have received little attention, although their role in bazaar capitalism has been recognized (see Smith 1997b). In this volume we have sought to unravel some of the complex changes involved in the uneven transformation from a strongly collectivist and partially closed (internationally) model of tourism to one increasingly shaped by market relationships and integration into an expanding global system of tourism. The main dimensions of change have centred on the role of the state, re-internationalization, privatization, consumption and uneven territorial development. These are strongly interrelated, both directly and through their insertion into broader processes of societal transformation.

8.2 TOURISM AND THE STATE: STRATEGIC SECTOR OR POLICY NEGLECT

The priority given to tourism by the state actually seemed to decline in the transition, especially in the first period. The Czechoslovakian government, and its successors, adopted broadly liberal tourism policies and allowed market forces to take the lead in the transformation of tourism. The pole position of tourism in privatization meant that most tourism establishments were transferred to private ownership. Other than the enabling legislation for privatization, there was little pro-active state intervention. There were few state funded development projects and, except for some relatively small scale programmes of subsidized loans, there were no significant changes in either the legislative or financial framework within which the newly privatized firms operated. In effect, there was a near institutional vacuum, and an incomplete shift to a market economy. This was no accident, for it was precisely this institutional opaqueness which allowed political capitalism (Staniszkis 1991) and all forms of corruption to flourish. State intervention was, at best, reactive. For example, the Czech Tourism Law was prepared as a reaction to the failure of a number of major travel agents who stranded large numbers of Czech tourists abroad. In Slovakia, the Tourism Law only attracted the attention of the state when the need to converge with EU practices of consumer protection became pressing.

Tourism also suffered from the weakness of the local state. Since 1990, there has been no legislative or regulatory framework for local and regional tourism development. While tourist associations were established in both republics, they lacked the active participation of local and regional governments. In other words, there was the antipathy of the associational economies (Cooke and Morgan 1998) and the learning regions (Malmberg and Maskell 1999) which have been extolled as models of economic development elsewhere in Western Europe.

The effective withdrawal of the state from the regulation of the tourism industry presents a clear example of the intersection of old and new pathways. On the one hand, it reflects the ideological legacy which prioritized material production and attached to tourism the role of supporting the reproduction of the labour force. On the other hand, it also reflects the neo-liberal economic policies of the transition which militated against the prioritization of particular sectors of the economy. These created the conditions under which the owners of some small and large privatized tourism firms could use the institutional vacuum to exploit the resources of their enterprises for purely short-term and, often, semi-legal or even illegal ends. Such a situation was not, of course, tenable other than in the very short term. In the second half of the transition, the state did begin to impose new forms of regulation on the tourism sector, and the emerging strategies for the sector paid at least lip-service to social and environmental considerations. Moreover, the stark stabilization policies of the first part of the transition period also began to provide a more favourable climate for economic expansion in the economy as a whole in the mid-1990s. This reinforces the need to analyse the dynamic nature of processes in the transition.

8.3 RE-INTERNATIONALIZATION: GLOBAL COMPETITION AND SPATIAL PROXIMITY

A distinctive and relatively closed model of international tourism had been created in Central Europe under state-socialism. National rather than international provision was prioritized, and the latter was structured around limited flows to politically 'friendly countries' especially to Hungary, and to the Black Sea region. This model was no longer viable after the liberalization of passport and visa controls. Instead, international tourism flows began to be redirected towards Western Europe, and there was strong growth in both incoming and outbound tourism.

The re-internationalization was shaped by broader economic conditions. At one level, the opening of borders did not lead to massive flows of long stay outbound international tourism; quite simply, the gap in wages and prices between Central and Western Europe precluded such tourism for all but a minority. However, uneven economic development also created the conditions for other types of international mobility, especially in terms of business, trade and retail flows. The most significant growth was in business tourism and visiting friends and relatives. The latter was stimulated by the desire to renew long-disrupted family and friendships ties, and by the 'velvet divorce' which transformed what had previously been intra-national into international flows. Trade and retail tourism was stimulated, at least in the initial phase, by shortages in the production and distribution of goods, and latterly by persistent price differentials. Indeed, international travel played a significant role in the growth and functioning of the informal sector. In this respect, the intensity and the direction of trans-border flows was a barometer of changes in the broader economic transition. Business tourism was promoted by changes not only in markets, as Western Europe was opened up, but also by fundamental changes in business practices. In contrast to central planning, international travel is intrinsic to what are increasingly globalised market economies.

There was also the growth of outbound holiday tourism. The lowering of barriers to international travel was followed by an understandable flush of informally organized curiosity travel to destinations such as Paris. However, international holiday tourism has subsequently been reorganized along lines which are similar to those in many Western European countries. Individual travel, especially using accommodation provided by friends and family, co-exists with an increasingly formalized and regulated inclusive holiday market; the latter has been facilitated by the arrival of international travel agencies, which now hold key positions in both the Slovak and the Czech markets. Access to such holidays is, however, socially constrained. The vast majority of the population can afford no more than day excursions or short tourist visits to neighbouring countries. However, the emerging middle class, and many of the self-employed, are able and choose to purchase foreign package holidays. While their overall preference is for the Mediterranean region, their choice of particular destinations is largely shaped by price considerations. Finally, a small elite group – mainly the new rich in the privatization process – are joining their Western counterparts in a genuinely global search for exotic and 'different' tourist destinations.

The two countries have also become destinations for international tourism, benefiting not only from 'the attraction of the new' but also from more general shifts in tourism consumption which have favoured more individualized holidays, and prime natural and cultural sites. The Czech Republic, and especially Prague, has been particularly successful, attracting more tourists than either Italy or the UK. The majority, however, have been on relatively short visits characterized by low spending. This reflects the fact that the vast majority of their tourists have been from neighbouring countries, both from Central Europe as well as from Austria and Germany.

226

Their trips also tend to be multi-purpose, so that it is increasingly difficult to refer to individual market segments. In this their international tourism is fundamentally different to that of, say Spain and Portugal, which attract holiday tourists from more distant countries of origin. Thus far, only Prague has demonstrated this level of more globalized tourist attraction, and it remains open to question whether any other regions, even the Tatras mountains, can achieve the same position in global markets. The tourism destinies of most regions are therefore likely to continue to be highly dependent on external conditions in neighbouring countries.

8.4 PRIVATISATION: PROPERTY RIGHTS AND PRODUCTION

Tourism was one of the most privatized industries in Slovakia and the Czech Republic. Most establishments were sold via public auction as part of the Small Privatization programme. This was broadly transparent and fair, and it created a relatively dynamic sector with relatively new *de facto* and *de jure* owners. As would be expected, however, there were also relatively large numbers of failures amongst small tourism firms. This reflected a combination of factors: a lack of experience amongst many owners, a lack of capital, difficulties in securing loans from the financial sector, and overpaying for enterprises (a function of the lack of historical market values). The net result was to create a relatively high degree of instability in the ownership of small firms, and it often took several transfers of ownership rights before effective proprietors were found who had both the resources and the commitment to develop these tourism assets. Therefore, as was stated previously, there was no simple linear process of converting public into private property rights, but rather there were changing forms of 'intersection of old and new pathways' (Smith and Pickles 1998, p 15).

Large hotels and the spas were privatized either via coupon privatization or direct sales. The former was more important in the Czech Republic, while there was apparently less transparency in the direct sales in Slovakia. There were two important implications of this process. First, many of the firms ended up in mixed forms of ownership, by virtue of the banks and other financial institutions remaining in state ownership. This has been characterized by Stark (1996) as 'recombinant' property. However, we believe that the importance of recombinant property has been overstated. The institutionalization and regulation of markets is notoriously weak in the transition economies, and corrupt practices in the 'tunnelling out' of firms' assets has reinforced a climate of suspicion. In these circumstances, sole or clear majority ownership was required for investors to exert effective control over their assets. Recombinant property has therefore been inherently unstable, and – as the case studies revealed – has tended to be replaced by dominant ownership forms. Privatization did not always produce recombinant property, and many firms were transferred into dominant ownership at extremely low prices compared to their real market evaluations. While this process was informed by the desire of politicians and enterprise managers to exploit the once-in-a-lifetime possibility to accumulate capital, it also – perhaps surprisingly – created favourable conditions for the development of these firms. The new owners were not excessively burdened by debts, and were able to use the capital generated by the firms to reinvest in their longer-term development. A highly inequitable redistribution of property rights therefore produced favourable conditions for the development of the tourism sector – in context of the realities of transition.

While the creation of new forms of property rights has mainly been viewed as the outcome of struggles between national interests and capitals, it has not – and could not – be immune from foreign intervention. The case studies have identified examples of both greenfield investments and acquisitions by foreign capital. There are also largely unconfirmed suspicions that foreign capital was instrumental in funding the wave of small-scale privatization. Whatever, the reality of the situation, it is likely that foreign capital will play an increasingly important role in the tourism industry in these countries in future. This may be realized either through direct investment in particular establishments, especially the spas and some of the leading urban hotels, or indirectly through the activities of foreign travel agencies and tour companies. This is a destiny they are likely to share with the tourism industry in Western Europe which has hitherto been largely dominated by national capital, with relatively few exceptions (Williams and Montanari 1995).

8.5 TOURISM AND UNEVEN DEVELOPMENT

The state-socialist period had been characterized by strong tendencies to regional convergence as the outcome of central planning. Market relationship, in combination with reduced state intervention, meant that after 1989 there was a sharp increase in regional divergence. In general terms, rural regions and some of the more heavily industrialized regions were the main losers while the capitals and other cities with diversified economic bases were the main winners (see Dunford and Smith 1998). Changes in tourism largely reinforced this overall patterns, although there were some exceptions, notably in selected border regions and in the Tatra mountain region.

The capitals and other larger cities tended to benefit from the growth in domestic and international business travel as part of the emergence of market economies; these flows have disproportional economic weight due to the higher expenditures of business as opposed to holiday tourists. Stark evidence for this can be found in hotel prices in Prague which rival those in most Western European capital cities. Prague has also benefited from its status as a global tourism attraction and its ability to attract tourists from relatively high income countries such as the USA and Japan. Border regions have also tended to benefit from international tourism expansion but their experiences are sharply differentiated. Almost all border regions have benefited from increases in VFR tourism, but especially those adjacent to Hungary and the new Czech–Slovak border. Excursionism has increased across most borders, but – not surprisingly – it is the regions which are adjacent to Germany and Austria which have been the main winners in terms of increased international expenditure. These are also the regions which have benefited most from integration into wider European trade and investment flows. The main losers have been those regions which were and are mostly dependent on relatively low-quality facilities which were used to providing for domestic holiday tourism. Economic recession, especially before 1993, and increasing competition meant that they lost market share whilst also lacking the investment to renew their tourism facilities and their images. The impact of all these changes has been to contribute to regional economic divergence, although they also contribute to diversifying the overall pattern of winners and losers. In the Tatra mountains, for example, decline in other sectors of the regional economy has meant that tourism has become relatively more important since 1989, and has made a substantial contribution to sustaining income and employment levels.

The tourism destinies of individual regions remains uncertain. However, it can reasonably be argued that continued economic growth, and increased European integration is likely to reinforce the position of Prague and Bratislava in business tourism. Prague is also likely to continue to benefits from its position as a world city in tourism attraction terms, whilst Bratislava's proximity to Vienna makes its future role as a tourism destination less certain. The reduction of price differentials, particularly if the two countries become members of the EU and of the Euro zone, will also serve to reduce the currently high level of trade and retailing tourism in most border regions. Therefore, the recovery in domestic tourism remains one of the most significant sources of future tourism expansion. The question is whether the regions with weaker tourism images will be able to compete effectively in what is likely to become an increasingly competitive and international market for both longer holidays and short breaks in Central Europe. The regions of the Slovak and the Czech Republics are not simple passive recipients of these global changes. Instead, they have the capacity to influence their trajectories as centres of both national and international tourism. Given appropriate policies, management strategies and investment programmes, they are capable of competing effectively and adding to global competition. In some cases, notably Prague and the Tatra mountains, they may even have a significant impact on the global scene.

8.6 CONSUMPTION: LEISURE TIME AND TOURISM AS CASUALTIES OF TRANSITION?

The consumption of tourism has been subject to apparently contradictory trends. On the one hand, the number of people taking long holidays has increased, while the number taking shorter holidays has decreased. Yet the numbers of short stays has increased and the total number of longer holidays has decreased during the transition. The reasons for this lie in logical responses to the economic challenges of transition, which above all has been characterized by a profound deepening of social cleavages. A regressive income redistribution, and an end to guaranteed and regulated sources of work and income have had an impact on the time and resources available to purchase holidays from an increasingly privatized tourism industry.

In general, the main losers have been those with fixed incomes, such as pensioners, and those who have lost their jobs. For them, as for many others on low wages, any kind of holiday has become a barely accessible good, whereas before 1989 it had been a right. Their response has been to reduce the total numbers of holidays taken, concentrating their resources on a single long holiday. Wherever possible, they have also relied on the reduced but still significant remnants of collective provision such as trade-union- or factory-owned holiday facilities. Elsewhere in the population, there are those who may have more income, perhaps as a result of multiple job-holding, but by the very nature of such work, they no longer have the time for taking several holidays a year. They also have tended to concentrate their holidays into a single unit, and to have reduced their number of (shorter) holidays. The real winners in terms of tourism have been either those who travel for business purposes or have sufficient income for a number of holidays each year. The two groups tend to coincide but they are not synonymous.

Tourism consumption, perhaps more than any other dimension of tourism, illustrates the changing path-dependent path-creating nature of the transition. There are strong elements of continuity, or the persistence of 'old pathways', evident in the importance of collective provision and in VFR tourism. But both of these also perform different functions and for different segments of the population than was the case in state-socialism. The removal of barriers to international travel and the privatization of many facilities has also produced a truncated geography of such 'old pathways'. At the same time, new pathways have been created by privatization, the development of commercial package holidays, and foreign travel. Moreover, as argued previously, the intersection of pathways does not follow a simple unilinear pattern with predictable logic. Instead, there have been sharp reversals in access to tourism, with consumption virtually collapsing in the first part of the transition but then recovering with the onset of economic growth in the later 1980s. The resulting shifting bricolage is a product of the intersection of dynamic social changes with equally dynamic changes in the ownership and management of tourism facilities. For these same reasons, it is difficult to predict the future course of changes in domestic tourism consumption. At one level, it can be argued that future increases in prosperity would be likely, given the positive elasticity of demand for tourism, to result in increased consumption. However, the levels of tourism consumption in the Czech and Slovak Republics is relatively high in comparison to the experiences of the Southern European economies at a similar stage in their development. This is in part due to the legacy of collective provision, and to institutionalized holiday practices. Therefore the future of tourism consumption will depend as much on the continued availability of collective provision, which will be a function of wider industrial restructuring, as on the growth and distribution of income.

BIBLIOGRAPHY

Adamec, V. and Jedličková, N. (1991), *Slovensko; Turistický Sprievodca, (Slovakia, Tourist Guide)*, Bratislava: Sport.

Ash T., Hare, P. and Canning, A. (1994), 'Privatization in the former centrally planned economies' in P.M. Jackson and C.M. Price (eds), *Privatization and Regulation: a Review of the Issues*, Harlow: Longman, pp 213–36.

Bacigalová, J. (1997), Vzdelanie v cestovnom ruchu ponúkajú tri slovenské univerzity, (Three Slovak universities offer education in tourism), TREND Weekly 4, No. 44, 29 October 1997.

Baláž, V. (1992), *Komparácia cestovného ruchu v Slovenskej a Rakúskej republike*, (A Comparison of Tourism in the Austrian and Slovak Republics). Bratislava: Institute of Forecasting, Slovak Academy of Science.

Baláž, V. (1994), 'Tourism and regional development problems in the Slovak Republic', *European Urban and Regional Studies*, 1(2), pp 171–7.

Baláž, V. (1995a), 'Regional development during economic transition. A case study of the Slovak Republic', *European Urban and Regional Studies*, 2(4), pp 353–62.

Baláž, V. (1995b), 'Five years of economic transition in Slovak tourism', *Tourism Management*, 1(2), pp 143–50.

Baláž, V. (1996a), 'The Wild East? Capital markets in the V4 countries', *European Urban and Regional Studies* 3(3), pp 251–66.

Baláž, V. (1996b), 'Coupon privatization and investor protection', *Journal of Interdisciplinary Economics*, 7(1), pp 3–25.

Baláž, V: (1996c), *Regional Tourism Management in the Slovak Republic*, Exeter: Tourism Research Group, University of Exeter, Discussion Paper No. 8.

Baláž, V: (1996d), *International tourism in the economies of central European countries*, Exeter: Tourism Research Group, University of Exeter, Discussion Paper No. 9.

Baláž, V. and Mitsutake, M. (1998), 'Japanese tourists in the transition countries of Central Europe', *Tourism Management*, 19(5), pp 433–43.

Bankové a zúčtovacie centrum Slovenska (1997): *Stredné hodnoty finančných ukazovateľov* (Banking and Clearing Centre of Slovakia, *Median values of the financial indicators of Slovak business*), Bratislava: Banking and Clearing Centre.

Beattie, R.M. (1991), 'Hospitality internationalization: an empirical investigation', *International Journal of Contemporary Hospitality Management*, 3, pp 14–20.

Böröcz, J. (1990), 'Hungary as a destination 1960–1984', *Annals of Tourism Research* 17(1), pp 18–35.

Böröcz, J. (1996), *Leisure Migration: a Sociological Study of Tourism*, Oxford: Pergamon.

Bujna, M. (1998), 'Návštevnosť Slovenska vlani klesla a menej cestovali aj občania SR' ('Decreases in incoming and outcoming tourism in Slovakia'), *TREND weekly*, No. 4, 1 April.

Burawoy M. and Krotov P. (1993), 'The economic basis of Russia's political crisis', *New Left Review* 198, pp 49–69.

Burns, P. (1998), 'Tourism in Russia: Background and structure', *Tourism Management* 19(6), pp 555–65.

Bútora. M. (1997): *Slovensko 1996, Súhrnná správa o stave spoločnosti a trendoch na rok 1997*, (*Slovakia, A Comprehensive Report on the Society Situation*), Bratislava: Inštitút pre verejné otázky.

Carter, F.W. (1991), 'Czechoslovakia' in D.R. Hall (ed.), *Tourism and Economic Development in Eastern Europe and the Soviet Union*, London: Belhaven.

Carter, F.W., Hall, D.R., Turnock, D. and Williams, A.M. (1995), *Interpreting the Balkans*, London: Royal Geographical Society, Geography Intelligence Paper No. 2.

Čech, J. (1994), '*Od obce po ministerstvo*', (*From village to Ministry*), in *Cestovníiruch*, a supplement of *Ekonom weekly*, No. 2.

Češka, R. (1995), 'Privatization in the Czech Republic' in *Privatization in Central and Eastern Europe –1994*, Ljublana: Central and Eastern European Privatization Centre, pp 108–20.

ČFNM, Český fond národního majetku (1996), 'Česká privatizace' (Czech National Property Fund, The Czech Privatization), *Ekonom weekly*, No. 19, pp 31–35.

Český statistický úřad (1989–1998a), *Kapacity a využití ubytovacích zařízení*, (Czech Statistical Office, *Capacities and outputs of the accommodation facilities*), Prague: Czech Statistical Office.

Český statistický úřad (1989–1998b), *Návštevnost v ubytovacích zařízení cestovního ruchu*, (Czech Statistical Office, *Visitors in the tourist accommodation facilities*), Prague: Czech Statistical Office.

Český statistický úřad (1993–1998a), *Statistická ročenka*, (Czech Statistical Office, *Statistical Yearbook*), Prague: Czech Statistical Office.

Český statistický úřad (1993–1998b), *Bulletin CSU, Statistické informace* (Czech Statistical Office, *the CSU Bulletin quarterly, Statistical information monthly*), Prague: Czech Statistical Office.

Český statistický úřad (1994–1998), *Národní účty*, (Czech Statistical Office, *National accounts*), Prague: Czech Statistical Office.

Cestat (1992–1998), *Statistical Bulletin*, a joint publication by the Czech Statistical Office, Hungarian Central Statistical Office, Central Statistical Office of Poland, Statistical Office of the Republic Slovenia, Statistical Office of the Slovak Republic: Prague, Budapest, Poland, Ljubljana and Bratislava.

Commission of the European Communities (1986): *Europeans and their holidays*, Brussels: Commission of the European Communities.

Commission of the European Communities (1992a), *Socio-economic Situation and*

Development of the Regions in the Neighbouring Countries of the Community in Central and Eastern Europe), Luxembourg and Brussels: Directorate-General for Regional Policies, Regional Development Studies 2.

Commission of the European Communities (1992b), *Europe at the Service of Regional Development*, Luxembourg and Brussels: Directorate-General for Regional Policies.

Commission of the European Communities (1997), *Commission Opinion on Slovakia's Application for Membership of the European Union*, Brussels: Commission of the European Communities, COM(97) 2004 final.

Cooke, P. and Morgan, K. (1998), *The Associational Economy*, Oxford: Oxford University Press.

Cox T. (1994), 'Privatization and social interests in Eastern Europe', *Journal of European Public Policy* 1(3), pp 395–412.

Croall, J. (1995), *Preserve or Destroy: Tourism and the Environment*, London: Calouste Gulbenkian Foundation.

Crouch, G.I. and Shaw, R.N. (1992), 'International tourism demand: a meta-analytical integration of research findings' in P. Johnson and B. Thomas (eds), *Choice and Demand in Tourism*, London: Mansell, pp 175–207.

Csontosová, M. (1998), 'České hotely hľadajú východisko z krízy', ('Czech hotels are looking for solution of a crisis'), *TREND weekly*, No. 4, 1 April 1998.

Dallago, B. (1995), 'Privatization in Europe: a comparison' in R. Daviddi (ed.), *Property Rights and Privatization in the Transition to a Market Economy*, Maastricht: European Institute of Public Administration, pp 231–65.

Dlouhý, V. and Mládek, J. (1994), 'Privatisation and corporate control in the Czech Republic, *Economic Policy*, Supplement, December 1994, pp 155–70.

Doering, T. R. (1976), 'A re-examination of the relative importance of tourism to state economies', *Journal of Travel Research*, 15(1), pp 15–17.

Dostálová, E. (1997), 'Křehké zdraví české ekonomiky', (Fragile health of the Czech economy), *Ekonom weekly*, 49, pp 22–3.

Dunford, M. and Smith, A. (1998), 'Uneven development in Europe' in D. Pinder (ed.), *The New Europe: Economy, Society and Environment*, Chichester: Wiley.

Dunning, J.H. and McQueen, M. (1982), 'The eclectic theory of the multinational and the international hotel industry' in A.M. Rugman (ed.), *New Theories of the Multinational Enterprise*, London: Croom Helm.

Economist Intelligence Unit (1993), 'The market for cultural tourism in Europe', *Travel and Tourism Analyst*, No. 6, pp 30–46.

Ekonom weekly (1994), 'Co říká statistika', ('What the statistics are saying'), *Cestovní ruch*, a supplement of the *Ekonom weekly*, No. 2.

Ekonom weekly (1997), 'Zmetek české transformace' ('Failure of the Czech transition'), *Ekonom weekly*, 45, pp 78–9.

Estrin, S. (1994), 'Economic transition and privatization: the issues' in S. Estrin (ed.), *Privatization in Central and Eastern Europe*, Harlow: Longman, pp 3–30.

Eurostat (1992), *Family Budgets. Comparative tables 1988*, Luxembourg: Office for Official Publications of the European Communities.

Evans, G. and Whitefield, S. (1998), 'The structuring of political cleavages in post-communist societies: The case of the Czech Republic and Slovakia', *Political Studies*, 46(1), pp 115–39.

Falt'an, L., Gajdoš, P. and Pašiak, J. (1995), 'Marginalised Territories in Slovakia: their current situation', *Sociológia*, 27(1–2), pp 106–13.

Fayos-Solá, E. (1996), 'Tourism policy: a midsummer night's dream?', *Tourism Management*, 17(6), pp 405–12.

Federální statistický úřad (1985), *Historická statistická ročenka ČSSR*, (Federal Statistical Office, *Historical Statistical Yearbook of the CSSR*), Prague: Federální statistický úřad.

Federální statistický úřad (1986–1993a), *Statistická ročenka ČSSR za roky 1985–1992*, (Federal Statistical Office, *Statistical yearbook of the CSSR for 1985–1992)*, Prague: Federální statistický úřad.

Federální statistický úřad (1990–1993b), *Cestovný ruch organizovany prostredníctvom cestovnych kancelárií*, (Federal Czechoslovak Statistical Office and Slovak Statistical Office, *Tourism Organized via Travel Agents*), Prague: Federální statistický úřad.

Fogel, D.S. and Etcheverry, S. (1994a), 'Reforming the economies of Central and Eastern Europe' in S.D. Fogel (ed.), *Managing in Emerging Market Economies, Cases from the Czech and Slovak Republics*, Colorado and Oxford: Westview Press, pp 3–33.

Fogel, D.S. and Etcheverry, S. (1994b), 'Economic and social reforms in the Czech and Slovak Republics' in S.D. Fogel, (ed.), *Managing in Emerging Market Economies, Cases from the Czech and Slovak Republics*, Colorado and Oxford: Westview Press, pp 34–66.

Freyer, W. (1990), *Tourism*, Munich: Oldenbourgh Verlag.

Gatnár, L. (1996), 'Transformácia a jej modernizačné elementy – porovnanie Českej a Slovenskej republiky', ('Transformation and its modernisation elements – comparing the Czech Republic with the Slovak Republics'), *Sociológia*, 28(4), pp 299–308.

GfK (1997), 'Výzkum: Příjezdový cestovní ruch', (The GfK agency, 'Research: Incoming tourism'), *Cestovní ruch*, No. 4, p. 2.

GfK (1998), 'Cizinci k nám jezdí nakupovat', (The GfK agency, 'Foreigners are coming for shopping'), *Hospodářské noviny*, 25 February (Prague).

Go, F.M. and Pine, R. (1995), *Globalization Strategy in the Hotel Industry*, London: Routledge.

Gowan, P. (1995), 'Neo-liberal theory and practice for Eastern Europe', *New Left Review*, 213, pp 3–60.

Grabher, G. and Stark, D. (1998), 'Organising diversity: evolutionary theory, network analysis and post-socialism' in J. Pickles and A. Smith (eds.), *Theorising Transition: the Political Economy of Post-Communist Transformations*, London: Routledge, pp 54–75.

Grabler, K. (ed.) (1997), *International City Tourism*, London: Pinter.

Grellnethová, M (1997), 'Tourism Area Central Europe – Danube Region', *Bulletin pre cestovný ruch*, No. 4, pp 2–3, Ministerstvo hospodárstva Slovenskej republiky, sekcia cestovného ruchu (Ministry of Economy of the Slovak Republic, Tourism Unit), Bratislava.

Guráň, P., Filadelfiová, J. and Ritomský, A. (1997), 'Tradičné a moderné: zmeny a život súčasnej rodiny', ('Traditional versus modern: Changes and life of present families'), *Sociológia* 29(1), pp 5–20.

Hájek, M. (1997), 'Makroekonomická analýza české ekonomiky 1996', ('The 1996 macroeconomic analysis for the Czech Republic'), *Politická ekonomie*, No. 3, pp 307–50.

Hajko, J. (1996), 'Hotel Carlton má po úspešnej súťaži nového majiteľa', ('A new owner for the Carlton hotel after a successful tender'), *TREND weekly*, No. 4, 31 January.

Hall, D.R. (1984), 'Foreign tourism under socialism: the Albanian "Stalinist" model', *Annals of Tourism Research* 11(4), pp 539–55.

Hall, D.R. (1991a), 'Evolutionary pattern of tourism development in Eastern Europe and the Soviet Union' in D.R. Hall (ed.), *Tourism and Economic Development in Eastern Europe and the Soviet Union*, London: Belhaven.

Hall, D.R. (1991b), 'Eastern Europe and the Soviet Union: overcoming tourism constraints' in D.R. Hall (ed.), *Tourism and Economic Development in Eastern Europe and the Soviet Union*, London: Belhaven.

Hall, D.R. (1991c), 'Introduction' in D.R. Hall (ed.), *Tourism and Economic Development in Eastern Europe and the Soviet Union*, London: Belhaven.

Hall, D.R. (1995), 'Tourism change in Central and Eastern Europe' in A. Montanari and A.M. Williams (eds), *European Tourism: Regions, Spaces and Restructuring*, Chichester: Wiley, pp 221–43.

Hospodářské noviny daily (1997), 'Ministr Kvapil předložil zákon o cestovním ruchu', ('Minister Kvapil has submitted the Tourism Law'), *Hospodářské noviny*, 10 October (Prague).

Hospodářské noviny daily (1998a), 'Devízové příjmy z turistiky loni klesli', ('International tourist receipts decreased last year'), *Hospodářské noviny*, 9 February (Prague).

Hospodářské noviny daily (1998b), 'ČNPF: V kauze lázní Třeboň jde o legální krádež', (The FNM says, the Třeboň spas cause is a legal fraud), *Hospodářské noviny*, 11 March (Prague).

Hospodářské noviny daily, (1998c), 'Vrtochy počasí zřejmě sníží přijímy horských středisk', ('The weather changes are likely to decrease the income of the mountain resorts'), *Hospodářské noviny*, 16 February (Prague).

Hudson, R, and Lewis, J.R. (1984), Capital accumulation: the industrialization of Southern Europe? in A.M. Williams, (ed.), *Southern Europe Transformed: Political and Economic Change in Greece, Italy, Portugal and Spain*, London: Harper and Row, pp 179–207.

Jáč, R. (1996), 'Ekonomická transformace v ČR', ('The Czech economic transition'), *Supplement of the Národní Hospodářství*, No. 6 I–IX.

Janegová, V. (1996), 'Pre kategorizáciu ubytovacích a pohostinských zariadení musia platiť jednotné pravidlá', ('Single rules for the accommodation and catering standards'), *TREND weekly*, No.14.

Janků, J. (1996a), 'Majitelia hotela Devín chcú, aby ho hostia vyh—adávali pre kvalitné služby a osobitnú atmosféru', ('The Hotel Devín's owners want to attract guests via high-quality services and a special atmosphere'), *TREND weekly*, No. 50, 11 December.

Janků, J. (1996b), 'V Terchovej si začali uvedomovať, že koľajnice cestovného ruchu si musia vybudovať predovšetkým sami', ('Terchová starts to realize that themselves must develop the tourism'), *TREND weekly*, No. 34, 21 August.

Jansen-Verbeke, M. (1995), 'A regional analysis of tourist flows within Europe', *Tourism Management*, 16(1), pp 73–82.

Johnson, M. (1997), 'Hungary's hotel industry in transition, 1960-1996', *Tourism Management* 18(7), pp 441-52.

Józsa P. (1998), 'Nový vlastník kúpeľov Dudince investuje do modernizácie', ('The Dudince Spas' new owner invests in modernisation'), *TREND weekly*, No. 7, 11 February.

Kainc, J. (1996), 'Promarila se velká šance. Promarní se i letos?', ('Big chance lost. Will it be lost this year again?'), *Světoběžník monthly* No. 8, pp 10–11.

Kaspar, C. (1986), 'Der Fremdenverkehr im Grundriss', *Auflage*, 3, pp 112–49, Bern and Stuttgart.

Klvačová, E. (1996), 'Kdo řídí české akciové společnosti?', ('Who is managing the Czech joint-stock companies?'), *Ekonom weekly* 27, pp 16–17.

Kopšo, E. (1985), *Ekonomika cestovného ruchu* (*Economics of Tourism*), Bratislava: Slovenské pedagogické nakladateľstvo.

Krivý, V. Feglová, V. and Balko D. (1997), *Slovensko a jeho regivny, (Slovakia and its regions)*, Bratislava: Nadácia Médiá.

Kuča, Š. (1997), 'Škrty v rozpočte SACR obmedzia pripravené aktivity', ('Reduced SACR budget will limit the prepared activities'), *TREND weekly*, No. 44, 29 October.

Kuminiaková, V. (1998), 'V plánoch rozvoja kúpeľov dominujú nové liečebné domy a technické vybavenie' ('New hotels and equipment prevail in the spa development plans'), *TREND weekly*, No. 7, 11 February.

Leško, M. (1997), 'Predseda HZDS dal, aby mohol dostať', ('The HZDS chairman gave in order to receive'), *The Sme daily*, 17 October.

Librová, H. (1997), 'Dekoncentrace osídlení – Vize a realita', ('The decentralization of settlements – Vision and reality'), *Sociologický časopis*, 33(1), pp 27–40.

Landesmann, M., and Székely, I.P. (1995a), 'Introduction', in M. Landesmann and I.P. Székely (eds), *Industrial Restructuring and Trade Reorientation in Eastern Europe*, Cambridge: Cambridge University Press, pp 1–22.

Landesmann, M., and I.P. Székely, I.P. (1995b), 'Industrial structural change in Central and Eastern European economies', in M. Landesmann, M., and I.P. Székely (eds), *Industrial Restructuring and Trade Reorientation in Eastern Europe*, Cambridge: Cambridge University Press, pp 23–68.

Law, C. (1993), *Urban Tourism*, London: Mansell.

Lury, C. (1996), *Consumer Culture*, Cambridge: Polity Press.

Macháček, L. (1997), 'Individualizácia prvej postkomunistickej generácie v Slovenskej republike', ('Individualisation of the first post-communist generation in the Slovak Republic') *Sociológia*, 29(1), pp 21–44.

Machonin, P. (1994), 'K sociologické komparaci české a slovenské společnosti', ('A sociological comparison of the Czech and Slovak societies') *Sociológia* No. 4, p. 342.

Malá, V. (1985), 'Teória potrieb a spotreby v cestovnom ruchu', in Kopšo (ed.), *Ekonomika Cestovného Ruchu*, ('Needs and consumption theory of tourism', in Kopšo (ed.), *Tourism Economics*) Bratislava: Slovenské pedagogické nakladateľstvo, pp 104–22.

Malmberg, A. and Maskell, P. (1999), 'Localized learning and regional economic development', *European Urban and Regional Studies* 6(1), pp 5–8.

Marcom (1996), 'Výzkum motivace zahraničnych turistů' (The Marcom agency, 'Foreign tourist travel motives survey'), *Cestovní ruch*, No. 4, pp 5–7.

McIntyre, J., Porter, L. and Wendelova, P. (1994), 'Ex-émigré entrepreneur Viktor Koženy and the Harvard Group', in S.D. Fogel, (ed.), *Managing in Emerging*

Market Economies, Cases from the Czech and Slovak Republics, Colorado and Oxford: Westview Press, pp 149–65.

Medved, J. (1984), *Financie v cestovnom ruchu* (vybrané kapitoly), (*Tourism finance, selected chapters*) Bratislava: Rektorát VŠE.

Ministerstvo hospodárstva Slovenskej republiky (1992), *Zásady zákona o cestovnom ruchu, 1. a 2. verzia návrhu*, (Ministry of Economy of the Slovak Republic, *The Principles of Tourism Development Act, First and Second Proposals*), Bratislava: Ministry of the Economy, unpublished papers, May 1992.

Ministerstvo hospodárstva Slovenskej republiky (1993), *Strategické možnosti rozvoja cestovného ruchu so zvláštnym zameraním na intenzifikáciu devízového prínosu cestovného ruchu*, (Ministry of Economy of the Slovak Republic, *Strategic Possibilities of the Tourism Development with a Special Respect to Developing and Intensifying of International Tourist Receipts; a report for the Economic Board of the Slovak Government*), Bratislava: Ministry of Economy, unpublished papers, January 1993.

Ministerstvo hospodárstva Slovenskej republiky (1994), *Zámery rozvoja cestovného ruchu*, (Ministry of Economy of the Slovak Republic, *Principles of the Tourism Development; a report for the Slovak Government*) Bratislava: Ministry of Economy, unpublished papers, March 1994; summarized in *TREND weekly*, Bratislava, 16 March 1994.

Ministerstvo hospodárstva Slovenskej republiky (1994–1996), *Ekonomické analýzy ekonomiky SR*, (Ministry of Economy of the Slovak Republic, Economic Analysis Section, *Analysis of the Slovak Economy*), Bratislava: Ministry of the Economy, unpublished reports.

Ministerstvo hospodárstva Slovenskej republiky (1995), *Program podpory rozvoja cestovného ruchu*, (Ministry of Economy of the Slovak Republic, *Tourism Development Programme*, Bratislava, 1991, 1993, 1994 and 1995), Bratislava: Ministry of the Economy, the full version was published in *TREND weekly*, Bratislava, 16 March 1994.

Ministerstvo hospodárstva Slovenskej republiky (1997a), *Program podpory rozvoja cestovného ruchu v Slovenskej republike po piatich rokoch*, (Ministry of Economy of the Slovak Republic, *Five years of the Tourism Development Programme in Slovakia*), Bratislava: Ministry of Economy, *Bulletin pre cestovný ruch*, 2/97.

Ministerstvo hospodárstva Slovenskej republiky (1997b), *Zlaté bane informácií*, (Ministry of Economy of the Slovak Republic, *Information gold mines*), Bratislava: Ministry of Economy, *Bulletin pre cestovny ruch*, 2/97.

Ministerstvo hospodárstva Slovenskej republiky (1998), *Návrh legislatívneho zámeru na vypracovanie zákona o cestovnom ruchu*, (Ministry of Economy of the Slovak Republic, *Proposal for the Tourism Law Concept*), Bratislava: Ministry of Economy, internal unpublished papers.

Ministerstvo obchodu a cestovného ruchu Slovenskej republiky (1990), *Interné materiály*, (Ministry of Trade and Tourism of the Slovak Republic, *Internal materials on commercial and non-commercial tourism*), Bratislava: Ministry of Trade and Tourism.

Ministerstvo životného prostredia Slovenskej republiky (1996), *Národná správa o rozvoji osídlenia a bývania v SR pre konferenciu OSN, Habitat II*, (Ministry of Environment of the Slovak Republic, *The National Report on the Dwelling and Settlement Development Conference of the UN, Habitat II*), Bratislava: Ministry of Environment.

Ministerstvo životného prostredia Slovenskej republiky (1997), *Koncepcia územného rozvoja Slovenska – II. návrh*, (Ministry of Environment of the Slovak Republic, *Concept of the territorial development of Slovakia*), published in *TREND weekly*, 27 August.

Ministry of Administration and Privatization of National Property of the Slovak Republic (1996), *Privatization Process in the Slovak Republic*, Bratislava: Ministry of Administration and Privatization of the National Property.

Montanari, A. (1995), 'The Mediterranean region : Europe's summer leisure space', in A. Montanari and A.M. Williams (eds), *European Tourism: Regions, Spaces and Restructuring*, Chichester: Wiley.

Myant, M. (1995), 'Transforming the Czech and Slovak economies: evidence at the district level', *Regional Studies* 29(8), pp 753–60.

Mygind, N. (1994), *Societies in transition, from plan to market, from party dictatorship to democracy, from 'socialism' to . . . ?*, Copenhagen: Institute of Economics, Copenhagen Business School.

Národná banka Slovenska (1993–1998a), *Platobná bilancia za roky 1993–1998*, (National Bank of Slovakia, *Balance of Payments 1993–1998*), Bratislava: National Bank of Slovakia.

Národná banka Slovenska (1993–1998b), *Štatistické informácie, 1993–1997*, (National Bank of Slovakia: Statistical Information monthly, 1993–1997), Bratislava: National Bank of Slovakia.

Národná banka Slovenska (1993–1998c), *Menový prehľad 1993–1998*, (National Bank of Slovakia, *Monetary survey monthly 1993–1998*); Bratislava: National Bank of Slovakia.

Nejdle, K. (1994), 'Česká centrála cestovního ruchu', (Czech Travel Centre), *Cestovní ruch, a supplement of the Ekonom weekly* No. 2.

NFHR (1996), Národní federace hotelů a restaurací ČR: Stanovisko NFHR ČR k problematice DPH z pohledu hotelových a restuaračních služeb, (National Federation of the Hotels and Restaurants of the Czech Republic, opinion given by the NFHR ČR about VAT in the hotel and restaurant services), pp 64–5, *Světoběžník monthly* 4, pp 64–5.

Nielsen, K., Jessop, B. and Hausner, J. (1995), 'Institutional change in post-socialism' in J. Hausner, B. Jessop and K. Nielsen (eds), *Strategic Choice and Path Dependency in Post Socialism: Institutional Dynamics in the Transformation Process*, Aldershot: Edward Elgar, pp 3–44.

Novák, J. and Zídková, H. (1997), 'Některé poznatky statistiky cestovního ruchu v roce 1996', ('Some results of the tourism statistics'), *Statistika* (the Czech Statistical Office monthly), 10, pp 398–403.

OECD (1989), *Tourism Policy and International Tourism in OECD Member Countries*, Paris: OECD.

OECD (1996a), *Financial Accounts of the OECD Countries, Part III: Non-financial Enterprises*, Paris: OECD.

OECD (1996b), *Tourism and Tourism Policy in the OECD Member Countries*, Paris: OECD.

OECD (1997), *Services. Statistics on Value Added and Employment*, Paris: OECD.

Okáli, I., Gabrielová, H., Hlavatý, E. and Outrata, R. (1997), 'Economic development in Slovakia in 1996', *Ekonomický časopis* pp 175–221.

Pearce, D. (1995), *Tourism Today. A Geographical Analysis. Second Edition*, Harlow: Longman.

Pekník, K. (1995), 'The overall changes in the structure of inhabitants' income during the period of economic transformation till the end of 1993', *Sociológia*, 27(1–2), pp 95–101.

Podoba, J. (1996), 'Niekoľko poznámok k diskontinuitám vo vývoji slovenského poľnohospodárstva a etnologického myslenia', ('Several comments on discontinuities in development of Slovak agriculture and ethnic thinking'), *Slovenský národopis*, 2 p 217.

Pohl, G., Anderson, R., Claessens, S. and Djankov, S. (1997), *Privatization and Restructuring in Central and Eastern Europe*, Washington World Bank, Technical Paper 386.

Polish Central Statistical Office (1995), *Rocznik Statisticzny 1995*, (*The 1995 Statistical Yearbook*), Warsaw: Polish Central Statistical Office.

Porvaznik, J. (1994), 'Privatization in the Slovak Republic' in *Privatization in Central and Eastern Europe – 1993, Central and Eastern European Privatization*, pp 254–64, No. 4, Ljublana.

Procházka, L. (1997), 'Hotel S.E.N.', *Úspěch monthly*, No. 4, pp 33–4.

SFNM, Slovensky fond národného majetku (1996a), 'Vyročná správa', (Slovak National Property Fund, 'The 1995 Annual Report'), *TREND weekly*, 27 March.

SFNM, Slovenský fond národného majetku (1996b), 'Vyťahy z vyročných správ fondu za roky 1992–1995', (Slovak National Property Fund, 'Abstracts from the 1992–1995 Annual Reports, *Hospodárske noviny daily*, 4 October.

Shaw, G. and Williams, A.M. (1987), 'Firm formation and operating characteristics in the Cornish tourism industry', *Tourism Management*, 8, pp 344–8.

Shaw, G. and Williams, A.M. (1994): *Critical Issues in Tourism, A Geographical Perspective*, Oxford: Blackwell.

Shaw, G. and Williams, A.M. (1998), 'Entrepreneurship, small business culture and economic development', in D. Ioannides and K.G. Debbage (eds), *The Economic Geography of the Tourist Industry: a Supply Side Analysis*, London: Routledge.

Simonian, A. (1995a), 'Zemský ráj to napohled, Úskalí cestovního ruchu', (look at the paradise on earth, problems of tourism'), *Ekonom weekly*, 21, pp 33–7.

Simonian, A. (1995b), 'Již nejen pro vejce, O polské zahraniční turistice' ('No.more travel just for egg-buying; about Polish international tourism'), *Ekonom weekly*, 36 p 58.

Sinclair, M.T. and Stabler, M. (1997), *The Economics of Tourism*, London: Routledge.

SIPRI Yearbook (1990): *World Armament and Disarmament*, Oxford: Oxford University Press.

Slovenská záručná banka (1998), 'Program podpora rozvoja cestovného ruchu v SR' (Slovak Guarantee Bank, Tourism Development Programme in the Slovak Republic'), *TREND weekly*, No. 14, 1 April.

Sme daily (1997), 'Prevádzkovateľ hotela Holiday Inn upisuje akcie v objeme 150 mil. Sk' ('The Holiday Inn hotel operator announces a public share offering of Sk 150 million'), *Sme daily*, 9 December.

Smith, A. (1994), 'Uneven development and the restructuring of the armaments industry in Slovakia', *Transactions of the Institute of British Geographers* 19(4), pp 404–24.

Smith, A. (1995), 'Regulation theory, strategies of enterprise integration and the political economy of regional economic restructuring in central and eastern Europe: the case of Slovakia', *Regional Studies* 29(8), 761–72.

Smith, A. (1997a), 'Constructing capitalism? Small and medium sized enterprises, industrial districts and regional policy in Slovakia', *European Urban and Regional Studies*, 4(1), pp 45–70.

Smith, A. (1997b), 'Breaking the old and constructing the new? Geographies of uneven development in Central and Eastern Europe' in R. Lee and J. Wills (eds), *Geographies of Economies*, London: Arnold.

Smith, A. and Ferenčíková, S. (1998), 'Inward investment, regional transformations and uneven development in eastern and central Europe: enterprise case studies from Slovakia', *European Urban and Regional Studies*, 5(2), pp 155–73.

Smith, A. and Pickles, J. (1998), 'Introduction: theorising transition and the political economy of transformation' in J. Pickles and A. Smith (eds), *Theorising Transition: the Political Economy of Post-Communist Transformations*, London: Routledge, pp 1–24.

Soane, J. (1992), 'The origin, growth and transformation of maritime resorts since 1840', *Built Environment*, 18, pp 13–26.

Špelinová, E. (1996), 'Novodobá historie hotelu Košík' (New history of the Košík hotel), p 64, *Světoběžník monthly*, No. 10.

Šporer P, (1997), 'Konkurenciu na Slovensku treba vítať, tvrdí liptovskohrádocký podnikateľ Pavel Kováč', ('Competition is desirable in Slovakia, says Mr. Kováč, an entrepreneur from Liptovský Hrádok'), *TREND weekly*, 13 August.

Staniszkis, J. (1991), 'Political capitalism in Poland', *East European Politics and Societies*, 5, pp 127–41.

Stark, D. (1992), 'Path dependence and privatization strategies in East-Central Europe', *East European Politics and Societies*, 6(1), pp 17–54.

Stark, D. (1994), 'Path dependence and privatization strategies in East-Central Europe', in E. Milov (ed.), *Changing Political Economies – Privatization in Post-Communist and Reforming Communist States*, New York: Lynne Rienner Publishers, pp 115–46.

Stark, D. (1996), 'Recombinant property in East European capitalism', *American Journal of Sociology*, 101(4), pp 993–1027.

Štatistický úrad Slovenskej republiky (1991–1998a), *Zahraniční návštevníci v ubytovacích zariadeniach Slovenskej republiky*, (Slovak Statistical Office, *Foreign Visitors in Slovak Accommodation Establishments*) Bratislava: Slovak Statistical Office.

Štatistický úrad Slovenskej republiky (1991–1998b), *Kapacity a výkony ubytovacích zariadení*, (Slovak Statistical Office, *Capacities and Outputs of Accommodation Facilities*), Bratislava: Slovak Statistical Office.

Štatistický úrad Slovenskej republiky (1991–1998c), *Ekonomicky monitor*, (Slovak Statistical Office, *Economics Monitor Monthly*), Bratislava: Slovak Statistical Office.

Štatistický úrad Slovenskej republiky: (1993–1998a), *Príjmy a výdavky domácností v Slovenskej republike*, (Slovak Statistical Office, *Income and expenditure of households in the Slovak Republic*), Bratislava: Slovak Statistical Office.

Štatistický úrad Slovenskej republiky (1993–1998b): *Cestovný ruch organizovaný prostredníctvom cestovných kancelárií*, (Federal Czechoslovak Statistical Office and Slovak Statistical Office (1990–1997): *Tourism Organised via Travel Agents*), Bratislava, Slovak Statistical Office 1993–1998.

Štatistický úrad Slovenskej republiky (1994–1998), *Štatistická ročenka Slovenskej republiky za roky 1993–1997*, (Slovak Statistical Office, *Statistical Yearbook of the Slovak Republic for 1993–1997*), Bratislava: Slovak Statistical Office.

TOURISM IN TRANSITION

Štatistický úrad Slovenskej republiky (1997a), *Základné ukazovatele veľkých organizácií v obchode, pohostinstve, ubytovaní a cestovných kancelariách, 1., 2., 3. a 4. štvrĺMrok 1996* (Slovak Statistical Office), Bratislava: Slovak Statistical Office.

Štatistický úrad Slovenskej republiky, (1997b), *Základné ukazovatele malých organizácií v obchode, pohostinstve, ubytovaní a cestovných kanceláriách, 1., 2., 3. a 4. štvrĺrok 1996*, (Slovak Statistical Office, *Basic Indicators for Large Enterprises in Trade, Catering and Accommodation and Travel Agencies for the 1st, 2nd, 3rd and 4th Quarters 1996)*, Bratislava: Slovak Statistical Office.

Štatistický úrad Slovenskej republiky (1997c): *Štatistická správa o základných vývojových tendenciách v prvom polroku 1997*, (Slovak Statistical Office, *Statistical Report on Main Developments During First Half of 1997*), Bratislava: Slovak Statistical Office.

Šucha, J. (1997), 'Vláda SR aktualizovala zámery cestovného ruchu', ('Slovak government amended the tourism development plans'), *TREND weekly*, No. 44, 29 October.

Šujan, I. (1996), 'Analýza a prognóza makroekonomického vývoje ČR v roce 1995–1997', ('The 1995–1997 macroeconomic analysis and forecast'), *Supplement of the Národní Hospodářství*, No. 7 and 8, pp X–XIV and I–VIII.

Světoběžník (1996), 'Otevřený dopis Komisii pro cestovní ruch Hospodářskeho výboru Parlamentu České republiky', ('An open letter to the Tourism Commission of the Economic Committee of the Czech Parliament'), *Světoběžník monthly* No. 8 p 4.

Svitana (1998), 'Hotelové akdémie rastú ako z vody', ('Hotel academies are quickly growing in numbers'), *TREND weekly*, No. 14, 1 April.

Syrovátka, J. (1997), *Čas Fischera* (The time of Fischer), *Mladý Svět weekly*, No. 48, pp 30–2.

TREND weekly (1996), Najvyznamnejšie priame predaje v rokoch 1995 a 1996, ('The most important direct sales in 1995 and 1996'), *TREND weekly*, No. 51.

TREND weekly (1997), 'Rebríčky TRENDU najúspešnejších slovenských cestovných kancelárií', ('The TREND list of the most successful Slovak Travel Agents'), *TREND weekly*, 2 April.

TREND weekly (1998a), 'Rebríčky TRENDU najúspešnejších slovenských cestovných kancelárií', ('The TREND weekly list of top Slovak travel agents'), *TREND weekly*, No. 14, 1 April.

TREND weekly (1998b), 'Priame predaje podľa rozhodnutia Fondu národného majetku SR', ('Direct sales based on decisions of the Slovak National Property Fund'), *TREND weekly*, No. 7.

TTG monthly (May 1997), 'S CK vycestovalo loni 1.5 milionu občanů ČR' ('1.5 million Czech citizens travelled abroad with travel agents last year'), *TTG monthly* May.

Urry, J. (1990), *The Tourist Gaze: Leisure and Travel in Contemporary Societies*, London: Sage.

Urry, J. (1995), *Consuming Places*, London: Routledge.

Ústav turizmu (1995–1998), *Cestovanie a dovolenkové aktivity obyvateľov Slovenska v roku 1994, 1995, 1996 a 1997* (Tourism Institute, 'Travel and holiday activities of the Slovak population in 1994, 1995, 1996 and 1997') Bratislava: Tourism Institute.

Ústav turizmu (1997), *Aktívny zahraničný cestovný ruch na Slovensku v roku 1996*

(Tourism Institute, 'Incoming tourism in Slovakia in 1996'), Bratislava: Tourism Institute.

ÚVVM (1996), *Názory. Informačný bulletin, Ústav pre výskum verejnej mienky pri Štatistickom úrade SR*, (*Opinions. Information Bulletin of the Public Opinion Research Institute of the Slovak Statistical Office*), No. 4.

Vechter, J. (1995), 'Privatizácia priniesla do českých hotelov investície', ('Privatization has brought investments to the Czech hotels'), *TREND weekly*, No. 5.

Veyret, P. (1963), 'Le tourisme en Tchécoslovaquie', *Revue Géographie de l'Est*, 3(2), pp 131–6.

Viceriat, P. (1993), 'Hotel chains', *European Economy*, 3, pp 365–79.

Vintrová, R. (1993), 'The general recession and the structural adaptation crisis', *Eastern European Economics* 31(3), pp 78–94.

Vitáková (1994), 'Informační a rezervační systém', ('Information and reservation system'), *Cestovní ruch*, a supplement of *Ekonom weekly* No. 2.

Vláda Slovenskej socialistickej republiky (1981): *Smery pre aktualizovanú realizáciu rajonizácie cestovného ruchu v zmysle uznesenia vlády SSR č.76/1981* (Government of the Slovak Socialist Republic, *Guidelines for the implementation of the amended Territorial Distribution of Tourism according to the 76/1981 regulation*) Bratislava: Government of the Slovak Socialist Republic.

Vládny výbor pre cestovný ruch ČSR (1974–1982): (Government committee for tourism of the ČSR): *Bulletin No. 3/1974, 1/1976, 2/1981, 2/1982*, Bratislava.

Všudybyl (1997), 'Cestovní ruch přináší stále větší částky', ('Tourism generates increasing amounts'), *Všudybyl monthly*, January.

Výzkumní ústav obchodu (1988), *Účasť čs. obyvateľstva na cestovnom ruchu v roku 1987*, (Trade Research Institute, *Participation of the Czechoslovak Population in Tourism Activities in 1987*), Prague: Trade Research Institute.

Williams, A.M. (ed.), (1984), *Southern Europe Transformed: Political and Economic Change in Greece, Italy, Portugal and Spain*. London: Harper and Row.

Williams, A.M. (1994), *The European Community*, Second edition, Oxford: Blackwell.

Williams, A.M. (1995), 'Capital and the internationalization of tourism' in A.M. Williams and A. Montanari (eds), *European Tourism: Regions, Spaces and Restructuring*. Chichester: Wiley, pp 163–76.

Williams, A.M. (1997), 'Tourism and uneven development in the Mediterranean' in R. King, L. Proudfoot, and B. Smith (eds), *The Mediterranean: Environment and Society*, London: Edward Arnold, pp 208–26.

Williams, A.M. and Baláž, V. (1998), 'Transformation and division in Central Europe' in R. Hudson and A.M. Williams (eds), *Divided Europe: Society and Territory*, London: Sage.

Williams, A.M. and Baláž, V. (1999), 'Privatization in Central Europe: Different legacies, methods and outcomes', *Environment and Planning C: Government and Policy*.

Williams A.M., Baláž, V. and Zajac, S. (1998), 'The EU and Central Europe: the remaking of economic relationships, *Tijdschrift voor Economische en Sociale Geografie* 89(2), pp 131–49.

Williams, A. M. and Montanari, A. (1995): *European Tourism. Regions Spaces and Restructuring*, p 13, Wiley, Chichester.

Williams, A.M. and Shaw, G. (1998a), 'Tourism policies in a changing economic environment' in A.M. Williams and G. Shaw (eds), *Tourism and Economic Development: European Experiences*, Chichester: Wiley.

Williams, A.M. and Shaw, G. (1998b), 'Western European tourism in perspective' in A.M. Williams and G. Shaw (eds), *Tourism and Economic Development: European Experiences*, Chichester: Wiley.

WTO (1994): *Compendium of Tourism Statistics*, Fourteenth edition, Madrid: WTO.

Würzl, A. (1988), *Fremdenverkehrspolitik*, Vienna: Wirtschaftsuniversität.

XVI. zjazd Komunistickej strany Československa (1981): *Dokumenty a materiály*, (XVI General Meeting of the Czechoslovak Communist Party, *Documents and Materials*), Bratislava, Pravda.

Zeman, D (1998a), 'Okresům chybějí nutné informace' ('Districts lacks information needed') *Hospodářské noviny daily*, 16 February.

Zeman, D (1998b) 'Top Spirit přecenil své schopnosti' ('The Top Spirit over-estimated its abilities') *Hospodářské noviny daily*, 10 March.

ANNEXES

ANNEX I: *Slovak districts: basic data for 1996*

District	Area (km²)	Population	GDP (Sk million)	GDP per capita (Sk)	International tourism receipts (% of GDP)
Banská Bystrica	2,075	178,770	25,690	143,702	3.7
Bardejov	1,014	81,279	6,836	84,101	1.5
Bratislava City	368	448,785	163,191	363,629	2.2
Bratislava District	1,261	147,965	11,351	76,712	4.4
Čadca	934	123,994	7,225	58,272	3.5
Dolný Kubín	1,659	123,394	6,427	52,086	8.4
Dunajská Streda	1,075	110,526	8,195	74,148	4.0
Galanta	965	143,322	10,786	75,257	0.8
Humenné	1,909	113,880	9,387	82,425	2.4
Komárno	1,100	109,206	8,388	76,808	2.3
Košice-City	244	238,886	41,520	173,807	1.3
Košice-District	1,533	100,683	3,392	33,694	1.1
Levice	1,551	121,047	8,867	73,255	0.8
Liptovský Mikuláš	1,968	133,546	12,848	96,204	14.7
Lučenec	1,304	95,847	6,798	70,926	0.9
Martin	1,128	114,224	10,118	88,584	1.4
Michalovce	1,310	112,749	6,344	56,267	9.9
Nitra	1,443	212,654	15,910	74,817	1.7
Nové Zámky	1,347	153,090	9,012	58,870	3.0
Poprad	1,963	158,344	16,036	102,981	24.8
Považská Bystrica	1,196	172,301	13,882	80,567	2.9
Prešov	1,418	205,658	15,531	75,520	1.1
Prievidza	960	140,494	12,056	85,811	4.1
Rimavská Sobota	1,823	99,242	4,364	43,978	0.7
Rožňava	1,621	87,370	5,386	61,650	0.7
Senica	1,691	147,720	12,916	87,437	1.4
Spišská nová Ves	1,529	148,016	11,611	78,443	3.2
Stará Ľubovňa	624	48,112	2,465	51,225	6.1
Svidník	862	44,724	2,799	62,582	3.4
Topoľčany	1,361	161,444	10,602	65,671	0.4
Trebišov	1,322	119,163	8,498	71,310	0.5
Trenčín	1,310	180,374	17,740	98,352	2.6
Trnava	1,390	235,138	31,146	132,458	10.5
Veľký Krtíš	848	46,927	2,562	54,595	0.1
Vranov nad Topľou	847	75,484	3,897	51,630	0.0
Zvolen	1,721	123,368	10,105	81,911	4.1
Žiar	1,264	94,441	9,700	102,709	1.0
Žilina	1,097	184,285	17,448	94,679	2.8
Slovak Republic	49,035	5,336,452	581,300	108,930	3.7

Source: Štatistický úrad Slovenskej republiky (1991–1998a); authors' own calculations.
Notes: Exchange rate: 1 US$ = 31.895 Sk, on 29.12.1996; the reported district GDP excludes VAT, sale taxes, the foreign trade balance and public and financial sector contributions. It was grossed by 10.7% to allow for the share of international tourist receipts in total district GDP. The total receipts (US$ 672.8 million) were distributed by districts according to the nights spent by foreign tourists.

ANNEX II: *Changes in the regional distribution of tourist nights in Slovakia in 1989–96*
(percentage distribution)

District	Nights spent by domestic tourists			Nights spent by foreign tourists		
	1989	1993	1996	1989	1993	1996
Banská Bystrica	4.7	7.2	5.7	6.9	7.4	4.5
Bardejov	0.4	0.7	7.1	0.1	0.2	0.5
Bratislava City	3.8	13.9	8.1	17.1	24.2	16.7
Bratislava District	3.2	0.8	1.2	2.2	0.6	2.3
Čadca	1.9	0.5	0.5	0.4	0.3	1.2
Dolný Kubín	3.5	2.0	2.1	2.4	3.1	2.5
Dunajská Streda	0.7	0.2	0.7	3.5	0.4	1.5
Galanta	2.1	1.2	0.5	0.5	0.6	0.4
Humenné	0.3	0.3	0.9	0.1	0.2	1.0
Komárno	1.2	1.1	0.8	1.3	1.2	0.9
Košice City	1.6	20.0	3.7	3.5	5.8	2.5
Košice District	1.3	0.0	1.5	0.8	0.0	0.2
Levice	1.6	0.8	0.3	0.3	0.8	0.3
Liptovský Mikuláš	6.5	2.8	6.9	9.3	7.8	8.8
Lučenec	1.3	1.4	0.5	0.6	0.3	0.3
Martin	2.1	0.9	3.3	2.6	1.3	0.7
Michalovce	9.9	11.3	2.6	2.4	1.9	2.9
Nitra	1.7	1.9	2.4	2.7	2.5	1.2
Nové Zámky	4.1	3.0	2.5	0.9	1.4	1.2
Poprad	14.8	8.9	10.9	19.6	20.0	18.8
Považská Bystrica	2.9	2.6	4.4	1.6	2.0	1.9
Prešov	1.3	1.6	1.1	1.1	1.5	0.8
Prievidza	1.6	1.7	4.1	0.8	1.0	2.3
Rimavská Sobota	0.9	1.9	0.8	0.4	0.4	0.1
Rožňava	1.4	0.9	0.3	1.4	0.8	0.2
Senica	2.4	0.4	1.0	1.2	1.5	0.8
Spišská nová Ves	3.1	1.2	1.3	2.9	1.7	1.7
Stará L'ubovňa	1.4	0.0	1.1	0.3	0.0	0.7
Svidník	0.8	0.0	0.3	0.4	0.0	0.4
Topol'čany	3.0	0.0	0.4	0.5	0.0	0.2
Trebišov	0.8	0.0	0.2	0.1	0.0	0.2
Trenčin	2.1	2.0	2.7	2.7	2.1	2.1
Trnava	3.2	2.2	2.3	2.8	3.1	15.3
Veľký Krtíš	0.2	0.0	0.2	0.0	0.0	0.0
Vranov nad Topl'ou	1.1	0.2	0.1	0.4	0.2	0.0
Zvolen	1.8	2.8	11.7	1.3	1.9	1.9
Žiar	1.4	0.6	1.4	0.4	0.6	0.5
Žilina	3.8	3.2	4.2	4.2	3.5	2.3
Slovak Republic	100.0	100.0	100.0	100.0	100.0	100.0

Source: Štatistický úrad Slovenskej republiky (1991–1998a).

ANNEX III: *Czech counties: basic data for 1996*

County	Area (km^2)	Population
Prague	496	1,215,771
Central Bohemia	11,013	1,108,236
Southern Bohemia	11,345	700,289
Western Bohemia	10,875	861,747
Northern Bohemia	7,990	1,777,310
Eastern Bohemia	11,240	1,236,756
Southern Moravia	15,028	2,057,539
Northern Moravia	11,068	1,972,870
Czech Republic	79,055	10,930,518

Source: Český statistický úřad (1993–1998a).

ANNEX IV: *Basic tourism indicators for Central Europe in 1996*

		Czech Rep.	Hungary	Poland	Slovakia
Foreign visitor arrivals[1]	*million*	109.4	39.8	87.4	33.1
Domestic citizens' departures[1]	*million*	48.6	12.1	44.7	22.9
Number of beds[2]	*thousands*	143	88	81	36
Nights spent by foreign tourists[2]	*thousands*	13,641	10,676	7,199[3]	8,683
Occupancy rates	*%*	51.9	47.2	44.4[3]	38.3
International tourist receipts	*US$ million*	4,075	2,228	7,000	672
Share in GDP	*%*	7.3	5.4	5.6	3.7
Share in exports	*%*	18.6	14.2	28.6	7.9

Source: Cestat (1998).
Notes: 1 = visitors at frontiers; 2 = in hotels and similar establishments; 3 = in 1995.

ANNEX V: *Registered units in the hotel and restaurant sector in Central Europe: by selected legal forms in 1997*

	Czech Rep.[1]	Hungary	Poland	Slovakia
	Absolute values			
Total	68,947	83,188	12,622	15,845
Personal businesses	63,637	70,155	x	14,521
Civil companies	x	x	10,160	x
Limited companies	4,272	5,235	1,986	919
Joint-stock companies	220	6,526	59	56
Co-operatives	47	x	40	11
State-owned	58	x	17	6
	Percentage of all businesses in each category			
Total	4.2	8.3	2.5	4.7
Personal businesses	4.4	10.6	x	5.4
Civil companies	x	x	4.1	x
Limited companies	3.3	3.7	1.7	2.6
Joint-stock companies	2.1	4.7	0.8	1.9
Co-operatives	0.6	0.4	0.2	0.6
State-owned	3.6	x	0.5	1.7

Source: Cestat (1988).
Note: 1 = 20 January 1998.

ANNEX VI: *Czech tourism accommodation and spas: capacity, facilities and performance by region, in 1996*

	Prague	CB	SB	WB	NB	EB	SM	NM	Total
	Accommodation: Basic indicators (absolute values)								
Establishments	825	782	1,876	1,017	1,044	2,493	988	1,002	10,018
Beds	63,947	26,335	42,376	34,049	36,729	73,957	47,267	44,647	369,307
Employees	11,570	3,550	6,059	7,868	4,442	10,047	7,318	8,520	59,374
Nights ('000)	6,939	2,066	3,514	4,368	2,884	7,217	4,898	5,460	37,286
Foreign tourist nights ('000)	5,950	626	660	1,764	1,075	2,178	964	968	14,186
	Accommodation: facilities and services available (absolute values)								
Restaurant	223	245	325	302	356	605	314	386	2,756
Bar, café	185	113	160	173	206	345	194	252	1,628
Congress facility	48	21	23	29	22	39	51	39	272
Seminar room	125	124	174	155	207	317	223	257	1,582
Business service	60	22	39	33	23	38	31	35	281
Souvenir sales	244	130	207	214	220	368	198	257	1,838
Swimming pool	34	72	77	52	64	141	64	100	604
Sauna, solarium	43	43	63	72	65	157	54	114	611
Fitness centre	32	33	30	35	27	71	37	63	328
Sports centre	41	140	237	123	173	330	162	258	1,464
Parking	310	361	668	448	514	1,008	436	545	4,290
Currency exchange	137	41	74	83	67	83	69	85	639
Laundry	161	78	120	102	84	98	106	116	865
	Spas: basic indicators (absolute values)								
Establishments	0	4	3	31	4	6	4	9	61
Beds	0	371	734	6,667	1,706	1,867	675	3,990	16,010
Employees	0	107	316	3,299	157	771	245	1,573	6,468
Nights ('000)	0	23	61	427	41	122	46	245	965
Foreign tourist nights ('000)	0	5	5	175	2	2	2	13	205
Average length of stay (days)	0	10.1	20.5	13.3	4.2	7.2	10.3	12.5	12.7

Sources: Český statistický úřad (1989–1998a); Český statistický úřad (1989–1998b).
Notes: The 1996 data were, for the first time, processed using the methodologies recommended by WTO and Eurostat. Data for tourist accommodation facilities includes individual facilities (tourist beds in flats, second homes, weekend houses, etc.) and spa facilities. The data include all commercial tourist facilities and were collected directly in the facilities and not from their owners, as in previous years. The data for 1996 were more complete than, and not fully comparable to, those for earlier years.

ANNEX VII: *Czech and Slovak accommodation in 1990–96: capacity and performance*

	1990	1991	1992	1993	1994	1995	1996
				Czech Republic			
Number of facilities	2,531	1,633	1,132	1,476	1,939	3,030	10,018
Number of beds	193,244	136,507	130,466	132,857	163,994	237,350	399,672
Nights spent ('000)	24,480	14,982	13,481	14,661	17,801	23,721	37,286
				Slovakia			
Number of facilities	890	793	811	578	1,009	704	1,194
Number of beds	69,834	61,267	72,960	47,843	58,276	54,090	72,762
Nights spent ('000)	10,256	6,405	4,286	4,717	6,349	5,835	8,683

Sources: Federální statistický úřad (1986–1993a); Štatistický úrad Slovenskej republiky (1991–1998b); Český statistický úřad (1993–1998a).
Notes: in 1991–3 only those facilities registered in the Business Register reported these data.

Index

Tatras mountains 51, 73, 74, 135, 161,
166, 170, 178, 179, 183, 192, 227,
229
Tatratour 150, 153
taxes 48, 55, 57, 141
Terchová 51, 118–119
Top Spirit 106, 154
tour operators 9, 151
Tourism Council 52
Tourism Development Programme 42,
46, 47, 50, 57, 69, 119, 166, 170
Tourism Fund 22
Tourism Information Programme 42,
48
Tourism Law 42, 43, 46, 54, 57, 156,
224–225
Tourism Marketing Agency 42
tourism policies 38–56, 58, 172
Tourism Units 40, 50–51
tourist gaze 69, 169
Tourist Information Offices 48
trade unions 100, 102, 148, 158, 198,
203
trading 87, 226, 229
transit tourism 61, 66, 78, 87
travel agencies 54, 64, 125–126, 150–
153, 155–156, 158
travel intensity 23

travel propensity 204, 213
Travela 54, 155
Třebon 106

Ukraine 64, 71, 72, 73, 76, 80, 87, 179
unemployment 26, 33, 34, 36, 119,
163, 164, 167, 168
urban areas 50, 165, 183, 197–198,
209–210, 213, 228
urban tourism 8, 77
USA 106,155

Vadium Group 116
'velvet divorce' 29, 45, 64, 82, 161,
178, 190, 224, 226
Vietnam 127
visas 41, 87, 176
visiting friends and relatives (VFR) 61,
71, 76, 78, 82, 85, 86, 87, 190,
220, 226, 229

wages 15, 28
wealth 207–208
Western Bohemia 34, 67, 78, 168, 170,
171, 172, 187, 188, 191, 194

Yield Ltd 116
Yugoslavia 178